LING SHU

or

THE SPIRITUAL PIVOT

Ling Shu

OR

The Spiritual Pivot

translated by

WU JING-NUAN

ASIAN SPIRITUALITY, TAOIST STUDIES SERIES

The Taoist Center • Washington, D.C.

PAPERBACK EDITION 2002

SECOND PRINTING 2004

ISBN 0-8248-2631-0

Camera ready copy prepared by the author

This publication is printed on acid-free paper and meets the
guidelines for permanence and durability of the Council on
Library Resources.

Distributed by
University of Hawai'i Press
2840 Kolowalu Street
Honolulu, Hawai'i 96822

Dedication

To Qi Bo
Shao Shi
Bo Gao
Lei Gong
my family
and Huang Di

Acknowledgements

My thanks and regards to all of my patients who over the years have shown the wisdom of the ways enunciated in the Spiritual Pivot.

I thank my associates and staff, Tina Pirrone, Fang Neng-Yu, Julie Taylor, Eric Serejski, Caroline Woods, and Beth McGrath Oness, for help, comments, editing and encouragement to make the published work more beautiful and readable.

Chapters 8 and 29 were printed in a limited edition for the Taoist Center Press in the Trees by Chad Oness at Sutton Hoo Press.

Contents

Scroll Twelve

Introduction

Transformation of human society comes from intuitive genius which sees design, beauty and harmony for the individual in relation to people, to earth, and to heaven, which can be expressed and taught.

Teachings recording such genius were attributed to Huang Di, The Yellow Emperor and his ministers. Chinese legend says Huang Di reigned from 2696 to 2598 B.C. He was third in the line of great men who helped to create the civilizations of China. These essays are collected in the book *Huang Di Nei Jing, The Yellow Emperor's Inner Classic* which forms one of the world's first medical texts. The book is divided into two parts: the first, the *Su Wen, Simple Questions* are discussions of heaven, earth and the nature of man. The second, the *Ling Shu, The Spiritual Pivot* is also called the *Canon of Acupuncture* since it is the first literature on this medical procedure.

The twelve scrolls which make up this work probably were compiled in the era of the Warring States, 480 to 222 B.C. even with the attribution to Huang Di, the Yellow Emperor. The language of the text leaves no doubt that different parts of the treatise were written or rewritten and edited at different times. There is no way of knowing how great the differences in time may be, a hundred or a thousand years.

Two great commentaries must be mentioned in conjunction with any historical analysis of the book. Wang Ping of the Tang Dynasty wrote in 762 A.D. that he had combined various texts to make one more meaningful whole. In the reign of Shen Cong, the Emperor of the Sung Dynasty in the years 1068 to 1078 A.D., the *Nei Jing* was re-edited under the guidance of the two scholars Gao Bao-heng and Lin Yi. Most of the texts in use today come from these two recompilations.

It is always safe to say that the written material in the book came from oral traditions which may well have stretched back to the Yellow Emperor. I like to think so, even though many of the chapters detailing the method of the Wu Xing, "Five Dynamic Elements," are reminiscent of the Han dynasty, 206 B.C. to 220 A.D. By now, as far as I am concerned, it makes little difference; the acute awareness and brilliant deductive reasoning of the authors of these books send shivers up my spine. The insight of these works is staggering. I find that when some aspect of traditional medicine is unclear, I will discover it wondrously illuminated by my re-reading of the book.

A new translation must bring fresh understanding of the classics. Thus, I do not adhere to many explanations which were made by ancient Chinese scholars. At the same time, I avoid as much as possible using modern western terms in translation. We live today but must go back to the age of Huang Di to see the insight of this great classic.

A modern translation must take into account the poetic nature of classical Chinese literature, even in a technical text. The clipped style allows for wide variations in interpretation, especially since many terms are of a technical nature and must be compared to Chinese medical thought as it existed some thousands of years ago.

Reality and its management focus on the interdependence and interactions between heaven, man and earth. The forces of nature move in their primal journey not in material structure but in the living spirit. My hope is that the *Ling Shu, The Spiritual Pivot* will be read first for its livable philosophy which maintains harmony within the Dao, and secondly as an illumination of the techniques of acupuncture in this, the era of its reflowering.

To facilitate reading, I have added my own commentary to many of the eighty-one chapters.

Words in parentheses within the text are my own additions, added for clarity.

The Vocabulary of the Ling Shu

In my translation of the *Ling Shu* I have tried to keep as close to the original Chinese as possible. However, one great stylistic difference between ancient Chinese literature and today must be recognized: In ancient times, punctuation was not used. The periods and commas are mine.

The poetics of the original come from the nuances and niceties of dialogue between a great emperor and his ministers. The kowtow of politeness and form did not detract from verbal barbs when communication was not clear. I have attempted to give a rendering of this in language which would be clear and precise. At times it has been necessary to use Latin nomenclature for anatomical features but in most instances I have avoided doing so. Within the realm of courtly dialogue the metacarpophalangeal joint seems out of place.

Many of the chapters pose questions and use theories which are not explained in that very chapter but are explained in another portion of the book. Chapter Three, for instance, explains many of the theories of chapter One. Chapter Eight defines certain vocabulary important to the study of Chinese medicine. Later chapters are referenced in earlier chapters. This book then stands as a nonlinear equation in its own right and is not set up to be studied in a linear a b c d e fashion.

An important feature of the *Ling Shu* is the notation for the acupuncture points and the twelve major channels of qi energy along which they lie.

I have capitalized the names of each such point and channel. By request from my students I have also included the modern number for each point (see appendix C) although they do not occur in the original.

Each major channel has three parts to its name: its association with the arm or leg; the yin or yang mode of energy coursing through it; and the inner organ to which it is related, for example, the Lung Channel of the Arm Major Yin. A symptom of our material philosophy of today is that we use the organ name of the channel as its identifying feature. Thus, the first acupuncture point which occurs on the above channel of energy, Middle Mansion, is marked today as the Lung One point. In the *Ling Shu* this was not the case. The channel in most instances would be mentioned as the Arm Major Yin or when the anatomical position was clear, simply as the Major Yin. I have followed this practice.

The names of the acupuncture points have remained the same in most cases. For those which have changed I have included the change in appendix C. The words describing the points are important. Holes, gaps, and hollows all contribute to the ancient belief that there were entrances into and exits out of the body. I look upon them as resonating cavities.

Certain Chinese ideograms have no exact translation into another language. Others have technical meanings within the theories of acupuncture. The important ones in the *Ling Shu* are as follows:

Qi, the vital breath, air, vapor, atmosphere, energy. *Qi* moving is like water moving. So there are many riverine analogies. I find the Chinese more expressible and easier to use, so in most occurrences the romanization *qi* is used instead of a translation.

Dao, the way, a road, a principle; the way of the universe.

Shun, to flow with the current, favorable, to agree, to obey.

Ni, to go against the current, to rebel, to oppose.

Lai, to come, is a smooth flowing with the current.

Wang, to depart, past, gone, is a counterflow against the current.

He, to enclose, to close, to join, side by side, in tune with.

The volume of qi decreases as it flows away from the torso to the extremities of the limbs and vice-versa, that is, increases as it flows from hands and feet towards the torso. Designated acupuncture points along this flow are descriptive in volume and are called the *shu* points. They are five: *jing*, well; *ying*, spring; *shu*, stream; *jing*, river; *he*, confluence or sea.

The qi in its flow like river water can be clear or muddy. Muddy does not mean bad. It is simply a description usually denoting the qi which comes from food. Nourishment from water and foodstuffs occurs as water and valleys.

Gu, valley, ravine, a hollow.

The pictographs for yin and yang depict yin, the dark, shady side of a hill or river bank; yang, the bright, sunny side of a hill or riverbank. By extension they became the symbols of the dualistic nature of the universe and the perceivable manifestations of the Dao. They are dynamic principles forever changing, forever contending like the passage of light and nonlight of day and night. As a binary unit they were able to be used to explain reality, a system of opposites but more precise definitions were needed. These definitions in the *Ling Shu* are the three modes of energy for Yin, Major Yin, Minor Yin and Shrinking Yin and the three modes for Yang, Major Yang, Minor Yang and Bright Yang. Major and Minor are simple. The other two adjectives come from the analog to light of yin and yang. Yin in movement retreats or shrinks. Yang in movement advances or brightens.

In addition to the modes of yin and yang are the forces known as the Wu Xing, the Five Dynamic Elements. I have included dynamic in the translation for *xing* instead of simply Five Elements because the theory is based again, on dynamic motion, not structure. Xing means to walk, to move. Two major movements are clear - the cycle of mutual production: Wood, Fire, Earth, Metal, Water, Wood, and so forth, and the cycle of mutual destruction: Wood, Earth, Water, Fire, Metal, Wood.

The use of this theory of the Five Dynamic Elements continues the dynamism of the Dao and yin and yang. In present day terms, I see the process as being akin to the wave continuum in a theoretical view of reality which has both particle-structural and wave-dynamic forms simultaneously.

In the *Ling Shu* text the valley energies mean foods, especially grains. I have kept the word valleys most times for there seem to be broader philosophical meanings to the character.

Chinese anatomical names have been kept in some instances simply because the English or Latin was more cumbersome. Examples are Broken Dish, the supraclavicular fossa; Fish, the base of the thumb; Crouching Rabbit, the upper surface of the thigh; Inch Mouth, the wrist pulse; Man's Receptor, the carotid pulse.

Measures for the body: the unit *cun*, an inch, the body inch normally the width of the thumb at the level of the cuticle. *Fen* is one-tenth of a *cun*.

Time: The ancient Chinese used a sexagenary, that is, sixty-unit cycle, based on the Twelve Earthly Branches and Ten Heavenly Stems as they meshed together. I see this sixty-day system as a major expression of the ancient interest in cycles and repetitions for in two months a recurring cycle can be plotted. The *Ling Shu* provides the foundation for therapy based on timing in accord with the sexagenary cycle.

In this book I use the pinyin system for romanization of Chinese characters.

SCROLL ONE
1. OF NINE NEEDLES AND TWELVE SOURCE POINTS
"The Laws of Heaven"

Huang Di said to Qi Bo, "I, the emperor of the people, receive revenues of rents and taxes to nourish the Hundred Families, but I am grieved by not being able to provide for those afflicted with disease. I wish they did not have to endure the poison of medicines and the use of stone probes. I prefer to use those fine needles which penetrate the channels, harmonize the blood and qi energy, manage the current and countercurrents, and assemble the exits and entrances. Please unravel this for future generations and enlighten them in the proper methods so this therapy will not be destroyed or severed for aeons. See that it is easy to use, difficult to forget, a classical record. Delineate the process, clarify the extrinsic and the intrinsic, define an end and a beginning. Please formalize the reality of each item. Begin with the fundamentals of classical acupuncture. I wish to hear of these essentials."

Qi Bo answered saying, "In accordance with your imperial request, I relate the following: You wish to have the principles and records. To begin with the first, there are a total of nine needles and the principles of their way. The principles of using these fine needles are easy to say but difficult to master. Ordinary skills of acupuncture maintain the physical body; high skills maintain the spirit, use spirit to reveal the spirit and the guest at the door.[1] Without careful observation of the disease, how can there be an understanding of its origin? To needle is a subtle action on the body, whether quick or slow. Ordinary techniques guard the gates; high techniques control the moving power.[2] The moving power is inseparable from its space. The moving power, at the center of this space, is clear, quiet, and subtle.[3] Its coming cannot be hurried; its going cannot be chased.

"On understanding the moving power and its way: the onset of a therapeutic effect is faster than shooting an arrow. Without understanding the moving power and the Dao, effects are wasted, like arrows failing to leave the bow. To understand their comings and goings, emphasize the appropriate cycle of time.[4] Ordinary doctors are in the dark; wondrous are the few who possess the unique skills. To go is to be in counterflow, to come is to be in the flow; clearly knowing this, the first action will be without hesitation. Oppose the counterflow through seizing it by force and how can dispersion fail? Follow the energy flow to stimulate it and how can tonification fail? To oppose or follow, one can combine the methods as one wishes. This is the way of acupuncture.

"All use of acupuncture is thus: to tonify hollowness, to disperse fullness, to dredge stasis; the evil to be overcome will thus weaken.

"Generally speaking, needling methods, 'slow then quick' produces tonification, 'quick then slow' produces dispersion. To speak of fullness and exhaustion of energy is like to be or not to be. Observe the 'post' and the 'pre' to detain or withdraw the needle. Empty or full, the nine needles are exceedingly wondrous. To tonify or to disperse, results will be reached through the needles. To disperse means one must support the inner being to allow a departure. Consequently, yang receives the needling and noxious qi flows out. Place and lead the needle, communicate in harmony with the inner being, and the blood will not scatter and the qi will not exit. To tonify means to follow, to assist, to agitate. Move the needle gently as if going or stopping, like a mosquito or gadfly bite. Detain the needle as if remaining or wandering. Remove the needle and withdraw fast, like the arrow leaves the bowstring. Command the left hand to follow the right. This will cause the qi to stop. The outer door will be blocked and the center qi will be solidified. One must not detain the blood. It should be eliminated quickly.

"This is the manipulation and the way of the needles. Firmness is precious. The primary fingers make a vertical insertion; do not needle to the left or right. The spirit seems to be at the tip of the needle. Focus awareness on the patient. Investigate the blood pulses and the needle will not be dangerous. When inserting the needle, it is necessary to harmonize the yang and control both the yin and the yang. The spirit will follow. Do not go away. Understand the existence and the ridding of disease. The blood pulses are widely distributed at the *shu* points.[5] They are clear to see and strong to touch.

"Each of the nine needles has a name and a distinct shape. The first is called the chisel needle. Its length is one *cun* six *fen*.[6] The second is called the round needle. Its length is one *cun* six *fen*. The third is called the spoon needle. Its length is three and one-half *cun*. The fourth is called the lance needle. Its length is one *cun* and six *fen*. The fifth is called the sword needle. Its length is four *cun* and its width is two and one-half *fen*. The sixth is called the round and sharp needle. Its length is one *cun* six *fen*. The seventh is called the hair fine needle. Its length is three *cun* six *fen*. The eighth is called the long needle. Its length is seven *cun*. The ninth is called the big needle. Its length is four *cun*.

"The chisel needle has a big head with a sharp tip. It may be used to disperse the yang qi. The round needle has the shape of an egg. It is used for rubbing and massage, to divide and to separate so as not to injure the muscles and flesh. It divides and disperses the qi. The spoon needle has a point which is as sharp as a grain of millet. It controls the channels by touch, not by penetration, so as to bring about the qi. The lance needle has three cutting edges and may be used to affect chronic illnesses. The sword needle tip is like a sword. It may be used to press out large pustules. The round and sharp needle is as large as a tuft of hair.[7] It is both round and sharp. The center of its body is a bit larger. Its use is to seize the abrupt, cruel qi. The hair-fine needle has a tip like a mosquito or a gadfly's beak. It can be inserted slowly and quietly and detained for a long time to nourish true qi. It may be used also to reach the sickness of painful rheumatism. The long needle has a lance-like edge and a thin body so that it may be used to reach distant paralysis and deep rheumatism. The big needle is tipped like a stick and its point is slightly round. It may be used to disperse water at the moving gates.[8] These are the nine needles.

"Qi is located in the channels. The evil qi is located at the top. The muddy qi is located at the middle. The clear qi is located at the bottom. The needle must sink into the channels in order to let the evil qi out. Needle the middle channels in order to let the muddy qi out. Needle too deeply, and the evil qi will reverse and sink and disease will increase. Thus it is said the skin, the flesh, the muscles, and the channels have their own proper dwelling. So, for diseases, each has that needle which is suitable. Each needle is a different shape. Each is indicated by the needle which is suitable. Do not tonify the solid, nor disperse the hollow. To injure the insufficient qi and augment the surplus is called to aggravate disease. The disease will worsen. In diseases of extreme fullness, needling five channels can cause death. Needling three channels can cause weakness. To seize the yin excessively can cause death; to seize the yang excessively can cause insanity. These are the injuries of acupuncture.

"In acupuncture, when the qi is reached, do not ask the measure, but needle until the qi is reached. Once reached, do not repeat. In acupuncture each needle has its function. Each has its distinct shape. Each has that which it governs. These make the methods of acupuncture. Only when the qi is reached, will acupuncture be effective. This effect, it is said, is as if the winds blow away the clouds and clear the azure sky. These all are the Dao of acupuncture."

Huang Di said, "I wish to hear about the qi channels from five viscera and the six bowels."

Qi Bo replied, "The five viscera have five *shu* acupuncture points each. Five times five is twenty-five points. The six bowels have six *shu* acupuncture points each. Six times six is thirty-six points. The major channels are twelve. The *luo* channels are fifteen. A total of twenty-seven qi channels ascend and descend. Those points of exit make the *jing* well points. Those in which there is a flow make the *ying* spring points. Those in which there is a large flow are the *shu* stream points. Those in which there is flow make the *jing* river points.[9] Those in which there is entrance in relation to other channels make the *he* confluence or sea points. The flow of the twenty-seven energies all are found in the positions of the five *shu* acupuncture points.

"The sections or junctions of the body consist of 365 meetings or acupuncture points. With a knowledge of its importance, each word can have a result. Without knowing its importance, we thoroughly scatter the flow. Those which are called sections or acupuncture points refer to the place where the spirit qi and its flowing movement, out and in, is unhampered by skin, flesh, muscle, or bone.[10]

"Look at the patient's color. Observe the eyes. Know how the qi disperses and returns. Each has its own form. Listen to the patient's movement or stillness. Know his imbalance and his balance. The right hand is used to hold and push the needle while the left hand assists and controls. When the qi is reached, then withdraw.

"All can be governed or controlled by acupuncture. One must begin by examining the pulses. Inspect the qi to see if it is heavy or easy. Then decide what will determine a cure. If the five viscera's qi is already exhausted internally, and a needle is used mistakenly to solidify the external, this is called 'to exacerbate exhaustion'. To exacerbate exhaustion will result in death. It is a quiet death. A cure was abruptly opposed by the qi being treated by the practitioner at the armpit and breast. If the five viscera are already exhausted from the outside, and acupuncture is used contrary to solidifying the insides, this is called 'to rebel and exhaust'. To 'rebel and exhaust' must cause death. This death is fierce. A cure was opposed by mistakenly treating the four limbs.

"In acupuncture, needling the injured center of the body and not withdrawing properly will drain the essence. Needling the injured center and withdrawing the needle immediately will block the qi. When the essence is drained, the disease will increase greatly, and furthermore, will weaken the patient. Blocked qi will cause inflammation and purulence.

"The five viscera have resonances with the six bowels. The six bowels have twelve source points. The twelve source points come out near the four gates.[11] The four gates control the cure of the five viscera. When the five viscera are diseased, seize the exact points of the twelve sources. From these twelve sources, the five viscera have that which can endow the three hundred sixty-five sections with qi and flavor.[12] When the five viscera are diseased, there must be a corresponding manifestation in the twelve sources, and particularly with the source point which has the manifestation of the disease. Understand clearly the source points. Examine their correspondences and know the illnesses of the five viscera.

"In the middle of the yang is the Minor Yin, the lungs. Its source point comes out in Great Abyss. The Great Abyss is bilateral. In the middle of the yang is the Major Yang, the heart. Its source point comes out in Great Mound. The Great Mound is bilateral. In the middle of the yin is the Minor Yang, the liver, while its source point comes out in Major Pivot. The Major Pivot is bilateral. In the middle of yin is the extreme yin, the spleen. Its source point comes out in Pure White. Pure White is bilateral. In the middle of yin is the Major Yin, the kidneys. Its source point comes out in Major Stream. Major Stream is bilateral.

"In the region below the heart is a source point. It comes out at the Dove Tail. Dove Tail occurs on the middle of the body and is singular. The vitals have a source point which comes out in Throat of the Umbilicus. Throat of the Umbilicus point is singular. All of the twelve source points can control the cure of the five viscera and six bowels when they have disease. For abdominal flatulence, grasp the three yang channels. For diarrhea from dyspepsia, grasp the three yin channels.

"When man's five viscera are diseased, they might be compared to conditions of thorns, stains, knots, or obstructions. Thorns, although embedded for a long time, still can be pulled out. Stains, although filthy for a long time, still can be washed away. Knots, although tied for a long time, still can be untied. Obstructions, although blocked for a long time, still can be opened up. Some people say chronic disease cannot be cured. This is speaking incorrectly. The skillful acupuncturist can take hold of the disease in the same way he pulls out thorns, washes out stains, unties knots, or breaches obstructions. Disease, although chronic, still can be ended. Those who say diseases are incurable have not mastered the technique of acupuncture.

"Needle all fevers like one using a hand to touch boiling water. Needle cold wasted diseases like a man who has no desire to move. When the yin part of body has yang diseases, grasp that point under the mound by three distances, Three Distances. The correct primary movement is to thwart the danger so that the qi will descend and stop.

If not descending, repeat and begin again. For diseases in the upper body and internal viscera, needle Yin Mound Spring. For diseases in the upper body and external bowels, needle Yang Mound Spring."

Notes

1. When refering to diseases, a "guest" has usually been thought of as an invader, however ancient rules of conduct may give us a different meaning. A guest must be honored and shown respect. The host, if timorous or rude, could find himself harboring an unruly and unwanted guest instead of a mindful and respectful one. I am reminded of cold viruses: when the host is strong, the guest is quiet, when the host is weak, the guest becomes the master.

2. The moving power is qi. Qi is the energy of the universe. It comes in many forms and shapes in nature and in the human body. The Chinese character for qi means "energy" or "essence". The picture shows air with a grain of rice within it, thus a moving force which contains an essence.

3. This first enunciation of the acupuncture point, "at the center of this space," describes its geometry, a space, which is later defined as a hole, a depression or a communications node. This concept of a nonmaterial geometric void may be likened to the Daoist idea of *wu wei*, which does nothing but accomplishes everything: *"Wu wei er wu bu wei"*.

4. All acts and things including qi move according to rhythms which may be understood as cycles of time.

5. *Shu* is used in two different contexts: as a general name and as a specific one, stream point.

6. One *cun* is defined as one body inch. It is equal in length to the width of the thumb at the level of the cuticle. One *fen* is one-tenth of one *cun*.

7. "A tuft of hair" refers to the shape of a Chinese writing brush made of hair.

8. "Water at the moving gates" in modern terms would be edema at the joints.

9. The sound of the word *jing* is two different words in Chinese: one means well, another means river.

10. I believe this is an ancient theory which describes an electromagnetic field through and around the body.

11. The wrists and the ankles.

12. "Flavor" is the essence of food and drink. In the notation of the Wu Xing, the Five Dynamic Actions, each organ is matched with a resonant flavor or taste: Liver, sour; Heart, bitter; Spleen, sweet; Lungs, pungent; Kidneys, salty. See appendix A for a discussion of the Wu Xing.

2. THE ROOTS OF THE ACUPUNCTURE POINTS
"The Laws of Earth"

Huang Di asked Qi Bo, saying, "The way of acupuncture must penetrate the twelve major channels and that which is at their ends and beginnings, the collateral channels and how they separate and dwell; where the five acupuncture points are detained and where the six hollow organs make their juncture; the four seasons and that which goes out and goes in; the five viscera, how they flow in their dwellings, the width and length of their limits; the shallowness or depth in the body, and where they reach high and low. I would like to hear an explanation of these subjects."

Qi Bo said, "If you please, it is as follows: The lung comes out at Minor Shang. Minor Shang is on the inner tip and margin of the thumb. This is the well and wood point. It flows to Fish Border. The Fish Border point is on the Fish at the base of the thumb. This is the spring point. It continues to Major Abyss. The Major Abyss point is one *cun* behind the Fish in the center of a depression. This is the stream point. It moves to Channel Ditch. The Channel Ditch point is centered on the Inch Mouth, the arterial pulse. This moves, does not stay, so it makes the river point. It enters into Cubit Marsh. The Cubit Marsh point is in the middle of the elbow, where there is a moving pulse, and is the confluence or sea point. These are on the Arm Major Yin Channel.

"The heart comes out at Middle Capillary. The Middle Capillary point is at the tip of the middle finger. This is the well and wood point. It glides to Labor's Palace. The Labor's Palace point is in the center of the palm, in the middle between the base of the middle finger and the innermost crease of the wrist. This is the spring point. It goes to Great Mound beyond the palm, on and under the crease of the wrist, and between the two bones. This is the stream point. It moves to Messenger Go Between. The Messenger Go Between point's path is between two tendons, three *cun* in the middle of the arm, above the crease of the wrist. When there is a trespass in the heart, it is reached at this point. When there is no trespass, it is stopped at this point. This is the river point, entering into Crooked Marsh. The Crooked Marsh point is on the inner side of the elbow and in the center underneath a depression. Bend the elbow to obtain it. This is the confluence or sea point. These are on the Arm Minor Yin.

"The liver appears out at Big Stump. The Big Stump point is at the tip of the big toe. Its center is three hairs away from the corner of the nail. This is the well and wood point. It flows to Walking In Between.

Walking In Between is on the crack between the big toe and the foot. This is the spring point, going forward to Major Pivot. The Major Pivot point is two *cun* above Walking In Between in the middle of a depression. This is a stream point, moving to Middle Seal. The Middle Seal point is towards the front of the inner anklebone by one and one-half *cun*, in the middle of a depression. Sending in counterflow with the needle causes stasis. Sending in harmony causes draining. Bend the foot to obtain the point. This is the river point. It enters into Bending Spring. The Bending Spring point is below the thigh bone and on top of a large tendon. Bend the knee to obtain the point. This is the confluence or sea point. These are on the Leg Shrinking Yin.

"The spleen appears at Hidden White. The Hidden White point is at the top of the medial side of the big toe. This is the well and wood point. It flows to Great Capital. The Great Capital point is behind the joint at the base of the big toe, centered in a depression. This is the spring point. It goes toward and into Pure White. The Pure White point is below the flexible metatarsal bone. This is the stream point. It moves to Shang Mound. The Shang Mound point is in the middle of a depression below the inner anklebone. This is the river point. It enters into Yin Mound Spring. The Yin Mound Spring point is in the middle of a depression below the Support Bone (tibia) of the leg. Stretch the leg to obtain the point. This is the confluence or sea point. These are on the Leg Major Yin.

"The kidney appears in Gushing Spring. The Gushing Spring point is at the center of the sole of the foot. This is the well and wood point. It flows to Blazing Valley. The Blazing Valley point is below the blazing or navicular bone. This is the spring point. It goes forward toward Major Stream. The Major Stream point is in the middle of a depression behind the inner anklebone and above the bone of the heel. This is the river point. It moves into Returning Stream. The Returning Stream point is two *cun* above the inner anklebone, where the pulse moves without stopping. This is the river point. It enters into Yin Valley. The Yin Valley point is behind the tibia, below the great tendon (sartorius), and above the small tendons (semitendinosus and semimembranosus). A pulse responds to pressure by hand. Bend the knee to obtain it. This is the confluence or sea point. These are on the Leg Minor Yin Channel.

"The bladder appears at the Extremity of Yin. The Extremity of Yin point is at the tip of the little toe. This is the well and metal point. It flows into Penetrating Valley. The Penetrating Valley point is to the front of the joint at the base of the little toe on the lateral side. This is the spring point. It goes forward to Bound Bone. The Bound Bone point is in the middle of a depression behind the joint at the base of the little toe. This is the stream point. It continues to Level Bone. The Level Bone point is at the lateral side of the foot below a large bone (fifth metatarsal). This is the source point. It moves into Kun Lun Mountain. The Kun Lun Mountain point is located behind the external anklebone and above the bone of the heel. This is the river point. It enters into Yielding Middle. The Yielding Middle point is in the center, on the crease at the back of the knee. This is the confluence or sea point. Bend the knee to grasp it. These are on the Leg Major Yang.

"The gallbladder comes out of Cavity of Yin. The Cavity of Yin point is at the top of the fourth toe. This is the well and metal point. It flows to Narrow Stream. The Narrow Stream point is on the crack between the little and fourth toes. This is the spring point. It goes forward to Descending Tears. The Descending Tears point is in the middle of a depression above the crack by one and one-half *cun*. This is the stream point. It goes to Mound Dwellings. The Mound Dwellings point is in the middle of a depression to the front of and below the external anklebone. This is the source point. It moves to Yang Support. The Yang Support point is above the external anklebone in front of the Support Bone and the tip of the end bone. This is the river point. It enters into Yang Mound Spring. The Yang Mound Spring point is located at the lateral surface of the knee in the middle of a depression. This is the confluence or sea point. Stretch the knee to locate it. These are on the Leg Minor Yang.

"The stomach comes out at Tip Exchange. The Tip Exchange point is at the tip of the second toe. This is the well and metal point. It flows to Inner Court. The Inner Court point is on the lateral side of the second toe in the web with the third toe. This is the spring point. It goes forward to Sinking Valley. The Sinking Valley point is in the middle of a depression two *cun* above the junction between the second and middle toes. This is the stream point. It goes to Rushing Yang. The Rushing Yang is in the center of a depression five *cun* up from the foot's instep. This is the source point. Bend the foot to obtain it. It moves into Released Stream. The Released Stream point is in the middle of a depression one and one-half *cun* above Rushing Yang. This is the river point. It enters Lower Mound. The Lower Mound point is three *cun* below the knee on the lateral side of the tibia. This point is also called Three Distances and is the confluence or sea point. Turn back, and below Three Distances by three *cun* is Great Hollow Upper Passage. Turn back, and below Upper Passage by three *cun* is Great

Hollow Lower Passage. The large intestine is subordinate to the upper, the small intestine is subordinate to the lower. The Leg Bright Yang, the large intestine, and small intestine all are subordinate to the stomach, which is the Leg Bright Yang.

"The Triple Heater rises and joins with the Arm Major Yang.[1] It comes out in Capillary Gate. The Capillary Gate point is at the tip of the fourth finger. This is the well and metal point. It flows into Fluid Door. The Fluid Door point is in the depression between the fourth finger and little finger and is the spring point. It goes to Middle Islet. The Middle Islet point is in the middle of a depression beyond the base and joint, and is the stream point. It goes forward to Yang Pond. The Yang Pond point is above the wrist in the middle of a depression, and is the source point. It moves to Branch Ditch. The Branch Ditch point is three *cun* above the wrist in the middle of a depression between two bones, and is the river point. It enters into Celestial Well. The Celestial Well point is in the middle of a depression above a big bone on the lateral side of the elbow. This is the confluence or sea point. Bend the elbow to locate it. The lower heater[2] appears at a point located to the front of the big toe on the foot. Behind the Gallbladder Channel of the Minor Yang, it comes out in the middle crease of the knee on the lateral side, and is named Yielding Yang. This is on the Major Yang Channel. The Arm Minor Yang Channel, the Triple Heater, the Leg Minor Yang and Major Yin are those commanded. The Major Yang continues five *cun* above the anklebone, separates and enters and links with the bladder coming out in Yielding Yang, where it is joined with the primary Major Yang, enters the *luo* path of the bladder, and is tied to the lower heater. Solidity means a retention of urine. For incontinence of urine, the rule is to tonify. For a retention of urine, the rule is to disperse.

"The Small Intestine Channel of the Arm Major Yang arises and resonates with the Major Yang. It comes out in Little Marsh. The Little Marsh point is at the tip of the little finger. This is the well and metal point. It flows to Front Valley. The Front Valley point is located in the middle of a depression on the lateral side of the hand in front of the base joint of the little finger. This is the spring point. It goes forward to Back Stream. The Back Stream point is located on the lateral side of the hand in back of the base joint of the little finger and is the stream point. It passes into Wrist Bone. The Wrist Bone point is located on the lateral side of the hand to the front of the wrist bone, and is the source point. It moves to Yang Valley. The Yang Valley point is located in the middle of a depression below the Sharp Bone (head of the ulna). This is the river point. It enters into Small Sea.

The Small Sea point is located on the medial side of the elbow, to the outside of the large bone, one-half *cun* away from the tip in the middle of a depression. Extend the arm to obtain it. This is the confluence or sea point. These are on the Arm Major Yang.

"The large intestine rises and joins the Arm Bright Yang. It comes out in Shang Yang. The Shang Yang point is at the tip of the forefinger and is the well and metal point. It flows to Second Interval, which is to the front of the joint at the base of the finger. This is the spring point. It goes forward to Third Interval, which is behind the joint at the base of the finger. This is the stream point. It passes to Joining Valleys. The Joining Valleys point is between the thumb and the bone which makes a fork with it. This is the source point. It moves to Yang Stream. The Yang Stream point is located in the middle of a depression between two tendons, and is the river point. It enters into Crooked Pond, which is in the middle of a depression located near the arm bone on the lateral side of the elbow. Bend the arm to find it. This is the confluence or sea point. These are on the Arm Bright Yang.

"From this it may be said that the acupuncture points of the five viscera and six bowels are grouped five times five, making twenty-five points, and six times six, making thirty-six points. The six bowels all come out in the three Yang channels of the legs and connect above in the arm.

"In the middle of the body between the Broken Dish (supraclavicular fossae), is the Conception Vessel. This point is called Celestial Chimney. On the first line following the sides of the Conception Vessel are beating pulses (carotid pulses) on the Leg Bright Yang at points called Man's Receptor. The second line from the channel of the Conception Vessel is the Arm Bright Yang at points called Supporting Chimney. The third line from the channel is the Arm Major Yang with points called Celestial Window. The fourth line from the channel is the Arm Minor Yang at points called Celestial Shutters. The sixth line from the channel is the Leg Major Yang at points called Celestial Pillar. The seventh line from the channel is on the Governing Vessel Channel right through the middle of the neck. The point is called Wind Mansion. In the fossa of the armpit is a beating pulse on the Arm Major Yin. These points are called Celestial Mansion. Below the armpit by three *cun* is the Arm Pericardium Channel. These points are called Celestial Pool.

"When Upper Gate is needled, the patient's mouth should be open, not closed. When Lower Gate is needled, the mouth should be closed, not open. When Calf's Nose is needled, the knee should be bent, not extended. When the two gates, Inner Gate or Outer Gate are needled, the arm should be extended, not bent.

"On the Leg Bright Yang on the sides of the throat are beating pulses. The acupuncture points are located in the center of the breasts. On the Arm Bright Yang there are acupuncture points that are lateral to these. One is located at a place which is nearly one ·cun from the angle of the jaw. The Arm Major Yang has a point just at the angle of the jaw. The Leg Minor Yang has a point located below the ear and behind the angle of the jaw. The Arm Minor Yang comes out behind the ear and above the Final Bone (mastoid process). The Leg Major Yang has a point on the center of a great tendon (splenius capitis) on the posterior hairline and both sides of the nape of the neck.

"On the yin side of the elbow is a beating pulse. Located in this region is Five Distances, a forbidden point for needling because it is adverse to the five *shu* acupuncture points.

"The lungs are coupled with the large intestine, the bowel which is the path for transport. The heart is coupled with the small intestine, the bowel which receives abundance. The liver is coupled with the gallbladder, the bowel of the central essences. The spleen is coupled with the stomach, the bowel of five grains. The kidneys are coupled with the bladder, the bowel for ferrying liquids. The Minor Yang Triple Heater follows the kidneys, which rise and link to the lungs, so that it commands both organs. The Triple Heater is the bowel of the central ditch, the path through which water runs and comes out, and is correlative to the bladder. The Triple Heater is unique among the bowels.[3] These are the six bowels and those viscera with which they are coupled.

"In springtime, treat using the *luo* channels and the spring *shu* points on the great channels in the divisions of the flesh in its openings. In extremes, use a deep insertion. In moderate cases, use a shallow insertion. In summer, treat with the stream *shu* points and the tiny collateral channels on the top surface of the muscles, flesh, and skin. In autumn, treat with the confluence or sea *shu* points and all those of the springtime rules. In winter, treat with the well *shu* points or the stream *shu* points. The object is to needle deeply and detain. This is the order of the four seasons and where the qi dwells, as well as the residences of disease and that which is appropriate for each organ. Concerning cramps, to treat when the patient is standing can cause compliance immediately. For muscular flaccidity and coldness, needling when the patient is stretched out can command sharp benefit immediately."

13

Notes

1. The Triple Heater is an artificial construct devised by the ancients to incorporate respiration, digestion, and elimination as a triple functioning unit. It was and is intended to be an analog to the metabolic system. Much later in Chinese medical literature, in the Ming Dynasty, theories were advanced to link this construct, the Triple Heater, to the fatty tissue around the kidneys - that is, the adrenals.

2. The lower heater in this case refers to the bowels.

3. The Triple Heater is unique among the bowels because it has no material structure.

3. AN EXPLANATION OF THE MINUTE NEEDLES
"The Laws of Man"

"In this discussion of the use of needles, it is easy to make statements. The words themselves are easy, but they are difficult to penetrate and difficult to apply to man. The unskilled physician grasps only the form when he uses the techniques of acupuncture. The superior physician understands the spirit. His understanding of man includes both the blood and qi, whether there is an excess or deficiency, whether he should tonify or disperse. The spirit and the guest, the primary and the evil, all meet. The spirit is the primary qi, the guest is the evil qi. Located at the door means that the evil qi pursues the primary qi at those places where it comes out and enters. Don't just stare at disease. Begin by knowing the evil and the primary qi and which channels are diseased. For illness, know its origins. First know which channels are diseased, then treat them at those locations.

"Acupuncture and needling depend on precise timing, slow or fast are the methods. The unskilled physician only guards the gates. He knows the four limbs, but does not understand the goings and comings of blood and qi. The superior physician knows the subtleties. He understands how to handle qi, how the movements of the subtle energies are never separate from the qi's center space. He knows whether the qi is hollow or solid, whether the needling should be slow or fast. In the center space are the subtle energies which are clear, quiet and minute. The needling is effective when it obtains the qi. Think closely about covering the qi without loss. When the qi is coming, do not collide with it. When the qi is full, do not tonify. When the qi is going, do not pursue it. When the qi is hollow, do not drain. The saying that needling is hung by a hair means that the qi is easily lost. The analogy of drawing the bow but failing to send the arrow to the target means that one does not understand the theory of tonification and dispersion, or the exhaustion of blood and qi, or the arrest of the noxious qi. To know the qi and how and when to treat it, one must know its comings and goings, its flow and counterflow, as well as its fullness or hollowness. The importance of cycles must be understood in the timing of obtaining qi. These doors are closed to the unskilled physician. Ignorance and darkness will not understand the qi's subtle secrets. Wonderful is one who has the unique techniques and who thoroughly understands the theory of the needle. To go is a counterflow, and means the qi is hollow and small. To diminish means a counterflow. To come is a smooth direct flow, and means the shape of the qi is balanced. To be balanced

15

is to be in the flow. To intelligently know counterflow and smooth flow means the primary acupuncture actions are without question, and requires the knowledge of therapy and location. To meet and to seize means to drain and disperse. To pursue and relieve means to augment and tonify.

"So when it is said that hollowness should be solidified, it means the opening of qi is hollow, and should be tonified at that point. Overflowing should be drained, which means the qi opening is full and should be dispersed at that point. When it is stagnant and spoiled, it should be removed, which means to drain from the blood channels. Evil to be overcome must be weakened, which means that when all the channels are overfull, they should be drained and dispersed of evil. Slow and quick causes a solidification, which means a slow insertion and a fast withdrawal. Quick and slow causes a hollowness which means a fast insertion and a slow withdrawal.[1] It is like saying solidity and hollowness are to be or not to be, meaning solidity is to have qi and hollowness is not to have qi. Examine 'pre' and 'post,' to see what is lost and what remains, whether the qi is hollow or solid. To know when to tonify or to disperse, and in which order, examine the patient's qi to see if it has lessened or if it still remains. So it is that hollow and solid is like gaining and losing. This means that to tonify causes a full heat, as if gaining, while to disperse causes a timid heat, as if losing.

"Because qi is in the channels, when evil qi is at the upper part of man, it is said that the evil qi attacks the highest point (the head), therefore the saying that evil qi is located on top. Because muddy qi is in the middle part of man, it is said that all the water and valley qi enter the stomach.[2] Clear qi arises and goes forward to the lungs; muddy qi flows into the intestines and stomach. It is said that when cold and heat are not agreeable, drink and food are not apportioned, and disease begins in the intestines and stomach. Therefore the saying that muddy qi resides in the middle. The clear qi resides below, so it is said that when the clear damp earth qi attacks man, it must begin in the feet. Therefore the saying that clear qi resides below.

"To needle the points on the channels will expel the evil qi when one treats the top. To needle the middle channels will cause the muddy qi to come out when treating the confluence or sea points of the Bright Yang.

"To needle too deeply will cause the evil qi to return to depth, which means that for shallow floating diseases, do not needle deeply. Deep insertion will allow the evil qi to follow and enter, which is the reason for saying it will return to depth. The skin, flesh, muscles and channels each have their respective dwellings, thus each of the major channels has that which it controls.

"Treating all five channels can cause death. When disease is in the center and qi is insufficient, death can be caused by using the needles in excess to drain all the yin channels. In treating three yang channels, to drain the three yang's qi excessively may allow only a tentative restoration of the patient's health. To snatch the yin can cause death, which means that to needle Five Distances near the elbow five times in error can cause death. To snatch the yang can cause madness is an axiom.

"Look at the colors, examine the eyes to know what is scattered or returned. Regard the body as a unity. Listen to what moves or is still. This means the superior physician knows the mutual correspondences of the five colors by sight as well as knowing the harmonies of the cubit or inch pulses: small, large, slow, hurried, slippery, and rough, and what relations they have to disease.[3] They know the evil and primary qi, the theory of hollow evil, and the primary directional evils of the wind.

"The right hand controls and pushes while the left hand supports and serves during insertion and withdrawal of the needle. When the qi is reached, then to leave means to tonify or to disperse the qi and harmonize before stopping. To harmonize qi at the end and the beginning is a unity. One must support this with the heart and mind.[4] The sections and junctions form three hundred sixty-five meetings. The major channels seep and pour into all the points.

"When the qi of the five viscera is exhausted internally, the internal qi at the Pulse Mouth cannot be reached. Then contrariwise, if the disease is treated as an external disease by sea points on the yang channels, deep needling will insert yang qi. This yang qi will then reach the exhausted interior. This severe exhaustion can cause death. This death is without breath or movement and is caused by stillness. When the qi of the five viscera is exhausted externally, the external qi at the Pulse Mouth cannot be reached. Then contrariwise, if the treatment uses the acupuncture points at the four extremities and detains the needle in accord with the effects of yin qi, the yin qi will reach to cause the yang qi to reverse and to enter. Entering for the yang qi is a counterflow. This rebellious counterflow can cause death. This death where the yin qi is in excess is caused by roughness.

"Use that which is in accord with an examination of the eyes means the five viscera have messages in the five colors and their subsequent brightness. The following brightness causes tones and changes in tones. Tones and tone changes are caused, it is said, by the tones and the colors being balanced or as they begin to differ."

Notes

1. "Slow and quick," "Quick and slow" describe needling techniques.

2. Valley qi is the qi from foodstuffs, especially from the eating of grains.

3. Cubit or inch pulses are pulses which are found on the wrists.

4. "One must support this with the heart and mind" means the practitioner must concentrate and help the patient with knowledge and understanding.

4. THE NOXIOUS QI'S DISEASE FORMS
IN THE VISCERA AND BOWELS

Huang Di asked of Qi Bo, saying, "What is the noxious qi which moves and attacks man?"

Qi Bo replied, "The noxious qi moves and hits at the upper part of man."

Huang Di asked, "High and low has what limits?"

Qi Bo replied, "The upper half of the body is hit by noxious qi, the lower half of the body is hit by humid qi, whence the saying that noxious qi moves and hits man without having a constant pattern. Hits in the yin will cause a flow into the bowels, hits in the yang will cause a flow into the channels."

Huang Di said, "Yin and yang are different names for the same species. In the upper and lower body they meet mutually. The major channels are mutually connected like a circle without an end. The noxious qi which moves and attacks man hits either in the yin or hits in the yang, upper or lower, left or right, without a constant pattern. What causes that?"

Qi Bo replied, "All the yang channels assemble in the face. The noxious qi attacks man in an area stricken with hollowness, or at a time when he is fresh from exertion, or when there is sweating, or at meal times, or when the pores are open between skin and flesh.[1] The noxious qi attacks the face, and will flow downward in the Stomach Channel of the Bright Yang. Hits in the neck will flow downward in the Bladder Channel of the Major Yang. Hits in the middle of the cheek result in a downward flow in the Gallbladder Channel of the Minor Yang. If the noxious qi hits in the breast, the back, and both flanks, it will also hit their channels."

Huang Di said, "When noxious qi attacks the yin, what is it?"

Qi Bo replied, "Hits in the yin usually begin in arms and legs. The underside of man's skin is thin there, and his flesh is moist and marshy. This results in susceptibility to the wind, and only injures the yin."

Huang Di asked, "Does this cause injury to the viscera?"

Qi Bo replied, "When the body is hit by the wind, the viscera are not necessarily affected. The noxious qi entering the yin channels causes the viscera's qi to solidify. The noxious qi enters, but is unable to stay; therefore, it returns to the bowels. The noxious qi hits the yang and causes a flow into the channels. It hits the yin and causes a flow into the bowels."

Huang Di said, "The noxious qi which attacks man's viscera, what is it?"

Qi Bo said, "Worry and fear can strain the heart. Chilling the body and cold drinks can injure the lungs. These two coldnesses have a combined effect: the interior and the exterior are both injured. This causes the qi to move in a counterflow and ascend with coughs and panting. A fall on land or water injures the blood, which may clot in the body. Also, when there is great anger, the qi ascends and does not descend. It accumulates below the flanks, causing injury to the liver. When one is struck or hit, or has sexual intercourse while drunk, or is exposed to wind while sweating, it can injure the spleen. When one uses effort in lifting heavy objects, or has unlimited sexual intercourse, or bathes while sweating, it can injure the kidneys."

Huang Di said, "When the five viscera are hit by the wind, what is it like?"

Qi Bo said, "The yin and the yang are mutually affected. The noxious qi then must go forward."

Huang Di said, "Well done! I am pleased."

Huang Di asked Qi Bo, saying, "The head and face and the shape of the body follow the bones and connect with the muscles as the blood joins and the qi unites. When the weather is cold and causes the earth to be covered with hoarfrost and ice, this sudden coldness reaches hands and feet with numbness, yet there is heat in the face, even though it is not covered. Why?"

Qi Bo replied, "There are twelve major channels, and three hundred sixty-five pathways.[2] The body's blood and qi both ascend into the face and travel to its hollows and holes. Its clear yang qi ascends and travels into the eye and causes the pupil to see. Another qi travels to the ear and makes hearing. Ancestral qi ascends into the nose and allows smelling. A turbid muddy qi comes out from the stomach and travels to the lips and tongue to sense the flavors. The body fluids' qi ascends and warms the face; moreover, the facial skin is thick, so that even though the weather is extremely cold, the face cannot be injured."

Huang Di said, "The noxious qi which attacks man, what is the form of the disease?"

Qi Bo said, "Hollow noxious qi hits the body with a shivering and change of form. When the orthodox noxious qi attacks man, it is minor, first seen in the color of the complexion, and not detectable in the body. It is not like a case of to be or not to be, or like not knowing whether it goes or stays. There is form and yet no form. The essentials are not detectable."

Huang Di said, "Well done."

Huang Di asked Qi Bo, saying, "I have heard that to see the patient's color is to know his illness. It is called a gift of vision. Taking the patient's pulse is to know his disease. It is called a gift of spirit. Questioning the patient about his disease is to know its location. It is called a gift of technique. I desire to hear how seeing is knowing the disease, how pulse reading is obtaining information of the disease, and how questioning is to understand the disease thoroughly."

Qi Bo replied, "Man's color and pulse are measures and have mutual resonances, like a drumstick and drum. The shape of the sounds are mutually resonating; without attainment, they are mutually lost.

"These relationships are like cause and effect, like the roots of a tree and the leaves which come out on it, for the death of the root causes the withered leaf. Color, pulse, form and flesh cannot be separated. To know one method is to possess technique, to know two methods is to possess spirit, and to know three methods is to possess spirit as well as vision."

Huang Di said, "I wish to hear all about it."

Qi Bo replied, "The color green's pulse is wiry; red's pulse is like a hook; yellow's pulse is intermittent; white's pulse is fine like a hair; black's pulse is like a stone. When seeing a patient's color and not feeling its corresponding pulse but on the contrary, getting a pulse which is destructive to the corresponding pulse can mean death. Getting that pulse which is mutually generating means the illness can be cured."[3]

Huang Di questioned Qi Bo, saying, "Concerning the five viscera, what are the beginning signs, changes, and transformations of disease forms?"

Qi Bo replied, "First, determine the resonances and correspondences between the five colors and five pulses. Their diseases then can be distinguished."

Huang Di said, "How may one distinguish and determine by colors and pulses?"

Qi Bo said, "Conform the pulses, whether they are slow, hurried, small, large, smooth, or rough, to the illness and its changing conditions."

Huang Di said, "To conform to what and how?"

Qi Bo replied, "A hurried pulse means the skin at the elbow is also hurried. A slow pulse means the skin at the elbow is also slow. A small pulse means the skin at the elbow is also thin and slow. A large pulse means the skin at the elbow is also thick and slow. A slippery pulse means the skin at the elbow is also slippery. A rough pulse means the skin at the elbow is also rough.[4]

"There are minor changes and extreme changes in the pulses. The result is that one who excels in the conforming at the elbow does not have to take the pulse at the wrist. One who excels in conforming the pulses does not need to examine the colors. The ability to combine three diagnostic methods signifies a physician of superior skills with a cure rate of nine patients in ten; the ability to use two diagnostic methods signifies a physician of middling skills with a cure rate of seven patients in ten; and the use of one method signifies a physician of lower skills with a cure rate of six patients in ten."

Huang Di said politely, "What are the forms of sickness which relate to the pulse being slow, hurried, small, large, slippery, and rough?"

Qi Bo said, "To your imperial request, I will reply and speak of the five viscera and their changes in disease. The heart pulse extremely hurried goes with madness and convulsions; slightly hurried goes with pains in the heart and strained back, and food does not descend. Extremely slow goes with wild laughter; moderately slow goes with being stiff as a board in the area below the heart and spitting of blood at the time of walking up and down. Extremely large goes with an obstruction of the throat; moderately large goes with cardiac pain syndrome and strained back, and often shedding tears. Extremely small goes with frequent hiccups; moderately small goes with exhaustion. Extremely slippery goes with the condition of thirst; moderately slippery goes with a hernia of the heart involving the navel, with noises in the abdomen. Extremely rough goes with aphasia; moderately rough goes with an overflow of blood, cold limbs, noises in the ear, and madness.

"The lung pulse extremely hurried goes with insanity; moderately hurried goes with the lungs being cold or hot, fatigue, the coughing and spitting of blood, strained loins, back, and chest, like polyps and obstructions of the nose. Extremely slow goes with much sweating; moderately slow goes with paralysis, scrofula, hemiplegia, and continuous sweating in the areas below the head. Extremely large goes with swollen shins; moderately large goes with a numbing of the lungs and strains of the chest and back and with the fear of seeing sunlight. Extremely small goes with diarrhea; moderately small goes with exhaustion. Extremely slippery goes with panting from a blockage of the ascending breath; moderately slippery goes with upper nose and lower rectal bleeding. Extremely rough goes with vomiting blood; moderately rough goes with scrofula which occurs between the neck and the armpits. The lower parts are not able to support the upper parts, which correspond to a febrile state.

"The liver pulse extremely hurried goes with evil speeches; moderately hurried goes with fatty qi energy below the flanks, like an inverted cup.   Extremely slow goes with a condition of vomiting; moderately slow goes with difficult urination or retention of urine. Extremely large goes with an internal ulcer, a condition of vomiting and nosebleed; moderately large goes with dysfunction of the liver with a contraction of the yin, and coughing with abdominal strain.   Extremely small goes with great thirst; moderately small goes with exhaustion. Extremely slippery goes with a hernia; moderately slippery goes with incontinence of urine.   Extremely rough goes with excessive water drinking; moderately rough goes with convulsions, cramps, and tightening of the muscles.

"The spleen pulse extremely hurried goes with convulsions and spasms; moderately hurried goes with fullness of the diaphragm with regurgitation of meals and appearances like saliva in the stools. Extremely slow goes with impotence and weakness; moderately slow goes with muscular weakness from the wind, and uselessness of the limbs; the mind is in a lucid fever as if there is no disease.   Extremely large goes with sudden fainting, as if hit; moderately large goes with hernias and enlargement of the abdomen, with pus and blood in the intestines and stomach, proceeding to the outside.   Extremely small goes with chills and fever; moderately small goes with exhaustion.   Extremely slippery goes with hernias and weakness of the scrotum; moderately slippery goes with parasites, the poison from intestinal ulcerations.   Extremely rough goes with prolapses and ulceration of the colon.   Moderately rough goes with interior ulcerations of the colon with much discharge of pus and blood.

"The kidney pulse extremely hurried goes with bone and mental diseases; moderately hurried goes with a sinking deficiency, called 'the running piglet',[5] stiffness in the feet, retention of urine, and constipation. Extremely slow goes with a bent spinal column; moderately slow goes with diarrhea of undigested food, and food which descends the throat and then is regurgitated.   Extremely large goes with impotence; moderately large goes with stone-like water edema, with swelling beginning at the navel and descending to the abdomen.   If it ascends to the stomach region it is incurable.   Extremely small goes with persistent diarrhea; moderately small goes with exhaustion.   Extremely slippery goes with hernias; moderately slippery goes with weakness of the bones so one cannot stand up.   If one rises one cannot see.   Extremely rough goes with a large ulcer; moderately rough goes with amenorrhea and bleeding piles."

Huang Di said, "Diseases have six metamorphoses. How is acupuncture used for them?"

Qi Bo replied, "For all hurried pulses there is much cold, for slow pulses there is much heat. A large pulse means excess qi and deficient blood; a small pulse means blood and qi are both deficient. A slippery pulse means the yang qi is overflowing with slight heat. A rough pulse means much blood and less qi with slight cold.

"Therefore, needle the hurried pulse deep inside and detain for a long time. Needle the slow pulse shallowly and quickly, withdraw the needle to let out the heat. To needle the large pulse disperse the qi slightly without bleeding. To needle the slippery pulse, insert the needle shallowly and quickly in order to disperse yang qi and dispel heat. To needle the rough pulse one must hit the channels, follow the flow or counterflow of qi, and detain for a long time. It is necessary to massage the channels first. When the needle is withdrawn, quickly press the needle holes to prevent bleeding and harmonize the channels.

"All small pulses mean that the yin and the yang, the physical form, and the dynamic qi are all deficient. Do not use acupuncture, but harmonize instead by using sweet herbs."

Huang Di said, "I hear the qi of the five viscera and six bowels moves through the *ying* spring points and *shu* stream points, then enters and makes a confluence of qi. What commands the path they follow? Entering quietly, how will they be connected and what will they pass by? I would like to hear the reasons."

Qi Bo replied, "The yang channels are separate when entering the inner being, and they correspond to the bowels."

Huang Di said, "The *ying* spring and *shu* stream and *he* confluence points, does each have a personality?"

Qi Bo replied, "The *ying* spring points and *shu* stream points control the exterior; the *jing* river and the *he* confluence points control the inside and the bowels."

Huang Di said, "How can one control the inside and bowels?"

Qi Bo said, "By using the *he* confluence points."

Huang Di said, "The confluence points, does each have a personality?"

Qi Bo replied, "The stomach confluence point is at Three Distances. The large intestine confluence point enters at Great Hollow Upper Passage. The small intestine confluence point is at Great Hollow Lower Passage. The Triple Heater confluence point enters at Yielding Yang. The bladder confluence point enters at the middle of Yielding Middle. The gallbladder confluence enters at Yang Mound Spring."

Huang Di said, "How does one find them?"

Qi Bo replied, "To find Three Distances, lower the instep of the foot and feel the depression. For Great Hollows, raise the foot. For Yielding Yang, bend, then stretch. For Yielding Middle, bend to find it. For Yang Mound Spring, first sit and have the knees erect, then find it below the yang lateral side beneath the Yielding Yang. Find all points on the exterior of the channels with this meritorious procedure."

Huang Di said, "I wish to hear of the diseases of the bowels."

Qi Bo replied, "When the face is feverish, it is a disease of the Leg Bright Yang. When the Fish is showing engorged veins, this is a disease of the Arm Bright Yang. Solid protuberances or hollow depressions above the pulse of both insteps is a disease of the Leg Bright Yang, which is the Stomach Channel. In diseases of the large intestine, there will be sharp pains in the center of the intestines, and the sound of washing. In winter days, a heavy cold leads to diarrhea, pain around the navel, and an inability to stand for long. Because there is a union with the stomach, use the Great Hollow Upper Passage point. In diseases of the stomach, the abdomen swells up and the stomach channels near the heart are painful, and the pain rises to the upper limbs and the two sides of the ribs. There is blockage in the diaphragm and throat; food and drink cannot descend. Use the Three Distances point.

"Diseases of the small intestine cause abdominal pain. Loins and spine are painful, involving the genitals. There are times of distress during the elimination processes. There can be heat or extreme cold in front of the ears, or extreme heat on each shoulder, or there can be heat on the hand between the little and ring fingers, or the pulse sinks. These are its symptoms. For the diseases of the Arm Major Yang, use the Great Hollow Lower Passage point.

"In diseases of the Triple Heater, the abdominal qi is excessive. The abdomen is especially hard, there is difficulty in urination, and distress and anxiety are in abundance, which cause water retention and swellings. The symptoms may be at the Leg Major Yang to the lateral side of the Great Luo. The Great Luo is between the Bladder Channel of the Major Yang and Gallbladder Channel of the Minor Yang.[6] It may also be seen in the pulse. Use the Yielding Yang point.

"In diseases of the bladder, the side of the abdomen is swollen and painful. If massaged with the hand, there is a desire but an inability to urinate. There is heat above the shoulders, a sinking pulse, and heat on the lateral side of the foot and behind the anklebone. If there is a sinking pulse, use the Yielding Middle point.

"For diseases of the gallbladder, there is frequent belching, bitter tastes in the mouth, and a vomiting of stale fluids. The mind is weak and dull, and there is fear of being seized. The middle of the throat is obstructed with numerous spittings. On the Leg Minor Yang, from its root to its end, if the channel is depressed, cauterize. Cold or hot, use the Yang Mound Spring point.

Huang Di said, "What is the Dao of acupuncture?"

Qi Bo replied, "In acupuncture, one must hit the qi holes[7] and not attack the flesh or its sections. In hitting the qi hole, the needling causes the qi to flow into the passages. Attacking the flesh and sections will pain the skin. When tonification or dispersion are used improperly the diseases will be more severe. Hitting the tendons the muscle will slow, the noxious qi will not exit, and this will cause a struggle between the genuine and attacking qi. The attacking qi will then reverse and return to the inner being of man. To use acupuncture improperly will make the smooth flow become counterflow."

Notes

1. Pores between the skin and the flesh, *zhou li*, may have been a technical term which meant not just the normal pores on the skin, but an interactive level in the subdermal layer which was activated by pressure, heat, or needling. These pores, which may have included the acupuncture locus, did not necessarily have the structure of a pore, yet they also served as an opening to the body for qi.

2. The number of named acupuncture points or openings classically was three hundred and sixty-five.

3. The destruction and generation cycles are the foundations of the five element theory. See appendix A, The Five Actions and Shen Ke Cycles.

4. The skin at the elbow and on the forearm on the intersection of medial and lateral surfaces was observed for color and tactile sensation to conform with other diagnostic features.

5. "The running piglet" is movement like a leaping heart.

6. The Great Luo auxillary channel connects the Major Yang and Minor Yang Channels.

7. Qi holes are acupuncture points.

SCROLL TWO
5. ROOTS AND ENDS

Qi Bo said, "Heaven and earth are in mutual resonance. Cold and warm are in mutual movement. Yin and yang are the Dao, where some are less and some are more. The way of yin is even; the way of yang is odd. For things which begin in spring and summer, the yin qi is sparse; the yang qi is plentiful. When yin and yang are not in harmony, one can tonify or disperse. For things which begin in fall and winter, the yang qi is sparse and the yin qi is plentiful. When the yin qi is abundant, and the yang qi is weak, stalks and leaves wither and dry up. As moisture and rain return below to earth, yin and yang move mutually, so one can disperse or tonify.

"There are an extraordinary number of diseases in the separate channels. They cannot be counted without knowing the roots and ends of the five viscera and six bowels. Disease can break open the gates and upset the pivots and travel through the gates and inner doors. Yin and yang would be lost and unable to find their way back. The nine needles' subtleties are found in chapter 9, 'From Beginning to End.' For one who comprehends ends and beginnings, one sentence is enough. For one who does not understand ends and beginnings, the way of the needle is completely cut off.

"The Major Yang's root is at Extremity of Yin, and ends at Destiny's Door. Destiny's Door is the eye, and refers to the bladder point now known as Eyes Bright. The Bright Yang's root is at Tip Exchange. The end is at Great Forehead or Head Border which forms a pincers with the ears. The Minor Yang's root is at Cavity of Yin. Its end is Window Basket. Window Basket is centered in the ear.

"The Major Yang makes the gates. The Bright Yang makes the inner door. The Minor Yang makes the pivots. Breaking the gate will cause a flow of disease to flesh and joints and a cruel disease will begin. Because of this cruel disease, one must treat the Major Yang and see if there is an excess or deficiency. This flow will weaken and emaciate the skin and flesh. Breaking the inner door will result in weakness because the qi is unable to stop and to rest. Thus, for weakness, treat the Bright Yang by seeing if there is an excess or deficiency. Without stop or rest, the genuine qi is delayed and detained while the evil qi takes residence. When the pivot is broken, the bones are shaken, and it is not possible to be balanced on the ground. Thus, when the bones are shaken, treat the Minor Yang by seeing if there is an excess or deficiency. Shaken bones cause the joints to be difficult to bend. Then discuss the bones shaking, the reasons for the shaking, and thoroughly examine that point at its roots.

"The Major Yin's root is at Hidden White. Its end is at Great Granary. The Minor Yin's root is at Gushing Spring. Its end is at Angular Spring. The Shrinking Yin's root is at Big Stump. Its end is at Beautiful Jade, which is connected to the Center of Breathing. The Major Yin makes the gates. The Shrinking Yin makes the inner door. The Minor Yin makes the pivot. So if the gates are broken, the result is that the granaries are without transportation, and the diaphragm leaks. When the diaphragm leaks, treat the Major Yin. See if there is an excess or deficiency. Therefore, when the gates are broken, the qi is insufficient and diseases occur. If the inner doors are broken, the liver qi becomes relaxed and one is easily sad. When the patient is sad, treat Shrinking Yin. See if there is an excess or deficiency. If the pivot is broken, the kidney channel becomes tied up. When there is a tie-up, treat Minor Yin. See if there is an excess or deficiency. A tie-up should always be treated as an insufficiency.

"The Leg Major Yang's root is at Extremity of Yin. It flows into Level Bone, goes forward into Kun Lun Mountain, enters Celestial Pillar and Flying About.

"Leg Minor Yang's root is at Cavity of Yin. It flows into Burial Mound, goes forward into Yang Support, enters Celestial Appearance, and Bright Light.

"The Leg Bright Yang's root is at Tip Exchange. It flows to Rushing Yang, goes forward to Lower Mound, enters Man's Receptor, and Abundant Mound.

"The Arm Major Yang's root is at Little Marsh. It flows to Yang Valley, goes forward to Minor Sea, enters Celestial Window and Branch Regulator.

"The Arm Minor Yang's root is at Capillary Gate. It flows to Yang Pond, goes forward to Branch Ditch, and enters Celestial Shutter and Outer Gate.

"The Arm Bright Yang's root is at Shang Yang. It flows to Joining Valleys, goes forward to Yang Stream, and enters Supporting Chimney and Side Passage.

"This discussion of the twelve channels explains the points for treatment when there is an overflow of energy in these channels.

"Within one day and one night, the nourishing qi circulates fifty times and nourishes the essence of the five viscera.[1] If it does not correspond to this count, it is called the beginning of chaos. It is said that when the nourishing energy circulates fifty times, the five viscera all

28

receive qi. By feeling the pulse at the Pulse Mouth, one can count to see if it is reached. Fifty movements without irregularity in one cycle, the five viscera all receive qi. Forty movements in one cycle, and one viscera is without qi. Thirty movements in one cycle, and two viscera are without qi. Twenty movements in one cycle, and three viscera are without qi. Ten movements in one cycle, and four viscera are without qi. Fewer than ten movements in one cycle, and five viscera are without qi. The individual's short rhythms can be located from beginning to end with the above. So it may be said that when there are fifty movements without fail in one cycle, this is a regular frequency. It is in accord with the time period of the five viscera. The death pulse means it is slow suddenly and then fast suddenly."

Huang Di said, "In the chapter on counterflow and flow in the five human body types (chapter 38), it is said man's bones and articulations are small or large. The flesh is solid or soft. The skin is thick or thin. The blood is clear or muddy. The qi is slippery or rough. The pulse is long or short. The blood is plentiful or sparse. The major channels may be counted. I know about these things. All this covers the common persons and scholars, but how about kings and dukes and the aristocracy, whose food is blood and flesh. Their bodies are weak and soft, their muscles and flesh pliable and weak. Their blood and qi flows are quick, intense, slippery, and sharp. Can similar techniques of acupuncture that are slow or quick, shallow or deep, plentiful or small, be used?"

Qi Bo replied, "Rich foods or millet, legumes and leaves all have their tastes. How can they be the same? When the qi is slippery, withdraw the needle quickly. When the patient's qi is rough, withdraw slowly. When the qi is intense, use a little needle and insert shallowly. When the qi is rough, use a large needle and insert deeply. A deep insertion means a detaining. A shallow insertion means a rapid withdrawal. In accord with their appearance, needle the commoners with a deep insertion and detain the needle. Needle the aristocracy slightly and slowly, since all of their origins of qi are quick, intense, slippery, and sharp."

Huang Di said, "The body's qi, what is meant by flow and counterflow?"

Qi Bo said, "When the body's qi is insufficient, the disease qi is in excess; therefore, the evil is dominant, so quickly drain. When the body's qi is in excess, and the disease qi deficient, quickly tonify. When the body's qi is insufficient and the disease qi is insufficient, both yin and yang qi are insufficient. Do not needle. Needling will cause a more severe insufficiency. When an insufficiency is made more severe, it may cause exhaustion in both yin and yang. The blood and qi will be totally depleted. The five viscera will become vacant and hollow. The tendons, bones, and marrow will wither. This will finish an old person, and even the strong might not return to health. When the body's qi has an excess and the disease qi has an excess, this is spoken of as yin and yang both being in excess. Quickly disperse the evil by harmonizing the hollow and the solid. So it is said, 'When there is an excess, disperse. When there is an insufficiency, tonify.'

"So it is said that when the genuine and evil qi battle with each other, if the acupuncturist does not know flow and counterflow, and tonifies when the qi is overflowing, it will result in yin and yang being excessively full. The intestines and stomach will be full to the brim. The liver and lungs will have internal obstructions. Yin and yang will be confused. If the qi is hollow and it is dispersed, it will result in the major channels becoming vacant and hollow. The blood and qi will wither and exhaust. The intestines and stomach will also be closed and weak. The skin will thin and wrinkle, the hairs and pores will wane and die young. The individual can measure these as chapters of death.

"So it is said, the essentials of using the needle lie in knowing how to harmonize yin and yang. In harmonizing yin and yang, the essence and qi will glow with the joining of the physical body and the qi energy. This will send spirit to the inner storage chambers. Therefore it is said, the superior doctor balances the qi. The middling doctor is confused by the pulse. So it is said, the inferior doctor exhausts the qi and endangers the life. The inferior doctor cannot be too cautious. He must examine the five viscera, the changes and transformations brought about by disease, the five corresponding pulses, whether the major channels are solid or hollow, whether the skin is soft or coarse, then afterward decide on the treatment."

Note

1. The clepsydra, or waterclock, in ancient China was divided into fifty units of time within one circadian cycle. Thus the individual's metabolic cycle should move in resonance to this cycle.

6. LONGEVITY OR PREMATURE DEATH,
TO BE HARD OR SOFT

Huang Di questioned Shao Shi, saying, "I have heard man is born to be hard or to be soft, to be weak or to be strong, to be short or to be tall, to be yin or to be yang. I wish to hear about these patterns."

Shao Shi replied, "In the center of yin there is yin. In the center of yang there is yang.[1] To examine and to understand yin and yang is to have the rules of acupuncture. When the beginning of disease has been located, needling will have a foundation. Understand the source of an illness and to which season it has a mutuality and resonance, how yin and yang are in tune internally with the five viscera and six bowels, and how they are in tune externally with bone, skin, and muscle. Thus, internally there are yin and yang, and externally there are also yin and yang. On the inside the five viscera are yin, the six bowels are yang. On the outside the muscle and bone are yin, the skin is yang. Thus it is said, when disease is located at yin within yin, one must needle the yin channel through the spring and stream *shu* points. When disease is located at yang within yang, one must needle the yang channel at the confluence *shu* point. When disease is located at yin within yang, one must needle the yin channel river *shu* point. When disease is located at yang within yin, one must needle the *luo* channels.

"Thus it is said, when disease is located at the yang, it is called wind. When disease is located at the yin, it is called rheumatism. When yin and yang are both diseased, it is called wind rheumatism. Disease that has form but no pain is of the yang type. Disease that has no form but pain is of the yin type. When disease is without form, but painful, the yang is intact but the yin is injured. Quickly treat and cure the yin, but do not attack the yang. When there is form but no pain, the yin is intact but the yang is injured. Quickly treat and cure the yang, but do not attack the yin. When yin and yang are both disturbed, disease will have form, at other times it will be without form. Additionally, if there is a distress of the heart and mind, it is called yin overcoming yang. This is said to be neither external nor internal, but its form will not be long in appearing."

Huang Di asked Bo Gao, saying, "I have heard that the sequence of disease in the body's qi corresponds to external and internal circumstances.[2] Why?"

Bo Gao replied, "Wind and cold injure the body. Grief, fear, indigestion, and anger injure the qi. The qi injures the viscera, then the viscera are diseased. When cold injures the body, it manifests in the physical body. When the wind injures the muscles and qi channels, it manifests in the muscles and qi channels. This states that the body and qi, or what is external and internal, are in mutual resonance."

Huang Di said, "What is the acupuncture technique for this?"

Bo Gao replied, "For a disease of nine days, three acupuncture treatments. For a disease of a month, ten acupuncture treatments. More or less, far or near, treat in accord with the dimensions of the disease. If there is a chronic rheumatism which does not leave the body, see to the blood channels. Bleed to exhaust the diseased blood."

Huang Di said, "External or internal diseases, why are some difficult and some easy to cure?"

Bo Gao replied, "When the body is first diseased but it has not penetrated to the viscera, the needling should be as half. If the viscera is first diseased and then the body responds, needle double.[3] This is the response to a month's illness as to whether it is easy or difficult."

Huang Di asked Bo Gao, saying, "I have heard the body is slow or quick, the qi is abundant or sparse, the bones are large or small, the flesh is firm or soft, the skin is thick or thin. How does this relate to and establish a long or short life?"

Bo Gao replied, "When the physical body and qi are governed mutually, it results in long life; when not governed mutually it results in premature death. When skin and flesh are mutually fruitful, it results in long life; when not mutually fruitful, it results in premature death. When blood and qi in the channels are balanced to the body, it results in long life; when not balanced to the body, it results in premature death."

Huang Di said, "What is meant by the body being slow or quick?"

Bo Gao replied, "When the body is solid and the skin slow and relaxed, it results in long life. When the body is solid and the skin is quick and tense, it results in early death. When the body is solid and the pulses are solid and large, it will be a smooth life. When the body is solid, and the pulses are small and feeble and the qi sparse, this sparseness can result in a dangerous life. When the body is solid, the cheekbones depressed and the bones small, it can result in a premature death because the bones are small. When the body is solid and the great flesh and major limbs are firm, and there are proper divisions of the firm flesh, there will be long life because of the firm flesh. When the body is solid but the great flesh is not firm, nor divided according to principle, and the flesh is weak, it can result in early death because the flesh is weak. These are the celestial edicts for life which are in accord with the physical archetype, as well as the primary qi, which sees to long life or early death. One must be clear in understanding these physical archetypes and the primary qi in order to use them when examining the patient to decide whether there will be life or death."

Huang Di said, "I have heard that longevity and premature death cannot be measured."

Bo Gao replied, "When the walls and foundations are so low that their height does not reach the level of the ground, then he will not complete thirty years.[4] If there is this base and illness, he will not reach twenty years before death."

Huang Di said, "When the physical form and the qi are relatively equal, what establishes long life or early death?"

Bo Gao relied, "The balanced man, where the qi is superior to the physical body, means longevity. When disease shrivels the flesh and body, the qi is superior to the physical form, it means death; if the body is superior to the qi, it means danger."

Huang Di said, "Acupuncture has three variations, what are they?"

Bo Gao replied, "Needle the nourishing energy, the protective energy and the cold rheumatism detained in the channels".[5]

Huang Di said, "How to make the three variations of needling?"

Bo Gao replied, "Needle the nourishing energy to draw blood. Needle the protective energy to draw qi. Needle cold rheumatism to heat the interior."

Huang Di said, "The diseases of the nourishing energy, protective energy, and cold rheumatism, what are they?"

Bo Gao replied, "When the nourishing energy gives rise to disease, there will be chills and fever, and sparse qi. The blood will fluctuate up and down. When the protective energy gives rise to disease, qi and pain have times when they come and go.[6] There are angry sighs and substantial noises, as wind and cold intrude into the middle of the stomach and intestines. When the cold rheumatism gives rise to disease, it is detained and does not depart. It is a time of pain, and the skin is numb."

Huang Di said, "How does one needle the cold rheumatism to heat the interior?"

Bo Gao replied, "In needling the commoner, use the fire needle. In needling the aristocrat, use herbs to iron things out."

Huang Di said, "What do you mean, 'herbs to iron things out'?"

Bo Gao replied, "Use twenty catties of good wine.[7] One catty of Sichuan pepper, one catty of dried ginger, and one catty of hearts of cinnamon. That is a total of four ingredients. Masticate them and soak them in the wine, then use one catty of silk floss and forty *chi* of white cotton cloth. Add all this to the wine. Cover the vessel and seal with paint, so there is no leakage. Put the wine in the middle of horse manure to heat it up. After five days and five nights, remove the cloth and silk floss and dry them in the sun. When they are dry, repeat the soaking process until the wine is exhausted. Each soaking should take one day and night before the cloth and silk floss are taken out to dry again. When they are dry, use all the dregs, the herbs, and the silk floss, and use the cloth to wrap them. From six or seven *chi* of material, make six or seven napkins as wrappings. Then use mulberry charcoal to roast the bags. At this point, these can be used to iron out the cold rheumatism where the needling has been done. This heat enters and reaches the illness. The cold responds to the heated bag and thus is ironed out. Repeat again thirty times, then stop. The patient may walk about in a room, but must not be exposed to a draft of wind. Each needling must be accompanied by an ironing out so that the disease will be finished. This is what is called heating the interior."

Notes

1. Shao Shi means "junior instructor," so a young instructor at the emperor's court.

2. Bo means "uncle" or "elder." Gao may be a surname. Another instructor at the emperor's court.

3. "Half" refers to five treatments, "double" is ten treatments. This is analagous to the previous paragraph, "For a disease of a month, ten acupuncture treatments."

4. That is, when a man's skull is so misshapen that the major bones are below the level of the flesh in front of the ears.

5. "Nourishing" means blood, "protective" means qi. In Chinese the word for "energy" is not written.

6. Qi in this instance may mean "breath."

7. One catty equals one and one-third pounds.

7. ON GOVERNING THE NEEDLES

"Within the totality of acupuncture, the rules governing the needles are exceedingly wondrous. Nine needles make the total; each has its respective identity. Long, short, large, small, each has its actions. Without proper use of the needles, disease cannot be moved. If the illness is superficial and the needling deep, it will penetrate and injure the good flesh, and the skin will swell. If the illness is deep and the needling shallow, the sick qi will not drain and there will be large suppurations on the limbs. If the disease is small and the needling big, the qi will drain too much, which will quickly cause further injury. If the disease is great and the needling small, the qi will not flow and drain, which will cause it to return and attack. So if one misses the appropriate needling, the big will disperse too much, while the small will not move. This finishes the speech on the transgressions. Now we will speak of appropriate actions.

"When disease is located on the skin without a definitive location, treat by using the engraver's needle for this disease, except at the white regions of the skin. When disease is located at the divisions between the flesh, treat using the round needle. When the disease is of the major channels, chronic illnesses or rheumatism, use the lance needle. When the disease is in the channels and the qi is sparse, tonify at that point. Treat by using the spoon needle at the well, spring, stream, and the river *shu* points. When the disease makes large pus-filled ulcers, treat by using the sword needle. When the disease is rheumatism with abrupt and cruel qi coming forth, treat by using the round needle. In the case of persistent rheumatism and pain, treat by using the hair-fine needle. When the disease is located in the center of the body, treat by using the long needle. When the disease is edema, which causes blockages at the gates and joints, treat by using the big needle. When the disease is located in the five viscera and is solidly established, use the lance needle. Disperse the well, stream, dividing and *shu* points, and treat in accord with the four seasons.

"The totality of acupuncture exists in nine methods which are in accord with the nine changes.

"The first is called to needle the *shu* points. This is to needle, for example, the river, spring, and stream *shu* points, and the viscera points.

"The second is called to needle the distant road. This is, for example, to needle the lower part of the body although the disease is on the upper part. The needling is done on the points of the bowels.

"The third is called to needle the channels. This is to needle the great channels where they tie and divide.

"The fourth is called to needle the *luo* collateral channels. This is to needle the blood veins and the small collateral channels.

"The fifth is called divided needling. This is to needle the divisions which occur between the flesh.

"The sixth is called the great draining needling. This is to needle for a great dispersion by using the sword needle for purulent ulcers.

"The seventh is called hair needling. This is used to float away rheumatism of the skin.

"The eighth is called opposite needling. For this, one treats the right when disease is on the left, and treats the left when disease is on the right.

"The ninth is called heated needling. This is when a heated needle is used to treat rheumatism.

"Within the totality of acupuncture, there exist twelve parts which are in response to the twelve channels. The first is called to needle evenly. Direct the hand to the heart as well as to the back. Directly where the pain is, use one needle in the front of the body and one needle in the back. This may be used to treat rheumatism of the heart. Needling in this manner calls for a slanting insertion.

"The second is called declarative needling. This is used for pain which has no fixed location, which moves up and down. Use a perpendicular insertion and do not immediately withdraw. Use the left hand to press around the afflicted area, then withdraw the needle. Repeat the needling for each place.

"The third is called to magnify the needling. Use a perpendicular insertion from the side, and manipulate the needle backward and forward to magnify the effect on the muscles. This is used to treat rheumatism of the muscles.

"The fourth is called balanced needling. This is when one needle is inserted straight on, and two needles are inserted one to each side. It is used to treat cold qi which is small but deep. It is also called triple needling. Triple needling treats rheumatic qi which is small but deep.

"The fifth is called scattered needling. This is when one needle is inserted in the center, and four needles are inserted around it. It calls for shallow needling, and is used to treat cold qi which is extensive and large.

"The sixth is called straight needling. For straight needling, raise the skin, then needle. This is used to treat shallow cold qi.

"The seventh is called transmitted needling. For transmitted needling, insert directly and withdraw directly. This scatters the qi with the withdrawal of the needle from depth and is used to treat qi which is abundant and hot.

"The eighth is called short needling. This is for rheumatism of the bones. Shake the needle slightly as it goes to depth and take the needle close to the bone, then up and down as if rubbing the bone.

"The ninth is called shallow needling. This calls for a slanting shallow insertion. It is used to treat muscles which are cold and in spasm.

"The tenth is called yin needling. This is to needle both the left and right sides. It is used to treat cold deficiencies. When the middle has a cold deficiency, it should be treated at the point behind the anklebone on the Minor Yin Channel.

"The eleventh is called needling to the side. This is to insert one needle directly, then to insert another to the side. It is used to treat chronic rheumatism which is located in an area.

"The twelfth is called supplemental needling. For supplemental needling, insert directly, then withdraw directly. In addition, repeated shallow needling should be done to cause bleeding. This is said to treat swellings.

"When the channels are situated deep and cannot be seen, needle with a slight insertion and detain for a long time to reach the qi through the hole in the channel.[1] When the channels are shallow, do not needle until the channel has been massaged so that the essence does not come out, then needle. In this way only the evil will come out.

"That which is spoken of as the three depths of acupuncture causes the valley qi to come out. First is the shallow needling through the skin to let out the yang evil, then the needling to let out the yin evil. Whether the qi is sparse or abundant, go deeply through the skin until reaching the muscles and flesh, but do not enter the divisions between the flesh. To complete entry into the divisions between the flesh will result in the valley qi coming out. Thus, the 'rule of acupuncture' says, to begin, needle shallowly in order to expel the evil qi and to let the blood and qi come forward. Afterwards, needle deeply in order to affect the yin qi's evil. Finally, needle extremely deeply in order to descend to the valley qi. This is the essay.

"Thus, one who uses the needles without knowing the correlations to the year's climate, or if the qi is abundant or sparse, hollow or solid, or the causes, cannot be a physician.

"In the totality of acupuncture, there are five methods which are in resonance with the five viscera. The first is called one-half needling. For one-half needling, shallowly insert, then quickly withdraw the needle without needling to injure the flesh. It is like removing fine hair and is used to treat the skin qi. It is in resonance with the lungs.

"The second is called the leopard's spots acupuncture. The leopard's spots form of needling involves needles in left and right, front and back. This affects the center of the channels, and is used to treat the blood of the major channels. It is in resonance with the heart.

"The third is called gate needling. Gate needling is to needle left and right directly to exhaust the upper muscles. This is used for rheumatism of the muscles. Take care not to draw blood. This is in resonance with the liver. It is also called needling the deep spring, or delighted needling.

"The fourth is called adjacent valleys acupuncture. Adjacent valleys acupuncture is to needle left then right from the same hole, like a chicken's foot. Needle to the division between the flesh. This treats rheumatism of the muscles. It is in resonance with the spleen.

"The fifth is called transmitted needling. Transmitted needling is to insert directly and withdraw directly. The depth of the insertion reaches the bones. This is used to treat rheumatism of the bones. It is in resonance with the kidneys."

Note

1. "Hole" means acupuncture point, and refers to the anatomical fact that each acupuncture point occurs in a depression on the body as well as being an opening to the inner qi.

8. THE ROOTS OF SPIRIT

Huang Di asked Qi Bo, saying, "All of acupuncture's laws first must be rooted in the spirit. The blood, the channels, the nourishing energy, the qi, the seminal essence and the spirit, all are stored in the five viscera. When they are reached by debauchery, this causes a loss of the seminal essence which overflows and separates from the viscera. The human soul and animal spirit fly about, and will and thought are confused and disorderly. Knowledge and plans leave the body.

"What are the reasons for this? Are these sins of heaven or trespasses of man? What is meant by virtue, qi, life, seminal essence, spirit, human soul, animal spirit, heart and mind, thought, will, consideration, wisdom, planning? Please explain these questions."

Qi Bo replied, "Heaven abides so that we have virtue. Earth abides so that we have qi. When virtue flows and qi is blended, there is life. Life comes from what is spoken of as the seminal essence. When two seminal essences strike each other, it is spoken of as the spirit. Following the spirit as it goes and comes is the animal spirit. Together with the seminal essence as it exits or enters is that which is spoken of as the human soul. Those which are in accord with control of myriad things are the heart and mind. The mind has recall, which is spoken of as thought. Thought is that which, when kept, is spoken of as will. From will and that which is kept and changed is spoken of as consideration. From consideration of distant longings comes planning. From planning, to the managing of myriad things, is that which is spoken of as wisdom. Thus the wise nourish life by flowing with the four seasons and adapting to cold or heat, by harmonizing joy and anger in a tranquil dwelling, by balancing yin and yang, and what is hard and soft. So it is that dissolute evil cannot reach the man of wisdom, and he will be witness to a long life.

"Therefore, fright, distress, thought, and planning can injure the spirit. The injured spirit can result in fear flowing without stop; therefore, sadness and grief can move the center, and with extreme exhaustion, can even mean a loss of life. Too much joy and happiness can cause the spirit to shrink and scatter and not stay stored. Sorrow and grief can cause the qi to be blocked in the foundations so it does not move. Great anger causes confusion and doubt and a lack of control. Fear and fearing cause the spirit to be unsettled, to shrink away and to be nonreceptive.

"The heart and mind with frightened and distressed thoughts and anxiety can result in injury to the spirit. When the spirit is injured, it

39

can result in fear and loss of self. There is a breakdown of the tissue and a stripping of the flesh. The hair becomes haggard and the colors die young. There will be death in the winter.

"When the spleen is not released from worry and fear, it results in injury to thought. When thought is injured, it results in congestion and confusion. The four limbs cannot be raised. The hair becomes haggard. The colors die young. There will be death in the spring.

"Grief and sadness move the center and the liver which can result in injury to the human soul. The injured soul can cause madness, forgetfulness, and negation of the seminal essence. Without seminal essence, there is no primal point for man. The yin withdraws and the muscles warp. Neither the sides of the ribs nor bones can be raised. The hair becomes haggard. The colors die young. There will be death in the autumn.

"Joy and happiness without limits can result in injury to the animal spirits which are stored in the lungs. The injured animal spirits can cause madness. Madness does not preserve man. The skin becomes like heated leather. The hair becomes haggard. The colors die young. There will be death in the summer.

"The kidneys, when full of rage which does not stop, can result in frequent forgetfulness of previous words. The loins and backbone can be impaired and cannot raise up, stretch, or bend over. The hair becomes haggard. The colors die young. There will be death in the long summer.

"Fear and fearing without release can result in injury to the seminal essence. The injured seminal essence can cause the bones to be diseased and deficient. At the time of reproduction, the seminal essence will not descend. Thus the five viscera, which are the controls and storehouses of the seminal essence, should not be harmed. If they are injured, it will result in loss of protection, and the yin will become hollow. The yin being hollow will result in a lack of qi. A lack of qi will cause death.

"Therefore, when using acupuncture, one should examine and look at the patient's aspect in accord with knowledge about the seminal essence, the spirit, the human soul, and the animal spirit, and whether they have been preserved or forgotten. If the therapy is obtained through loss of thought, the five will be injured, and the needling will not be able to cure.

"The liver is the storehouse of blood. Blood is the shelter of the human soul. The liver qi being hollow can result in fear, being solid can result in anger.

"The spleen is the storehouse of nourishment. Nourishment is the shelter of thought. The spleen qi being hollow can result in the four limbs not functioning and an imbalance of the five viscera. When the qi is solid, the abdomen becomes swollen. The menses and urine will be diminished.

"The heart is the storehouse for the channels. The channels are the shelter of the spirit. When the heart qi is hollow, it results in sorrow. When the qi is solid, it causes laughter without stopping.

"The lung is the storehouse of qi. The qi is the shelter of the animal spirit. When the lung qi is hollow, it results in the nose being blocked, difficulty and sparseness of breath. When the qi is solid, it results in panting, a congested chest, and blowing with the face looking up.

"The kidneys are the storehouse of the seminal essence. The seminal essence is the shelter of the will. When the kidney qi is hollow, it results in a deficiency. When the qi is solid, it results in swellings. When the five viscera are not balanced, one must investigate the five viscera and the form of the disease in order to know whether the qi is hollow or solid, and to be attentive to the harmonies."

9. FROM BEGINNING TO END

"The totality of acupuncture includes in its way a completeness of beginning to end. To understand intelligently the beginning to end, one must know about the five viscera's principles and the primal yin and yang. Yin governs the viscera. Yang governs the bowels. Yang receives qi from the four extremities. Yin receives qi from the five viscera; therefore, to disperse and meet means to move in counterflow. To tonify and follow means to move with the flow of energy. Understand how to meet and how to follow to harmonize the qi. The rules on harmonizing the qi must depend on yin and yang. The five viscera are yin. The six bowels are yang. This should be transmitted to future generations with contracts of blood. With respect, it will be prosperous; with neglect, it will wane. Without the way of the Dao, actions will be selfish and necessitate premature death and calamities.

"Respect and serve Heaven's way. Please discuss, from beginning to end, the regulations of the major channels. One should know by taking the pulse at the Pulse Mouth, and the Man's Receptor, whether yin and yang are in excess or deficient, balanced or not balanced, according to the wholeness of Heaven's way.[1] So it is said the balanced man is not ill. Not ill means the pulses at the wrist and at the Man's Receptor point are in resonance with the four seasons, that top and bottom are mutually responsive and together with the comings and goings. The six channels' pulses are neither blocked nor agitated. The body's branches are mutually controlled and managed as to cold or heat. The physical form, the flesh, blood and qi must be mutually appropriate. This is said to be a balanced man.

"When the qi is sparse, the wrist pulse and the Man's Receptor pulse are also sparse, and the foot and inch pulses are not balanced. Thus both yin and yang are deficient, and if the yang is tonified, the yin will become exhausted. If the yin is dispersed, the yang will be overcome. If this is the case, it is necessary to use sweet medicines, but to drink one of the proper dose. Moxibustion should not be used. If dispersion is used before recovery, it will result in the imbalance of all five viscera.

"If the Man's Receptor pulse is twice as full, disease is located in the Leg Minor Yang.[2] If it is twice as full and rough, disease is located in the Arm Minor Yang. If the Man's Receptor pulse is three times as full, disease is located in the Leg Major Yang. If it is three times as full and rough, disease is located in the Arm Major Yang. If the Man's Receptor pulse is four times as full, disease is located in the Leg Bright Yang. If it is four times as full and rough, disease is located in the Arm

Bright Yang. If the pulse at Man's Receptor is five times as full and is, moreover, both large and fast, it is called an overflowing yang. An overflow of yang means out of bounds.

"If the pulse at the Inch Mouth is twice as full, disease is located on the Leg Shrinking Yin.[3] If the Shrinking Yin pulse is twice as full and rough, disease will be located in the Heart Master Pericardium Channel. If the Pulse Mouth is three times as full, disease is located in the Leg Minor Yin. If it is three times as full and rough, it is located in the Arm Minor Yin. If the Pulse Mouth is four times as full, disease is located in the Leg Minor Yin. If it is four times as full and rough, disease is located in the Arm Major Yin. If the Pulse Mouth is five times as full and is, moreover, both big and fast, it is called overflowing yin. Overflowing yin concerns the inner gates. If these inner gates are blocked it means death from an incurable disease.

"If the Man's Receptor pulse and the Major Yin wrist pulse are both five times fuller than normal, it is called locked and barred. This means there is only a short period before death.

"If the pulse at Man's Receptor on the neck is twice as full as the pulse at the wrist, disperse the Leg Minor Yang and tonify the Leg Shrinking Yin. Use two dispersion points for one tonification. Treat once a day in accordance with examination and diagnosis. Treat distant points. When the ascending qi harmonizes, stop.

"If the Man's Receptor pulse is three times as full, disperse the Leg Major Yang and tonify the Leg Minor Yin. Use two dispersion points for one tonification. Treat every other day in accordance with examination and diagnosis. Treat distant points. When the ascending qi harmonizes, stop.

"When the Man's Receptor pulse is four times as full, disperse the Leg Bright Yang and tonify the Leg Major Yin. Use two dispersion points for one tonification. Treat twice a day in accordance with examination and diagnosis. Use distant points. When the ascending qi harmonizes, stop. If the pulse at the Inch Mouth on the wrist is twice as full as the neck pulse, disperse the Leg Shrinking Yin and tonify the Leg Minor Yang. Use two tonification points for one dispersion. Treat once a day in accordance with examination and diagnosis. Treat distant points. When the ascending qi harmonizes, stop. If the Pulse Mouth is three times as full, disperse the Leg Minor Yin and tonify the Leg Minor Yang. Use two tonification points for one dispersion. Treat every other day in accordance with inspection and diagnosis. Treat distant points. When the ascending qi harmonizes, stop. If the Pulse Mouth is four times as full, disperse the Leg Major Yin and tonify the Leg Bright

Yang. Use two tonification points for one dispersion. Treat twice a day in accordance with inspection and diagnosis. Treat distant points. When the ascending qi harmonizes, stop. The reason for treating twice a day is that the Major Yin controls the stomach, where there is a great abundance of valley qi, so it is necessary to treat twice a day.

"If the Man's Receptor and Pulse Mouth are both four times more abundant than normal, it is said yin and yang are both overflowing. If this is so, there will be no openings, which will result in the blood channels being blocked and obstructed. The qi will be unable to move, the overflow will be debauched to the middle, and the five viscera will be harmed internally. If this is treated by moxibustion, it will result in changes which will lead to another disease.

"The total way of acupuncture is to harmonize the qi and then stop. To tonify yin and to disperse yang will make the tones of qi full of excellence. The ears will hear, the eyes will see brightly. The opposite of this is when the blood and qi do not move. Therefore it is said when the qi is reached, there will be an effect. Dispersing will cause fullness to be hollowed out. Then if the pulse is as large as before, but the treatment has caused it not to be as firm, it is a sign of recovery. If, however, it is as firm as before the treatment, the disease will not depart even though one's words are encouraging. To tonify results in increased solidity. The solidified pulse is large, but if the treatment has increased its firmness, it is a sign of recovery. If it has not caused a firming up, the disease will not depart, although there be fast and suitable words. Therefore, tonification should cause solidity, and dispersion should cause hollowness. Although pain may not lessen following the needle, disease must lessen to depart. One must begin by penetrating the twelve major channels and that which gives birth to disease. Afterwards what can be transmitted is the knowledge of acupuncture from beginning to end, for yin and yang are not the same movements. Hollowness and solidity are not similarly inclined, but treatment for both is through the channels.

"All acupuncture has a sequence, three depths to reach the valley qi. It treats evil qi which is reckless or converges, yin and yang when they change their positions, flow and counterflow when reversed, evil qi when deep or shallow in different organs and being nonresponsive to the four seasons, and the detention in the body of the debauched overflow of qi. Needling will cause all these to depart; consequently, the first depth, a shallow insertion, will cause the evil yang to go out. The second depth of acupuncture, the middle insertion, causes the evil yin to go away. The third depth of acupuncture results in reaching the valley qi. When the valley qi is reached, stop, for it is said that when the valley qi is reached, tonification has completed solidification and dispersion has completed hollowing; thus, it must be in accord with the knowledge that the valley qi has been reached. When the evil qi alone departs, the disease knows it has been overcome, even though yin and yang are not able to harmonize yet. Therefore it is said that tonification will result in solidity, and dispersion will result in hollowness. Even though pain does not follow the withdrawal of the needle, disease must depart when lessened.

"When the yin is abundant and the yang is hollow, first tonify the yang and afterwards disperse the yin to harmonize. When the yin is hollow and the yang is abundant, first tonify the yin and afterwards disperse the yang to harmonize.

"The three channels which move on the foot around the big toe must be examined for solidity or hollowness. If they are hollow and dispersion is applied, this is spoken of as intensifying hollowness. Intensifying the hollowness means the disease will worsen.

"All acupuncture is like this. Use the fingers and press. If the moving pulse is solid as well as fast, disperse quickly. If the pulse is hollow and slow, tonify. If the procedures are improperly reversed, disease will worsen. For each moving pulse, the Bright Yang is on top, the Shrinking Yin is in the middle of the foot, the Minor Yin is to the bottom.

"The chest points treat in the middle of the chest. The back points treat in the middle of the back. When the shoulder and upper part of the arm are hollow, use the points in the area. Treat until the qi ascends. For a heaviness of the tongue, needle the root of the tongue with the sword needle.

"If the hands can bend but not stretch, disease is located in the tendons. If they can stretch but not bend, disease is located in the bones. When at the bones, treat the bones. When at the tendons, treat the tendons.

"Tonification will result in solidity in an area. Treat with a deep insertion. Slowly press the bruise when the needle is withdrawn to get most of the evil qi to flow out. In an area which is hollow, treat with a shallow insertion in accord with nourishing the channels. Quickly press the bruise when the needle is withdrawn so that the evil qi sent from the exterior cannot obtain an entrance.

"In needling, when the evil qi comes out, it is tight and urgent. When the valley qi comes, it is slow and harmonious. When the pulse is hard, needle deeply in order to drain the qi. When the pulse is hollow, needle shallowly so that the seminal essence and qi are not drained out, and needle in accord with nourishing the channels. Only the evil qi should be removed from the body. When needling all pain, use dispersion if the pulses all reflect a solidity. So it is said, in following that which is above the waist, all is governed by the Arm Major Yin and Bright Yang, that which is below the waist, all is governed by the Leg Major Yin and Bright Yang.

"If disease is located in the upper body, treat the lower body. If disease is located in the lower part, treat the upper. If disease is located in the head, treat the foot. If disease is located in the loins, treat the crease of the knee.

"If disease begins in the head, the head becomes heavy. If disease begins in the hand, the arms become heavy. If it begins in the foot, the foot becomes heavy. To control disease, first needle the region in which it begins.

"Spring qi is located in the hair. Summer qi is located in the skin. Autumn qi is located in the divisions of the flesh. Winter qi is located in the tendons and bones. To needle these diseases, each should be treated in accord and balance with its season. Thus, needling fat people should be in accord and balance with autumn and winter. Needling thin people should be in accord and balance with spring and summer.[4]

"A disease which is painful is yin. A disease which is painful but cannot be located by pressure of the hand is yin. Needle deeply. The diseases located at the upper regions are yang. The diseases located at the lower regions are yin. Itching is yang. Needle shallowly.

"For disease which first begins in yin, first control the yin, then afterwards control the yang. For disease which first begins in yang, first control yang then afterwards control the yin.

"To needle a hot disease which is perverse, detain the needle to reverse it and make cold. To needle a cold disease which is perverse, detain the needle to reverse it and make heat. To needle a hot perverse disease, use two yin and one yang. To needle a cold perverse disease, use two yang and one yin. What is meant by two yin is to needle the yin twice. One yang is to needle the yang once.

"A chronic disease is when the evil qi has penetrated deeply. To needle this disease, insert deeply and detain for a long time. Every other day repeat the needling. One must first harmonize the body's left and right to remove disease from the blood and channels. This is the complete way of acupuncture.

"In all acupuncture there are rules. One must examine the physical body and the qi. One must see that the body's flesh is not stripped, and whether the qi is sparse and the pulse rough. If it is rough and deficient, one must use a misleading form of acupuncture.[5] Then the scattered qi can be retrieved, the assembled qi can be covered.

"At the time of acupuncture, one should be in an inner room in a quiet dwelling. Divine whether the spirit comes or goes in a place, as if the doors were closed and the shutters blocked, so that the human soul and animal spirit will not scatter. Give special thought to one spirit, to the seminal essence, and to the qi and their divisions, in a place without the noise of mankind in order to receive this essence. One must be one unity with the spirit. This is the will of the needle.

"For a first time, needle shallowly and detain, then slightly float the needle in accord with moving the spirit. The qi will be reached and then stop.

"Men in the inner chamber, women in the outer chamber will on the one hand prevent the qi from leaving the outer room, and on the other hand bar the qi from entering the inner room. This will allow the obtaining of qi.

"Acupuncture has its prohibitions. Fresh from sexual intercourse, do not needle; fresh from needling, do not have sexual intercourse. Already drunk, do not needle; already needled, do not drink. Fresh from labor, do not needle; already needled, do not labor. Already full of food, do not needle; already needled, do not eat to excess. Already starving, do not needle; already needled, do not fast. Already thirsty, do not needle; already needled, do not make thirsty. For great surprise or great anger, one must center the patient's qi, then needle. If the patient rides a carriage to come, have him lie down and rest for a time equal to eating a meal, then needle. If the patient comes by walking, have him sit and rest for a time equal to walking ten *li*,[6] then needle.

"These are the twelve prohibitions for those whose channels are disordered and qi scattered, whose nourishing and protective qi is in counterflow, and whose channels of qi are not in order. In these cases, needling will result in a yang disease penetrating the yin, and a yin disease penetrating the yang, which causes the evil qi to recycle. The coarse ordinary doctor does not examine, and this is spoken of as cutting the body, which can cause the physical body to overflow with debauched qi, muddy the brain and marrow, stop the transformation and transportation of the body fluids, and strip the five flavors. This is spoken of as losing qi.

"When the Major Yang Channels are cut off, the eyes roll up, the body bends backwards and suffers spasms and convulsions. The skin turns a pallid white, and the skin being white means that it cuts off sweating. When the ability to sweat is cut off, it means the end.

"When the Minor Yang is cut off, there will be deafness. The hundred joints will become totally loose. The connections of the eyes will be cut off. When the connections of the eyes are cut off, it results in death in a day and a half. In this death, the color will turn a greenish white before death.

"When the Bright Yang is cut off, the mouth and eyes will move and twitch. There will be frequent fear and absurd words. The color will be yellow. The patient's upper and lower regions will have full channels and will not move. This will cause the end.

"When the Minor Yin is cut off, the face becomes black. The teeth are extended and look dirty. The abdomen becomes swollen and blocked. The upper and lower regions become blocked. This will cause the end.

"When the Shrinking Yin is cut off, the middle will be feverish, the throat dry. There will be frequent urination. The heart and mind will be annoyed. These extremes cause the tongue to roll up, the testes to withdraw upwards. This will cause the end.

"When the Major Yin is cut off, the abdomen swells and is blocked. One cannot obtain breath. There is panting with frequent vomiting. Vomiting results in a rebellious counterflow. This causes the face to redden. When this rebellious counterflow does not occur, the upper and lower channels are blocked. This in turn causes the face to blacken, the skin and hair to be scorched, and the end to come."

Notes

1. The ancient Chinese system of pulse taking referred to in this chapter includes pulses on the radial artery on both right and left wrists, and pulses on the carotid artery (Man's Receptor) on the neck.

On each wrist, six pulses are identified. Three superficial (yang) and three deep (yin) by location and attribution to an organ.

There are three locations: inch, gate, and foot. Place the first three fingers on the radial pulse of the wrist. When the digit finger is proximal to the crease of the wrist, it is directly over the inch pulse. The second finger is directly over the gate pulse. The fourth, or ring finger, is directly over the foot pulse.

Pulses

Left		Right	
yang	yin	yang	yin
small intestine	heart	large intestine	lung
gallbladder	liver	stomach	spleen
bladder	kidney	Triple Heater	pericardium

In ancient times, the ratio of beats between the carotid pulse (Man's Receptor) and the wrist pulses was measured as a diagnostic feature for one's balance of energy.

2. Twice as full as the usual pulse.

3. Twice as full as the usual pulse.

4. Needling fat people should be in accord and balance with autumn and winter, that is, deeply. Needling thin people should be in accord and balance with spring and summer, that is, shallowly.

5. "A misleading form of acupuncture" means to use the opposite side, that is, use the left to treat the right, the right to treat the left.

6. Five kilometers.

SCROLL THREE
10. THE MAJOR CHANNELS

Lei Gong questioned Huang Di, saying "In the 'Restrictions and the Major Channels' it is said, 'Of all the principles of acupuncture, the major channels make the beginning.[1] They manage and nourish that which moves in the body. They make the body's limits and quantities. Internally, they follow the five viscera. Externally, they are divided between the six bowels.' I would like to hear all about their way."

Huang Di said, "Man begins at birth. First is the completion of the seminal essence. When the seminal essence is complete, it gives birth to brain and marrow. Then the bones solidify. The channels begin to nourish. The muscles begin to strengthen. The flesh begins to become a wall. The skin becomes firm and the hair begins to grow. The valley enters the stomach. The path of the channels is penetrated, and blood and qi begin to move."

Lei Gong said, "I would like to hear everything about the beginnings and birth of the major channels."

Huang Di said, "The major channels are able to decide life and death. They are the dwellings of the hundred diseases, but also the harmonizers of hollowness and solidity. This cannot be done if they cannot be understood.

"The Lung Channel of the Arm Major Yin starts in the middle heater. There is a lower auxiliary path to the large intestine. Returning, it follows the mouth of the stomach, ascends the diaphragm and the lungs which it subordinates. It follows the lungs and goes horizontally, coming out below the armpit. Descending, it follows the inside of the upper arm, travels to the front of the Heart Master Pericardium Channel of Minor Yin. It then descends to the middle of the elbow, follows the inside of the lower arm on top of the bone along its lower border. It enters the Inch Mouth and ascends the Fish, the base of the thumb. Following the border of the Fish, it comes out at the tip of the thumb. A branch follows the back of the wrist, goes straight out along the medial side of the digit finger, and comes out at its tip. When this channel is shaken it results in fullness and swelling in the lung, gasping and coughing, and pain in the Broken Dish.[2] When extreme, it results in crossing of the two arms, and dim vision. This comes about because of a deficiency of the arms.

"When that which is master of the lungs gives rise to disease, there is coughing, an ascent of qi, panting and thirst, an anxious heart, a congested chest, pain and spasms in the shoulder bone and medial anterior surface of the upper arm, and heat in the center of the palm.

"When the qi is full and there is an excess, it results in the shoulder and back being painful from wind and cold. There will be sweating from the attacking wind. Urination is frequent but scanty. When qi is hollow, it results in the shoulder and back being painful from cold. Sparse qi is in accord with an insufficiency of breathing. There will be change in the color of urine. For all these ills, if the qi is full, disperse; if hollow, tonify. If it is hot, use rapid techniques; if cold, use detaining techniques. If it is sinking and depressed, use moxibustion; if neither full nor hollow, treat the channel. When the qi is full, the Inch Mouth pulse is four times as large as the Man's Receptor pulse. When it is hollow, the Inch Mouth pulse is smaller than the Man's Receptor pulse.

"The Large Intestine Channel of the Arm Bright Yang begins on the top of the index finger next to the thumb. It follows the finger up along the side, comes out at Joining Valleys between two bones. It ascends, penetrates the middle of two muscles, follows the outer surface of the arm along the upper side, enters the elbow on the lateral side and goes up the upper arm on the anterior lateral side. It mounts the shoulder, coming out at Shoulder Bone on the front side. It continues up, coming out at an assembly point in the Support Bone.[3] It descends, enters the Broken Dish, and connects with the lungs. It goes down through the diaphragm to subordinate the large intestine. A branch follows the Broken Dish, ascends the neck, goes through the cheeks, enters the middle of the lower gums, returns and comes out at the pinch of the mouth. It crosses Middle of Man left to right, right to left, and goes up to the pinch next to the holes of the nose.

"When this channel is shaken, it results in toothaches and swelling of the neck. This channel is the master of ferrying the body fluids, and may be the source of diseases where the symptoms are yellow eyes, a dry mouth, a runny nose, nose bleed, sore throat, pain in the anterior part of the shoulder or upper arm, and pain and nonfunctioning of the thumb and index finger. When the qi is in excess, the areas the channel passes through are hot and swollen. When the qi is hollow, the result is cold, chills, and no circulation. As for these diseases, if qi is hot, use a fast insertion; if cold, detain the needle. If qi is sinking and descending, use moxibustion; neither abundant nor hollow, treat the channel. When the qi is abundant, the Man's Receptor pulse is four times greater than the Inch Mouth pulse. When the qi is hollow, the Man's Receptor pulse is smaller than the Inch Mouth pulse.

"The Stomach Channel of the Leg Bright Yang begins at the center of the junction of the nose and cheekbone. To the side, it receives the Bladder Channel of the Major Yang and descending, it follows the lateral portion of the nose and penetrates the center of the upper gums, returns and comes out at the pinch of the mouth, and circles the lips. It descends, making a junction at Receiving Fluids, retreats and follows the qi backwards along the lower side, and comes out at Great Welcome and then at Jaw Carriage. It ascends in front of the ear to Guest and Master, follows the front of the hairline, and reaches the forehead at the temples. A branch of the channel goes from the front of Great Welcome and descends to Man's Receptor. It follows the throat to enter the Broken Dish and descends to the diaphragm, subordinates to the stomach and connects with the spleen. Its straight branch descends from the Broken Dish on the inner side of the nipple and along the sides of the navel, where it enters Qi Rushing. Another branch begins in the mouth of the stomach and descends, following the fundus of the abdomen until it meets the Qi Rushing point. It continues to descend to Thigh Gate, touches Crouching Rabbit, descends through the knee and knee cap, then follows the lateral side of the leg bone to the foot and ankle, where it enters the medial crack of the middle toe. Another branch diverges at a point three *cun* below the knee on the lateral side and enters the lateral crack of the middle toe.[4] Yet another branch separates at the dorsum of the foot, enters the big toe and comes out at the tip.

"When this channel is shaken, it results in diseases where there is a shaking from cold as if one is sprinkled with water, frequent groaning, frequent yawning, and the forehead being black. A disease state causes the person to feel sick from fire and to be timid and fearful when hearing tones resonant to wood. While the heart desires motion, one stays alone behind blocked doors and closed shutters. In extremes, it results in the desire to ascend heights and sing and cast off one's clothes while walking outside. There are energetic noises in the abdomen, and swelling caused by a deficiency around the shinbone. This channel controls the blood and the diseases which arise from it: madness, fevers, warm diseases, debauchery, abnormal sweating, bleeding from the nose, a wry mouth, canker of the lips, swelling of the neck, numbness in the throat, water swelling abdomen, swelling and pain in the knee and knee cap. There is also pain along the shoulder and breast, Qi Rushing, the abdomen, the thighs, the front of the thigh, Crouching Rabbit point, the lateral side of the legbone, the upper part of the foot and ankle, and the middle toe does not function. When the qi is abundant, it results in the front of the body being all hot. So when there is an excess of qi in the stomach, it results in a melting of grains, frequent hunger, and yellow-colored urine. When the qi is insufficient, it causes the front of the body to shiver with cold. When the middle of the stomach is cold, it results in swelling and fullness.

"In all of these diseases, if the qi is abundant, disperse; if hollow, tonify. If it is hot, use a fast insertion; if cold, detain the needle. If it is depressed and sinking, use moxa; neither full nor hollow, treat in accord with the channel. When the qi is abundant, the Man's Receptor pulse is four times greater than the Inch Mouth pulse. When the qi is hollow, the Man's Receptor pulse is smaller than the Inch Mouth pulse.

"The Spleen Channel of the Leg Major Yin begins at the tip of the big toe. It follows the medial side of the toe along the border of the white flesh, passes by the metatarsal bone, and ascends the medial side of the ankle toward the front. It ascends along the medial side of the lower leg, following a line to the rear of the tibia bone, where it crosses and comes out to the front of the Liver Channel of the Shrinking Yin. It continues up along the diaphragm to under the arms and then the throat, where it connects with the root of the tongue and disperses in the lower part of the tongue. A branch returns and follows the stomach, separates as it ascends the diaphragm, and flows to the center of the heart.

"When this channel is shaken, it results in the root of the tongue being rigid, vomiting after eating, pain in the ducts of the stomach, swelling of the abdomen, frequent regurgitation, a gaseous discharge after a bowel movement, and great ease but weakness: an entire body heaviness.

"This channel controls the spleen and gives rise to disease where the root of the tongue is painful, the body is unable to move or swing, and food does not descend. There is anxiety in the heart, acute pain below the heart, watery stools, water is blocked, yellow jaundice, an inability to lie down, rigidity in standing, swelling and deficiency of the interior of the thighs and knees, and the big toes do not function. For all of these diseases, if the qi is abundant, disperse; if hollow, tonify. If it is hot, use a fast insertion; if cold, detain the needle. If it is depressed and sinking, use moxa; neither full nor hollow, treat the channel. When the qi is abundant, the Inch Mouth pulse is four times greater than the Man's Receptor pulse. When it is hollow, the Inch Mouth pulse is smaller than the Man's Receptor pulse.

"The Heart Channel of the Arm Minor Yin begins in the center of the heart and comes out, subordinating the heart and its connections.

It descends the diaphragm to connect with the small intestine. A branch follows the heart-connecting channels, ascends to the throat, and connects with the eye-connecting channels. Another straight channel returns, follows the heart-connecting channel, slopes up to the top of the lung, and descends to come out under the armpit. It descends following the medial surface of the upper arm along the back side of the surface. It travels to the back of the Lung Channel of the Major Yin and the Pericardium, descends the medial side of the elbow and follows the medial posterior area of the forearm. It reaches the wrist, behind which there is a sharp bone which comes to a point. Then it enters the inside of the palm along the medial posterior surface and follows the inside of the little fingers, where it comes out at the tip.

"When this channel is shaken, it results in disease where the throat is dry and the heart is painful. There is thirst with the desire to drink. There is a deficiency of the upper arm. When that which controls the heart gives rise to disease, the eyes are yellow, the ribs hurt, and the medial posterior surface of the upper arm is painful and cold. The center of the palm is hot and painful. For all of these diseases, if the qi is abundant, disperse; if hollow, tonify. If it is hot, use a fast insertion; if cold, detain the needle. If it is depressed and sinking, use moxa; neither full nor hollow, treat the channel. When the qi is abundant, the Inch Mouth pulse is three times greater than the Man's Receptor pulse. When the qi is hollow, the Inch Mouth pulse is smaller than the Man's Receptor pulse.

"The Small Intestine Channel of the Arm Major Yang begins at the tip of the little finger, follows the edge of the hand, ascends the wrist, comes out in the center of the wrist bone, goes straight up along the bone of the forearm along the lower edge of the arm, and comes out in the inner part of the elbow between two muscles. It ascends the lateral posterior surface of the upper arm, comes out at the shoulder joint, and winds around the shoulder blade. It crosses at the top of the shoulder and enters the Broken Dish, where it connects with the heart, travels along the neck and descends the diaphragm to reach the stomach and to subordinate the small intestine. A branch follows the Broken Dish, ascends the neck, jaws, and cheeks to reach the lateral point of the eye, then retreats and enters the middle ear. Another branch separates at the jaw, ascends the cheek, reaches the nose, and then reaches the inner angle of the eye with a slanting connection in the cheekbone.

"When this channel is shaken, it results in disease where the throat is sore, the chin and jaws are swollen, the neck is stiff and immobile, the shoulder feels as if it is pulled apart, the upper part of the arm feels as if it is broken.

"This channel controls the body fluids and may give rise to deafness, yellow eyes, swollen cheeks and pain in the neck, jaws, shoulder, upper arm, elbow, and the lateral posterior side of the arm. For all of these diseases, if the qi is abundant, disperse; if hollow, tonify. If it is hot, use a fast insertion; if cold, detain the needle. If it is depressed and descending, use moxa; neither full nor hollow, treat the channel. When the qi is abundant, the Man's Receptor pulse is three times greater than the Inch Mouth pulse. When it is hollow, the Man's Receptor pulse is smaller than the Inch Mouth pulse.

"The Bladder Channel of the Leg Major Yang begins at the medial corner of the eye, goes up the forehead, and crosses the top of the head. A branch goes from the top of the head to reach the upper angle of the ear. A straight branch goes from the top of the head to enter and connect with the brain, turns around, then comes out and separates below the nape of the neck. It follows the inside of the shoulder blade along the pinch of the backbone until it reaches the middle of the loins. There it enters, and follows the muscles of the backbone to connect with the kidney and subordinate the bladder. Another branch follows the middle of the loins, descends along the pinch of the backbone, goes through the buttocks, and enters the middle of the knee. Another branch goes from the interior of the shoulder blade both left and right, separates as it descends through the scapula along the pinch of the backbone, and passes into and through the pivot of the hip joint. It follows the outside of the rump along the posterior edge. Descending, it meets at the middle of the crease of the knee, continues through the interior of the calf, and comes out at the lateral posterior area behind the ankle, then follows the fifth metatarsal bone, to reach the lateral edge of the little toe.

"When this channel is shaken, it results in diseases where pain rushes to the head, the eyes feel as if stripped off, the nape of the neck feels as if bunched together, the spine is painful, the loins feel as if broken, the hips are unable to bend, the knee feels tied up, the calf feels as if it were separated. There is a deficiency of qi at the ankle.

"This channel controls the tendons and gives rise to diseases such as piles, fevers, madness and insanity, pain in the top of the head and in the nape of the neck, yellow eyes, tearing, nose bleeds. There can be pain in the back, loins, buttocks, knees, calves, and feet. The little toe does not function. For all these diseases, if the qi is abundant, disperse; if hollow, tonify. If it is hot, use a quick insertion; if cold, detain the needle. If it is depressed and descending, use moxa; neither abundant nor hollow, treat the channel. When the qi is abundant, the Man's Receptor pulse is three times greater than the Inch Mouth pulse. When it is hollow, the Man's Receptor pulse is smaller than the Inch Mouth pulse.

"The Kidney Channel of the Leg Minor Yin begins on the bottom of the little toe, travels diagonally to the heart of the sole, comes out below Blazing Valley, and travels to the rear of the inner anklebone. It separates to enter the middle of the heel, ascends to the medial side of the calf, and comes out at the medial side of the crease of the knee. It goes up the medial posterior area of the thigh, goes through the spine, subordinates the kidney, and connects to the bladder. A straight channel goes from the kidneys, ascends and passes through the liver and diaphragm, enters the center of the lungs, and goes to the throat, then to the root of the tongue. A branch follows the lungs, comes out and connects with the heart, and flows to the middle of the breast.

"When this channel is shaken, it results in the diseases where one is hungry but does not desire to eat, the face is as black as charcoal, there is blood from coughing or spitting, a 'he-he' sound and panting, a desire to arise when sitting. The eyes are blurred so that they are without perception, the heart is in suspension as if emaciated. When the qi is insufficient, it results in fear. The heart is frightened and distressed like a man who is about to be arrested. This is a deficiency in the bones.

"This channel controls the kidneys and gives rise to diseases where there is fever in the mouth, a dry tongue, a swollen throat, an upward flow of qi, the throat dry and sore, anxiety in the heart, pain in the heart, jaundice, diarrhea, pain in the spine and in the medial posterior area of the thighs, flaccidity, a fondness for lying down, and the bottom of the foot is hot and painful.

"For all these diseases, if the qi is abundant, disperse; if hollow, tonify. If it is hot, use a fast insertion; if cold, detain the needle. If it is depressed and descending, use moxa; neither abundant nor hollow, treat the channel. Moxibustion should result in a strong appetite and the growth of flesh. For treatment, loosen the belt and release the hair. A large staff and heavy shoes should be used in walking. When qi is abundant, the Inch Mouth pulse is three times greater than the Man's Receptor pulse. When the qi is hollow, the Inch Mouth pulse is smaller than Man's Receptor pulse.

"The Pericardium Channel of the Arm Shrinking Yin is the master of the heart. It begins in the middle of the breast, comes out and subordinates the pericardium and its connections. Then it descends the diaphragm, passes through, and connects the Triple Heater. A branch goes through the breast and comes out at the ribs three *cun* below the armpit. It mounts to reach the bottom of the armpit, follows the medial surface of the upper arm, travels between the Major Yin and Minor Yin, and enters the elbow. It descends the forearm, travels between two tendons, enters the middle of the palm, goes to the middle finger, and comes out at the tip. A branch separates at the middle of the palm, goes to the ring finger, and comes out at the tip.

"When this channel is shaken, it results in the palm of the hand being hot, the forearm and elbow being warped and stiff, and swelling in the armpit. In extreme cases, it results in fullness in the chest and ribs, palpitations of the heart, the face becoming red, yellow eyes and incessant laughter.

"This channel controls the blood channels and pulses, and may give rise to diseases such as anxiety in the heart, pains in the heart, and heat in the middle of the palm.

"For all these diseases, if the qi is abundant, disperse; if it is hollow, tonify. If it is hot, use a quick insertion; if cold, detain the needle. If it is sunken and descending, use moxa; neither full nor hollow, treat the channel. When the qi is abundant, the Inch Mouth pulse is twice as great as the Man's Receptor pulse. When the qi is hollow, the Inch Mouth is smaller than Man's Receptor pulse.

"The Triple Heater Channel of the Arm Minor Yang begins at the tip of the ring finger, goes up between the little finger and ring finger, follows the back of the wrist, and comes out on the lateral surface of the forearm between the two bones. It ascends and passes through the elbow along the lateral area of the upper arm, then goes up to the shoulder, where it crosses and comes out behind the Leg Minor Yang. It enters the Broken Dish, extends to the middle of the breasts, spreads around the pericardium, descends the diaphragm, and subordinates the Triple Heater. A branch goes from the center of the chest, ascends and comes out at the Broken Dish. It goes up the neck, connects to a line behind the ears, goes straight up to come out at the upper angle of the ear, then bends down and descends to the jaw, and reaches to the cheek. Another branch goes from behind the ear and enters the middle ear, then comes out to pass in front of the ear. It then passes to the front of the Guest and Master, and crosses the cheek until it reaches the lateral corner of the eye.

"When this channel is shaken, it results in diseases such as deafness, tinnitus with sounds like 'hun-hun' and 'tun-tun', swelling of the throat, and sore throat.

"This channel controls the qi and may give rise to diseases where there is abnormal sweating, pain at the lateral corner of the eye, in the cheek or jaw behind the ear, in the shoulder, in the upper arm, in the elbow, in the lateral area of the forearm, and a dysfunctioning of the ring finger.

"For all of these diseases, if the qi is abundant, disperse; if hollow, tonify. If it is hot, use a quick insertion; if cold, detain the needle. If it is depressed and descending, use moxa; neither abundant nor hollow, treat the channel. When the qi is abundant, the Man's Receptor pulse is twice as big as the Inch Mouth pulse. When the qi is hollow, the Man's Receptor pulse is smaller than the Inch Mouth pulse.

"The Gallbladder Channel of the Leg Minor Yang begins at the lateral corner of the eye. It ascends to reach the angle of the head's hairline, then descends behind the ear. It follows the neck and travels in front of the Arm Minor Yang, reaches the top of the shoulder, retreats and crosses to behind the Arm Minor Yang. Then it enters the Broken Dish. A branch goes from behind the ear to enter the center of the ear, then comes out and travels to the front of the ear, and goes to an area behind the lateral corner of the eye. Another branch separates at the lateral corner and descends to Great Welcome, and meets with the Arm Minor Yang, which reaches the lower cheek and continues to Jaw Carriage. Descending the neck, it meets the other branch at the Broken Dish, then goes down to the middle of the breast, goes through the diaphragm, connects with the liver, and subordinates the gallbladder. It follows the base of the ribs, comes out at Qi Rushing, winds around the border of the pubic hair, and goes horizontally to the center of the suspension of the hip. Another line goes straight from the Broken Dish and down to the ribs, passes along the breast, passes through the last rib, and descends to join the former branch at the center of suspension of the hip. It descends, follows the yang side of the thigh, and comes out at the lateral side of the knee, continues downward along the lateral side to the front of the leg bone and straight down until it reaches the end of the Binding Bone (the lower end of the fibula). It continues down and comes out to the front of the lateral anklebone, then follows the top of the foot to enter the space between the little toe and the fourth toe. Another branch separates at the top of the dorsum of the foot, enters the gap of the big toe, and follows the big toe on the inside of the bone which makes a fork with the next toe to come out at the tip, then it returns and passes through the toenail to come out at the Three Hairs.

"When this channel is shaken, it results in disease where there are bitter tastes in the mouth, frequent belching, pain in the heart and ribs, and inability to turn or to lean. When extreme, it results in the face looking slightly ashen, the body being without oil and dry, and the lateral side of the foot being hot. This is from the yang being deficient.

"This channel controls the bones and can give rise to diseases such as headache, pains in the chin and jaw, pain at the lateral corner of the eyes, swelling and pain in the center of the Broken Dish, swelling below armpits, horse beans or goiters under the arms, abnormal sweating caused by chills, fevers, and pains in the breast, ribs, buttocks, and knees along the lateral surface of the fibula to the lower end and the area in front of the lateral anklebone and every joint. It may also result in the fourth toe not functioning.

"For all these diseases, if the qi is abundant, disperse; if it is hollow, tonify. If it is hot, use a fast insertion; if cold, then detain the needle. If it is depressed and descending, use moxa; neither full nor hollow, treat the channel. When the qi is abundant, the Man's Receptor pulse is twice as large as the Inch Mouth pulse. When it is hollow, Man's Receptor is smaller than the Inch Mouth.

"The Liver Channel of the Leg Shrinking Yin begins in the big toe where the hair makes a border. It ascends the foot along the upper surface to reach a point one *cun* away from the medial anklebone, then goes up above the anklebone for eight *cun*, crosses and comes out behind the Major Yin, ascends to the crease of the knee along the medial side, then follows the yin side of the thigh to enter into the middle of the pubic hair, goes through the sexual organs until it reaches the abdomen, holds the stomach, subordinates the liver, and connects with the gallbladder. It then goes up through the diaphragm, extends to the ribs, follows the back of the throat to ascend and to enter the pharynx, then links with the eye connections, and ascends to come out on the temple, where it proceeds to meet with the Governing Vessel at the top of the head. A branch goes from the eye connections, descends to the inner part of the cheek, and circles the inner area of the lips. Another branch goes from the liver, separates and goes through the diaphragm to ascend and flow to the lungs.

"When this channel is shaken, it results in diseases where there are pains in the loins so that one cannot bend down or look up, hernias in men, and abdominal swellings in women. In extreme cases, it causes a dry throat, an ashen face and a complexion which looks pale.

"This channel controls the liver and may give rise to diseases such as fullness of the breast, vomiting, hiccups, diarrhea, fox (recurrent hernia), and weak or blocked urine.

"For all these diseases, when the qi is abundant, disperse; when hollow, tonify. When it is hot, use a quick insertion; when cold, detain the needle. When it is depressed and descending, use moxa; neither abundant nor hollow, treat the channel. When the qi is abundant, the Inch Mouth pulse is twice as big as the Man's Receptor pulse. When it is hollow, the Inch Mouth is smaller than the Man's Receptor.

"When the Arm Major Yin qi is cut off, it results in the skin and hair being scorched, for the Major Yin moves the qi to warm and moisten the skin and hair. Thus when the qi does not nourish, it results in the skin and hair being scorched. If the skin and hair are scorched, it causes the body fluids to move away from the skin and sections. When the body fluids move away from skin and sections, it causes the nails to wither and the hair to break. When hair is broken, it is the result of the hair already having died. On the third day, there will be worsening. On the fourth day, there will be death, for on that day fire overcomes metal.

"When the Arm Minor Yin qi is cut off, it results in the blood channels being obstructed. The channels not flowing result in blood not circulating. The blood not circulating causes the hair and color to be without lustre. This will cause the face to blacken like varnished charcoal, and the blood to begin to die. On the ninth day, there will be a worsening. On the tenth day there will be death, for on that day water overcomes fire.

"When the Leg Major Yin qi is cut off, it results in the channels not nourishing the muscles and flesh. The lips and the tongue are the roots of the muscles and the flesh, so that when the channels do not nourish, it causes a weakening of muscles and flesh. When muscles and flesh are weak, the tongue withers and the Center of Man swells (philtrum). When the philtrum swells, it causes the lips to reverse onto themselves. When the lips reverse, the flesh begins to die. In the first day, there will be a worsening. On the second day, there will be death, for on that day wood overcomes earth.

"When the Leg Minor Yin qi is cut off, it results in the bones withering. The Minor Yin causes the Kidney Channel. It nourishes the bones; when the bones are not nourished, it results in the flesh weakening and shrinking. The flesh weakening and shrinking causes the teeth to protrude and to have plaque. The hair will be without gloss. If one's hair is without gloss, the bones will begin to die. On the fifth day, there will be a worsening. On the sixth day, there will be death, for on that day earth will overcome water.

"When the Leg Shrinking Yin qi is cut off, it results in the tendons being cut off, for the Shrinking Yin is the Liver Channel, and the liver and tendons are in tune. The tendon and muscle channel is assembled by the yin qi and has a channel which is connected with the root of the tongue. When the tendons tighten, it causes the tongue to curl and the testicles to regress, so that blue lips, a curled tongue, and shrinking testicles are a result of the tendons beginning to die. On the seventh day, there will be a worsening. On the eighth day, there will be death, for on that day metal will overcome wood.

"When the five yin qi are cut off, it results in a whirling of the connections of the eye. This turning causes the eyes to wander. The eyes wandering cause the will to begin to die. The will beginning to die results in death within one and one-half days.

"When the six yang qi are cut off, it results in the yin and yang being separated one from the other. If they are separated, it causes the foundation between skin and flesh to leak so that this separation causes sweats. When this happens in the morning, the divination is death that evening. When it occurs in the evening, the divination is death in the morning.

"The twelve major channels lie hidden while travelling between the divisions of the flesh. They are deep and invisible, except for the Leg Major Yin, which passes through the upper part of the lateral anklebone and may be frequently seen because it has no place to hide.

"Those channels which float may be seen frequently and are the *luo* or linking channels. Of the six *luo* channels, the great *luo* of the Arm Bright Yang and Minor Yang are most visible because they begin among the five fingers and travel up to join the middle of the elbow.

"With the drinking of liquor, the protective qi will begin to move in the skin. Then the liquor qi and protective qi will flow into the *luo* linking channels, and these channels will begin to fill up; consequently, the protective qi will fill up to the brim, and the nourishing qi will be full, and so the major channels will have a great abundance. The channels become subject to heated movement because the evil qi resides and remains in the body and its extremities. If the channels are stagnant, it results in fever. If the *luo* channels are not firm, it results in a shrinking which is an emptiness. All of these channels are different, so this knowledge can be used to distinguish that channel which has been shaken."

Lei Gong said, "How does one know the difference between the major channels and the *luo* linking channels?"

Huang Di said, "The major channels cannot be seen. Whether they are hollow or solid, one must use the Inch Mouth pulse to know. The channels which can be seen are all *luo* channels."

Lei Gong said, "This insignificant self does not understand that."

Huang Di said, "The *luo* linking channels are unable to flow through the great joints. They must move by alternate routes to exit and enter; then they join again in the center of the skin. Their assemblies all can be seen from the outside. Consequently, for all acupuncture of the *luo* linking channels, one must needle their connections on top where there may be an extreme amount of blood. Even though there are no concentrations, one should treat quickly in order to disperse the evil and to let out its blood. If allowed to remain, it will become rheumatism.

"The complete examination of the *luo* linking channels is as follows. When the channels are blue or green, it indicates cold and also pain. When they are red, it indicates heat and fever. When the middle of the stomach is cold, the Fish on the hand, the base of the thumb's linking channels will be mostly green-blue. When the middle of the stomach is hot, the channels along the border of the Fish will be red. If there is an abrupt blackening of the *luo* channels, it is a sign of prolonged and chronic rheumatism. When they are red, black and green, it means both cold and hot qi. When they are green and short, it means a sparseness of qi.

"To use acupuncture for these cold and hot diseases, draw much blood from the *luo* channels. Treat once every other day. When this exhaustive bloodletting stops, then harmonize the hollow and the solid. When the channel is small and short, it means sparse qi. In extreme cases, to disperse results in depression. When depression is severe, it can result in fainting and in loss of speech; therefore, if there is depression, quickly seat the patient.

"For the Arm Major Yin Channel, the separation of the *luo* linking channel is at the point called Crack of Lightning.[5] This linking channel starts in the space on top of the wrist, goes along with the Major Yin Channel, and enters straight into the center of the palm and scatters as it enters the Fish Border. When this suffers from a solid disease, it causes the wrist bone and palm to be hot. When it is hollow, it results in yawning with the mouth open and an increasing frequency of urine. Treat by going to one and one-half *cun* beyond the wrist (at Lung 7). At this point, a separate branch travels to the Bright Yang.

"The *luo* linking channel to the Arm Minor Yin separates at the point called Penetrating Inside, which is beyond the crease of the wrist by one *cun*. After the separation, it travels up and follows the major channel to enter the middle of the heart, connects with the root of the tongue, and subordinates the eye connections. A solid disease results in a stick-like feeling in the chest. A hollow disease causes an inability to speak. Treat the point one *cun* beyond the palm. A separate branch travels to the Major Yang.

"The *luo* linking channel to the Arm Pericardium Channel separates at a point called Inner Gate, which is beyond the crease of the wrist by two *cun* and comes out between two tendons. It goes upwards along the major channel to connect with the pericardium. When the linking channel of the pericardium has a solid disease, it causes pain in the heart. A hollow disease causes rigidity of the head. Treat the point between the two tendons.

"The *luo* linking channel of the Arm Major Yang separates at the point called Branch Regulator. It is above the wrist by five *cun*. It flows inside to the Minor Yin. A branch goes up to the elbow and connects with the Shoulder Bone point. A solid disease results in a loosening of the joints and a wasting away of the elbow. A hollow disease results in the growth of small swellings and the smallest is like itching scabs. Treat by using the point of separation.

"The *luo* linking channel of the Arm Bright Yang separates at a point called Side Passage, which is beyond the wrist by three *cun*. There it separates and enters the Major Yin. Another branch separates and ascends, follows the upper arm, and rides on to the Shoulder Bone. It goes up along the curve of the jaw to slant into the teeth. Another branch enters the ear to join with the primary channel. A solid disease results in toothaches and deafness. A hollow disease results in coldness of the teeth and numbing of the diaphragm. Treat at the point of separation.

"The *luo* linking channel to the Arm Minor Yang separates at a point called Outer Gate. It is beyond the wrist by two *cun*. Continuing on the outside, it winds around the upper arm and shoulder to flow to the middle of the breast, and joins the pericardium. A solid disease results in warping of the elbow. A hollow disease results in the inability to crook. Treat at the point of separation.

"The *luo* linking channel to the Leg Major Yang separates at a point called Flying About. It is beyond the ankle bone by seven *cun*. It separates and travels to the Minor Yin. A solid disease results in a stuffed up nose and pains in the head and back. A hollow disease results in a bloody nose. Treat at the point of separation.

"The *luo* linking channel to the Leg Minor Yang separates at the point called Bright Light. It is beyond the ankle bone by five *cun*. It separates and travels to the Shrinking Yin, and goes down to connect with the dorsum of foot. A solid disease results in deficiencies. A hollow disease results in paralysis and lameness and an inability to rise from a sitting position. Treat at the point of separation.

"The *luo* linking channel to the Leg Bright Yang separates at the point called Abundant Mound. It is beyond the ankle bone by eight *cun*. It separates and travels to the Major Yin. The separation follows the lateral side of the leg bone, and ascends to connect at the top of the head to join with all the qi of the major channels in that area. It then descends to connect with the throat. When the diseased qi moves rebelliously in counterflow, it results in a numb throat and a sudden loss of voice. A solid disease causes madness. A hollow disease causes the foot to be inflexible and the shin to wither. Treat at the point of separation.

"The *luo* linking channel to the Leg Major Yin separates at the point called Grandfather Grandson. It is beyond the first metatarsophalangeal joint by one *cun*. It separates and travels to the Rushing Yang. This separation enters and connects the intestines and stomach. When deficient qi goes up in a counterflow it results in cholera. A solid disease causes the middle of the intestines to have sharp pains. A hollow disease causes a drum-like swelling of the intestines. Treat at the separation point.

"The *luo* linking channel to the Leg Minor Yin separates at a point called the Big Bell. It is behind the ankle bone, and from there winds around the heel. This separate channel travels to the Major Yang. A branch, together with the major channel, ascends and travels to below the pericardium, then goes externally through the loins and backbone. When its diseased qi is rebellious and in counterflow, it causes annoyance and depression. A solid disease causes constipation and a blockage of urine. A hollow disease causes pain in the loins. Treat the point of separation.

"The *luo* linking channel to the Leg Shrinking Yin separates at the point called Insect Groove, which is beyond the medial anklebone by five *cun*. It separates and travels to the Minor Yang. A branch flows along the leg, goes up to the testicles, and connects to the penis. When its diseased qi is rebellious and in counterflow, it results in swelling of the testicles and hernia. A solid disease results in an abnormal erection. A hollow disease results in cruel itching. Treat at the point of separation.

"The *luo* linking channel to the Conception Vessel separates at the point called Dove Tail. It is below the xiphoid process, and disperses to the abdomen. A solid disease results in pain in the skin of the abdomen. A hollow disease results in itching in that area. Treat at the point of separation.

"The *luo* linking channel to the Governing Vessel is at a point called Long and Strong. The point is below the coccyx. The channel goes clasping the backbone up to the neck and spreads at the top of the head. Then it descends both right and left along the medial side of the shoulder blades, branches to the Major Yang *luo* linking channel, then enters and goes through the backbone. A solid disease causes a rigidity of the backbone. A hollow disease causes the head to feel heavy, as well as a shaking from the top. This is from a trespass in the channel which clasps around the backbone. Treat at the point of separation.

"The great *luo* linking channel of the spleen starts at a point called Big Envelope, which is three *cun* below the Abyss of the Armpit. It extends to the breast and the ribs. A solid disease causes pain in the whole body. A hollow disease causes all of the hundred joints to loosen. This linking channel is the control for the network of *luo* linking channels and their blood. These can be treated by using the point of the great *luo* linking channel of the spleen.

"In all, there are fifteen *luo* channels. When they suffer from a solid disease they become visible. When they suffer from a hollow disease, they sink. Whether they are visible or invisible, one must investigate the complete circle, as well as top and bottom. People and channels both have their variations, so the *luo* linking channels have their differences and separations as well."

Notes

1. Chapter 48.
2. The Chinese word *dong* means "to move, to affect, to influence, to shake."
3. Here it means the seventh cervical vertebra.
4. One *cun* is approximately an inch. It is equal to .03581 meters.
5. The Chinese name, "Lie Que" can be translated as broken line, but I believe the point to have been associated with lightning and electrical discharge.

11. THE SEPARATE CHANNELS

Huang Di requested of Qi Bo, "I wish to hear how man is in tune with the Dao of Heaven and how internally the five viscera are in accord and resonate with the five tones, the five colors, the five seasons, the five flavors, the five positions, and also how externally the six bowels are in accord and resonate with the six pitch pipes. How do the six pitch pipes establish yin and yang and all the channels and join them with the twelve months, the twelve constellations, the twelve climatic divisions, the twelve river channels, the twelve daily time periods, and the twelve major channels? These are the resonances for the five viscera and the six bowels to be in accord with the Dao of heaven. For the twelve major channels in man are involved in the birth and the attack of disease, and also in the cures and causes of disease. Study these first. Work it out to the finish. The unskilled think it is easy; the superior know it is difficult. Please explain these separations and joinings, these exits and entrances."

Qi Bo kowtowed again and said, "How illuminating are these questions. The skilled pass right by them, while they are the very breath of the superior physician. Please listen to these words.

"The separate channel of the primary Leg Major Yang separates and enters into the middle of the crease of the knee. One path goes to a point five *cun* below the hip joint, and branches to enter the anus. It is allied with the bladder, spreads to the kidneys, then follows the backbone along both sides to enter and spread in the region of the heart. Straight branches follow the backbone up, come out in the neck and again are allied with the Major Yang. Here they join and make one channel.

"The separate channel of the primary Leg Minor Yin reaches the middle of the crease of the knee, separates and travels and joins the Major Yang, then goes up to reach the kidneys. At the point of the fourteenth vertebra, the second lumbar, it comes out and subordinates the Girdle Channel.[1] A straight branch connects with the root of the tongue, reverses, and comes out in the neck, where it joins the Major Yang to make the first junction. All of the yin separate channels are complete entities and may be compared to the primary channels.

"The separate channel of the primary Leg Minor Yang winds around the buttocks and enters the border of the pubic hair to join the Shrinking Yin. A branch enters the space between the lowest ribs and follows the base of the diaphragm to subordinate the gallbladder. It then spreads to the top of the liver, passes through the heart, and ascends

66

along the pinch of the throat to come out in the middle of the chin and jaw to spread into the face. It connects with the eye connections, then joins the Minor Yang at the lateral corner of the eye.

"The separate channel of the primary Leg Shrinking Yin separates at the top of the foot, then goes up to reach the border of the pubic hair, where it joins the Minor Yang. There they travel together and make the second junction.

"The separate channel of the primary Leg Bright Yang goes up to reach the buttocks, enters the base of the abdomen and subordinates the stomach. It then spreads to the spleen, goes up and penetrates the heart. It ascends, follows the throat to come out in the mouth, then continues up to the junctions of the nose and forehead to pass through and connect with the eye connections, and joins in the Rushing Yang.

"The primary Leg Major Yin travels up to reach the buttocks, where it joins the Rushing Yang. There they travel together, ascend to connect in the throat, and pass through the middle of the tongue. This is the third junction.

"The separate channel of the primary Arm Major Yang points to the earth and separates from the scapula to enter the armpit, travels the heart and subordinates the small intestine.

"The separate channel of the primary Arm Minor Yin separates from between two tendons to enter the Abyss of the Armpit and subordinate the heart. It goes up and travels to the throat, then comes out in the face. There it joins the Minor Yin at the medial corner of the eye and makes the fourth junction.

"The separate channel of the primary Arm Minor Yang points to heaven. It separates at the top of the head to enter the Broken Dish and descending, travels through the Triple Heater and spreads in the middle of the chest.

"The separate channel of the primary Arm Pericardium separates three *cun* below the Abyss of the Armpit to enter the center of the chest, where it separates to subordinate the Triple Heater. It comes out and follows the throat, then comes out behind the ear. It joins the Minor Yang below the Final Bone. This makes the fifth junction.

"The separate channel of the primary Arm Bright Yang goes from the hand to the chest and nipple. There it separates to go to Shoulder Bone and enters the Pillar Bone, the first cervical vertebra. Then it descends and travels to the large intestine. It subordinates the lungs, ascends and goes along the throat, and comes out in the Broken Dish to join the Bright Yang.

"The separate channel of the primary Arm Major Yin separates and enters the Abyss of the Armpit in front of the Minor Yin, then enters and travels to the lungs. It spreads around the Major Yang.[2] It ascends to come out in the Broken Dish, goes along the throat, then returns to join the Rushing Yang. This makes the sixth junction."

Notes

1. The Girdle Channel is one of the eight collateral channels.
2. The text is probably incorrect. The words should be "Rushing Yang" in reference to the Large Intestine Channel described in the previous paragraph, which would follow the system employed in the general format of this chapter.

12. RIVERS AND CHANNELS

Huang Di questioned Qi Bo, saying, "There are twelve major channels which externally are in resonance with the twelve rivers of water, while internally they subordinate the five viscera and six bowels. However, the twelve rivers of water are large or small, deep or shallow, wide or narrow, long or short. Each is unique. The five viscera and six bowels are high or low, large or small, and differ in the amount of valley qi they receive and distribute. What are their correspondences and harmonies? The rivers of water receive water and move. The five viscera resonate with spirit, qi, the human soul and the animal spirits, and store them. The six bowels receive the valley energy and move it. They also receive qi and spread it. The major channels receive blood and nourish with it. How may the above be coupled in making a cure? Please explain what depth of needling should be used, that is, deep or shallow, and the number and strength of the moxa cones."

Qi Bo replied, "How felicitous are these questions! For while it is said that the height of heaven is unlimited and the width of earth is immeasurable, and man is born in between heaven and earth and inside the six cardinal points, so for the height of heaven or the width of the earth, it is beyond man's strength to reach these boundaries and limits.

"For man who is on the average eight *chi*, the skin and flesh, and the external boundaries and limits may be measured, and the pulse taken.[1] Upon death, examination can reveal and disclose. There are great standard measures to the existence of the viscera being strong or weak; the bowels being large or small; the valleys being plentiful or sparse; the channels being long or short; the blood being clear or turbid; the qi being plentiful or sparse; the twelve major channels having much blood and little qi, or having little blood and much qi, or having much blood and qi, or having little blood and qi. Therefore, treatment in accord with acupuncture and moxibustion in each harmonizes the channel qi and is established by these constants having resonances."

Huang Di said, "I am pleased with what I hear, but it is still not clear in my mind. I would like to hear more of the origins."

Qi Bo replied, "In this, man is that which makes a triad with heaven and earth and has resonances with yin and yang. If one cannot comprehend this, one cannot make an examination. The Leg Major Yang externally is in resonance with the Qing River, and internally subordinates the bladder and penetrates the water ways. The Leg Minor Yang externally is in resonance with Wei River, and internally it subordinates the gallbladder. The Leg Bright Yang externally is in resonance with Hai River, and internally it subordinates the stomach. The Leg Major Yin externally is in resonance with the Hu River, while internally it subordinates the spleen. The Leg Minor Yin externally is in resonance with the Ru River, while internally it subordinates the kidney. The Leg Shrinking Yin externally is in resonance with the Mien River, while internally it subordinates the liver. The Arm Major Yang externally is in resonance with Huai River, while internally it subordinates the small intestine, which is the exit for the waterways. The Arm Minor Yang externally is in resonance with the Luo River, while internally it subordinates the Triple Heater. The Arm Bright Yang externally is in resonance with the Jiang River, the Yangtze, while internally it subordinates the large intestine. The Arm Major Yin externally is in resonance with the He River, the Yellow River, while internally it subordinates the lung. The Arm Minor Yin externally is in resonance with the Ji River, while internally it subordinates the heart. The Arm Pericardium externally is in resonance with the Zhang River, while internally it subordinates the pericardium.

"All of these, the five viscera, the six bowels, the twelve channels and river waters, externally have their headwaters, and internally have that which they subordinate, for all internally and externally are tied together, like a circle without end. This is also the case with man's channels.

"Therefore, since heaven is yang and the earth is yin, the area above the waist is comparable to heaven, while the area below the waist is comparable to earth. Therefore, north of the Hai River is yin, north of the Hu River is yin within yin. South of the Zhang River is yang. North of the He, or Yellow River, to the Zhang River is yin within yang. South of the Luo River until it reaches the Jiang, or Yangtze River, is the major yang in yang. This is one geographic rendering of yin and yang which is in accord with the mutual triad of man with heaven and earth."

Huang Di said, "There are correspondences and resonances between the major channels of qi and the rivers of water as to whether they are long or short, shallow or deep, and whether water or blood is plentiful or sparse, yet each is different. How can these resonances be applied to acupuncture?"

Qi Bo replied, "The Leg Bright Yang is like the sea to the five viscera and six bowels. Its channel is large, its blood plentiful, its qi abundant, and its heat strong. So if needling does not go deep, it will not disperse. If the needle is not detained, it will not disperse. On the Leg Bright Yang, needle to a depth of six *fen* and detain for ten exhalations of breath. For the Leg Major Yang, a depth of five *fen*, and detain for seven exhalations. For the Leg Minor Yang, a depth of four *fen*, and detain for five exhalations. For the Leg Major Yin, a depth of three *fen*, and detain for four exhalations. For the Leg Minor Yin, a depth of two *fen*, and detain for three exhalations. For the Leg Shrinking Yin, a depth of one *fen*, and detain for two exhalations.

"The yin and yang of the arm receive their qi from very close pathways, so their qi comes quickly. Do not needle beyond two *fen*, and do not detain the needle beyond one exhalation. One must keep in mind whether the person is young or old, large or small, fat or thin in accord with the laws of heaven, which are constant. Moxibustion also follows these rules. When moxa is excessive, it causes the illness of fire where the bones wither and the channels become rough. Excessive needling causes a stripping of the qi."

Huang Di said, "How can one determine the boundaries and limits, whether the major channels are large or small, the blood is plentiful or sparse, the skin is thick or thin, the flesh is firm or weak, and the crease of the knee large or small?"

Qi Bo replied, "These can be measured by taking an average person who is neither excessively lean or fleshy, and whose blood and qi are not weak. But how can one determine the boundaries of acupuncture if the criterion is a man who is emaciated, with a body and flesh looking stripped? To judge and to examine, follow the pulse with the hand. See if the patient is cold or warm, full or small, then harmonize. So it is said, the appropriateness of the treatment makes right."

Note

1. Eight *chi* (chinese foot) was the classic height for a gnomon, the upright pillar used to measure the sun's rays and thus the passage of time. In modern measure it equals approximately 1.84 meters. However, due to the ancient practice of using unique standards of measure for each individual person (e.g., the width of the thumb across the cuticle is a body inch or *cun*), every person could in fact be eight feet tall by his or her own standard of measurement. (See chapter 14, note 1.)

SCROLL FOUR
13. THE MUSCLE CHANNELS

"The muscle channel of the Leg Major Yang begins in the little toe of the foot, goes up to connect to the anklebone, then goes diagonally up to connect to the knee. A lower branch follows the lateral side of the foot to connect at the anklebone, then mounts and follows the heel to connect in the crease of the knee. A separate branch connects to the lateral part of the leg and ascends to the crease of the knee along the medial side, then goes from the center of the crease of the knee to connect to the buttocks. It continues up along the pinch of the backbone on both sides to the neck. A branch separates and enters to connect with the root of the tongue. A straight branch connects the neck to the Pillow Bone to the top of the head, then travels down in the space between eyebrows and eyes to connect in the nose. Another branch goes along the upper net of the eye and eyelid, then descends to connect with the cheekbone. Another branch goes from behind the armpit on the lateral side to connect at Shoulder Bone. Another branch enters the armpit, goes up to emerge at the Broken Dish, then moves up to connect to the Final Bone (mastoid process). Another branch comes out in the Broken Dish, and goes diagonally up into the cheekbones.

"The diseases of this muscle channel include swelling and pain in the little toe and the heel, spasms at the crease of the knee, a backward bent backbone, spasms in the neck muscles, an inability to raise the shoulders, cramps and pain in the branch from the armpit to the center of the Broken Dish, and inability to swing left or right. To treat, needle rapidly with a heated needle. The number of times should be in accord with knowledge and experience. Use the acupuncture points which are painful. These problems are called February rheumatism.

"The muscle channel of the Leg Minor Yang begins in the fourth toe, then travels up to the lateral anklebone and ascends along the lateral side of the leg to connect at the lateral side of the knee. A branch separates beginning on the lateral side of the thigh bone, then travels up through the thigh, where in the front it connects with Crouching Rabbit and in the back it connects with the buttocks. A straight branch ascends and rises to the depression under the bottom rib. It then travels up to the front side of the armpit, links with the region of the chest, and connects in the Broken Dish. A straight branch goes up and comes out at the armpit, goes through the Broken Dish to come out in front of the Leg Major Yang, and then travels to behind the ear. It goes up to the corner of the forehead and makes a junction at the top of the head, descends and travels to the chin, and goes up to connect with the cheekbones. A branch connects in the lateral corner of the eye and is the lateral connective.

"The diseases of this channel include muscle spasms of the fourth toe, muscle spasms of the lateral side of the knee so that the knee cannot bend or stretch, muscle spasms at the crease of the knee which to the front involves the thigh and to the back the buttocks. They can mount or ascend to cause pain in the depression under the bottom ribs, and continue up to cause pains in the Broken Dish, the region of the chest, as well as cramped muscles in the neck. If muscle cramps go from the left to the right, the right eye will be unable to open, because as the channel goes up, it passes through the right corner of the forehead travelling together with the Anklebone Channel. Because left is connected to right, an injury to the left corner will cause the right foot not to function. This is called the mutual intercourse of connected muscles. To cure, needle rapidly with a heated needle. The number of times should be in accord with knowledge and experience. Use the acupuncture points which are painful. This is called January rheumatism.

"The muscle channel of the Leg Bright Yang begins in the second toe and connects with the third toe, goes to the top of the foot, goes diagonally upward and laterally along the leg bone. It continues up to connect to the lateral side of the knee, and goes straight up to connect to the pivot of the thigh, ascends to follow the flanks, and is attached to the backbone. A straight branch goes up and follows the leg bone to connect with the knee. A branch connection goes along the leg bone and joins the Leg Minor Yang. Another straight branch goes up, follows the Crouching Rabbit, ascends and connects to the thigh, then assembles in the yin organs. Then it ascends and spreads in the abdomen to reach and connect to the Broken Dish. It goes up the neck and the pinch of the mouth on both sides to meet in the cheekbones, descends to connect with the nose, then goes up to meet the Leg Major Yang. The Major Yang is the upper eyelid. The Rushing Yang is the lower eyelid. Another branch goes from the cheek to connect with the front of the ear.

"The diseases of this muscle channel include muscle spasms of the middle toe and the leg, jumping hard feelings in the foot, muscle spasms of the Crouching Rabbit, swelling of the front part of the thigh, hernia, muscle spasms of the abdomen which can involve the Broken Dish and cheek, a sudden twisted mouth and eyes which will not shut. If heat causes relaxed muscles, the eyes will not open. If the muscles of the cheek are cold, it causes spasms and will induce twisting of cheek and mouth. If there is heat, it will cause the muscles to relax deeply. This makes the muscle unable to contract and causes a distortion. To treat, use an ointment of horse fat to apply in case of spasm. Use white wine and cinnamon to smear over flaccid areas and use a mulberry hook at the corner of the mouth. The use of this hook is immediately in resonance with the fresh mulberry coals placed in the middle of the pit. The depth of the pit should be determined by sitting. Use the ointment as if ironing out the contracted cheek; moreover, drink good wine, and chew some good broiled meat. For those who do not drink wine, try to strengthen the self with a small amount, then give three-slap massage to try to cure the problem. To treat, needle rapidly with a heated needle. The number of times should be in accord with knowledge and experience. Use the acupuncture points which are painful. This is called March rheumatism.

"The muscle channel of the Leg Major Yin begins at the tip of the big toe on its medial side. Then it goes up to connect to the medial anklebone. A straight branch makes a path up along the leg bone to the medial side of the knee, ascends to the yin side of the thigh to connect with the upper thigh and assemble in the yin organs. It goes up the abdomen to connect in the navel, follows the base of the abdomen to connect with the flanks, then spreads in the middle of the breast. An internal branch is attached to the backbone.

"The diseases of this muscle channel are pains in the big toe and the medial anklebone, pain and spasms of the muscles, pain along the leg bone and the medial side of the knee, pain in the yin side of the thigh where it leads to the upper thigh, knotting pain in the sexual organs, which can lead up to the navel and both flanks and cause pain in the chest and the center of the spine. To treat, needle rapidly with a heated needle. The number of times should be in accord with knowledge and experience. Use the acupuncture points which are painful. This is called August rheumatism.[1]

"The muscle channel of the Leg Minor Yin begins in the bottom of the foot on a line with the little toe. Then it goes together with the muscle channel of the Leg Major Yin and travels diagonally to below the medial anklebone to connect with the heel and join the muscle channel of the Major Yang. Then it goes up to connect with the medial side of the leg and goes together with the muscle channel of the Major Yin to ascend to the yin side of the thigh. It continues to the yin organs, then follows the backbone along the inner pinch of the spine along both sides until it reaches the back of the neck and connects to the Pillow Bone, and joins the muscle channel of the Leg Major Yang.

"The diseases of this muscle channel include muscle spasms in the bottom of the foot, and painful spasms where there is a trespass at the connection points. Other diseases include epilepsy, spasms, and cramps. When the back is affected, one cannot bend forward. When the front is affected, one cannot bend backward. Consequently, if it is a yang disease, the waist opposes a bending and one is unable to bow down. If it is a yin disease, one is unable to bend backwards and look up. To control, needle rapidly with a heated needle. The number of times should be in accord with knowledge and experience. Use the acupuncture points which are painful. When the disease is internal, use an ointment to iron it out, and drink some medicine. When this muscle channel is bent and tied up, this tying up, if frequent and extreme, means death, an incurable disease. This is called July rheumatism.

"The muscle channel of the Leg Shrinking Yin begins on the top of the big toe, then goes up to connect to the front of the medial anklebone, ascends and follows the leg bone. It continues up along the inside to connect below the tibia, then continues up along the yin side of the thigh to connect with the yin organs, where it connects with all of the muscle channels.

"The diseases of this channel include pain in the big toe and along the channel up to the front of the medial anklebone, pain along the medial side of the leg, pain and spasms in the muscles in the inner thigh. Malfunction of the sexual organs from an internal injury will result in no erection; injury from cold will result in contractions of the sexual organs; injury from heat will result in an abnormally long erection. Treat the organs where there is movement of water and clear the yin qi. When the disease is muscle spasms, treat by needling rapidly with a heated needle. The number of times should be in accord with knowledge and experience. Use the acupuncture points which are painful. This is called September rheumatism.

"The muscle channel of the Arm Major Yang begins on the top of the little finger, connects with the wrist, follows the medial side of the arm to connect with the elbow behind the Inner Pointed Bone (medial epicondyle), which, when snapped, has corresponding sensations on the top of the little finger. It continues by entering and connecting to the bottom of the armpit. A branch travels behind the armpit to ascend and to wind around the shoulder blade, then follows the neck to come out and travel to the front of the Leg Major Yang, and connects behind the ear on the Final Bone. Another branch enters the middle of the ear. Another straight branch comes out above the ear, descends to connect to the chin and jaws, then goes up to subordinate the lateral corner of the eye.

"The diseases of this muscle channel include pain in the little finger, along the branch to the elbow on the medial side, and behind the medial epicondyle, as well as pain along the yin side of the upper arm, the area below the armpit, the bottom of the armpit, on the surface behind the armpit, and pain which winds around the shoulder blade, which in turn includes pain in the neck. There are correspondences between ringing in the middle of the ear and pain in the chin and jaws, delayed vision after prolonged closing of the eyes, and spasms in the neck muscles, which can cause ulcers and swellings in the neck, and chills and heat at the neck. To treat, needle rapidly with the heated needle. The number of times should be in accord with knowledge and experience. Use the acupuncture points which are painful. When there is swelling, repeat treatment with the sharp needle. A branch goes up through the curve of the teeth and jaws and goes in front of the ear to subordinate the lateral corner of the eye. Then it goes up along a line above the jaws to connect with the corner of the forehead. When there are spasms in the muscles along this branch, there will be pain at points where this line passes through. To treat, needle rapidly with heated needle. The number of times should be in accord with knowledge and experience. Use the acupuncture points which are painful. This is called May rheumatism.

"The muscle channel of the Arm Minor Yang begins on the tip of the ring finger on the side of the little finger and goes to connect at the wrist. It ascends along the middle of the arm and connects to the elbow, goes up around the lateral side of the upper arm, and ascends to the shoulder. It travels to the neck to join with the Arm Major Yang. A branch from the point at the bend of the jaw enters to connect with the root of the tongue. Another branch goes up to the bend of the teeth and jaws, goes along in front of the ear, then subordinates the lateral angle of the eye. Then it ascends, mounting a line above the jaw to connect with the corner of the forehead.

"The diseases of this muscle channel include cramps of the muscles at the points which pass through this branch, and a rolled-up tongue. To treat, needle rapidly with a heated needle. The number of times should be in accord with knowledge and experience. Use the acupuncture points which are painful. This is called June rheumatism.

"The muscle channel of the Arm Bright Yang begins on the tip of the forefinger on the side next to the thumb. It connects with the wrist and moves up, follows the forearm, then goes up to connect with the outside of the elbow. It ascends the upper arm to connect with the shoulder. A branch winds around the shoulder bone to the pinch along both sides of the backbone. A straight branch goes along the shoulder bone and ascends the neck. Another branch goes up the cheek to connect the cheekbones. A straight branch ascends and comes out in front of the Arm Major Yang, mounts to the left corner of the forehead, links with the channel of the head, and moves down to the right chin and jaws.

"The diseases of this channel include pain and cramping of the muscles at the points through which this branch passes, and an inability to raise the shoulder or to turn the neck either to the left or right to look. To treat, needle rapidly with a heated needle. The number of times should be in accord with knowledge and experience. Use the acupuncture points which are painful. This is called April rheumatism.

"The muscle channel of the Arm Major Yin begins on the top of the thumb, then travels along the thumb to connect to the rear of the Fish, then moves to the lateral side of the Inch Mouth and ascends along the arm to connect to the center of the elbow. Then it mounts the medial surface of the upper arm to enter the bottom of the armpit, comes out in the Broken Dish, and connects to the front of the shoulder joint. On top there is a connection in the Broken Dish, below there is a connection in the base of the chest, where it spreads and goes through the cardiac orifice, assembles, then goes down to the lowest rib.

"The diseases of this muscle channel include cramping of the muscles at the points where this channel passes through. Extreme pain in the cardiac orifice may cause panting. Spasms in the ribs may cause the spitting of blood. To treat, needle rapidly with a heated needle. The number of times should be in accord with knowledge and experience. Use the acupuncture points which are painful. This is called November rheumatism.

"The muscle channel of the Arm Pericardium begins in the middle finger, then travels together with the muscle channel of the Major Yin to connect to the medial side of the elbow. It then ascends the yin side of the upper arm to connect with the bottom of the armpit, and spreads down both to the front and back by clasping the ribs. A branch enters the armpit and spreads to the center of the chest to connect with the cardiac orifice.[2]

"The diseases of this muscle channel include cramping of the muscles on the points along which this channel passes, pain in the sternum, and throbbing of the cardiac area. To treat, needle rapidly with the heated needle. The number of times should be in accord with knowledge and experience. Use the acupuncture points which are painful. This is called October rheumatism.

"The muscle channel of the Arm Minor Yin begins on the inner side of the little finger, then connects to the Pointed Bone (pisiform bone), the ulna, and goes up to connect to the medial side of the elbow. Then it goes up to enter the armpit, intersects with the Major Yin, and clasps the base of the nipple to connect with the center of the chest. Then it goes along the cardiac orifice and descends to connect with the navel.[3]

"These diseases internally are spasms of the heart which rise and fall like wooden beams.[4] Below, they may make the elbow feel as if it is in a net. The diseases of this muscle channel include pain and cramping of the muscles at the points along which its branches pass through. To treat, needle rapidly with a heated needle. The number of times should be in accord with knowledge and experience. Use the acupuncture points which are painful. When the symptoms of prostrated wooden beams occur with the spitting of blood and pus, it is death, there is no cure.

"For the diseases of the muscle channels, cold will cause a violent contraction and spasms of the muscles, heat will cause muscle relaxation weakness and malfunction of the yin organs. When the yang is in spasm, it will cause a bending backwards. When the yin is in spasm, it will cause a bending forward and an inability to stretch.[5] The fire needle may be used to needle cold spasms. Do not use the heated needle when heat causes muscles to relax and to be weak. This is called December rheumatism.

"When muscle spasms of the Leg Bright Yang and the Arm Major Yang cause the mouth and eyes to be twisted, and spasms of the eyes make one unable to see quickly, treat all of these with the proper methods as outlined above."

Notes

1. The text reads "July," which is probably an error, since the next section is about "July." "August" would be in conformation with later texts.

2. The original text reads "the upper arm" instead of "cardiac orifice" which is probably an error. Most Chinese commentaries believe this line

should have "cardiac orifice" replace the word for arm since this is the channel of the pericardium.

3. The text says "the upper arm", probably an error. See note 2.

4. Probably a heart attack.

5. The back is yang. The front is yin.

14. MEASUREMENTS IN REFERENCE TO THE BONES

Huang Di questioned Bo Gao, saying, "The limits of the major channels may be long or short. How is this established?"

Bo Gao said, "First, measure the bones from their joints, whether they are large or small, wide or narrow, long or short, to establish the limits of the channels."

Huang Di said, "I have heard there is an average unit of measure for man, that man's length is seven *chi* five *cun*, but the sections of the bones are large and small, long and short.[1] How many individual items are there?"

Bo Gao said, "The circumference of the head at its great bones is two *chi* six *cun*.[2] The circumference of the chest is four *chi* five *cun*. The circumference of the waist is four *chi* two *cun*. Going from the hairline on the front forehead to the hairline on the back of the neck is one *chi* two *cun*. From the front hairline down to the jaws is one *chi*. So is a gentleman tied and bound by these measurements. Going down from the throat where it connects to the middle between the two Broken Dish points is a length of four *cun*. Descending from this point, between the two Broken Dish points on the jugular notch to the tip of the sternum, is a length of nine *cun*. When this length is excessive, it is because the lungs are large. When it is not very full, it is because the lungs are small. From the tip of the sternum to the navel in between the Celestial Pivot is eight *cun*. When excessive, it is because the stomach is large. When it is not excessive, it is because the stomach is small. From the Celestial Pivot down to the Horizontal Bone (pelvic bone) is a length of six and one-half *cun*. When it is very long, it is because the curvature of the intestines is wide and long; when not very full, it is because they are narrow and short. The Horizontal Bone from side to side is six and one-half *cun*. From the upper edge of the Horizontal Bone down to the upper edge of the medial side of the Support Bone (tibia), the medial condyle of the femur is one *chi* eight *cun*. From the medial condyle of femur to the point below the medial condyle of the tibia is three and one-half *cun*. From the lower edge of the medial condyle of the tibia to the medial malleolus is a length of one *chi* three *cun*. From the medial malleolus to the ground is a length of three *cun*. From the popliteal fossa of the knee down to the tuberosity of the heel is one *chi* six *cun*. From the upper edge of the tuberosity of the heel to the ground is a length of three *cun*. Therefore, if the circumference of a bone is great, it will exceed the average size, while if the circumference is small, it will not reach the average size. From the corner down to the Support Bone is a length of one *chi*. Moving from there invisibly to the center of the armpits is a length of four *cun*.[3] From the armpit down to the lowest rib, is a length of one *chi* two *cun*. From the lowest rib to the pivot of the thigh (greater trochanter) is a length of six *cun*.

"From the pivot of the thigh down to the center of the knee on the lateral side is one *chi* nine *cun*. From the knee down to the lateral malleolus is one *chi* six *cun*. From the lateral malleolus down to the Level Bone, the tuberosity of the fifth metatarsal bone, is a length of three *cun*. From the Level Bone down to the ground is one *cun*.

"The width is nine *cun* between the points on the Final Bone[4] and the mastoid process which is behind the ears. In front of the ears, between the points called Ear Door is a width of one *chi* three *cun*. The width between the cheekbones, zygomas, is seven *cun*. Between the two nipples is a width of nine and one-half *cun*. Between the two thighs, the medial edges, is a width of six and one-half *cun*. The length of the foot is one *chi* two *cun*, the width is four and one-half *cun*. The shoulder to the elbow is a length of one *chi* seven *cun*. The elbow to the wrist is a length of one *chi* and one-half *cun*. The wrist to the base joint of the middle finger (metacarpophalangeal joint) is a length of four *cun*. From the base joint of the middle finger to the tip is a length of four and one-half *cun*.

"From the nape of the neck at the lower edge of the hairline to the backbone is a length of two and one-half *cun*.[5] The backbone, from beginning to the tail bone, which includes twenty-one vertebrae, is a length of three *chi*. Each upper vertebrae is 1.41 *cun* long. The remainder are divided among those beneath, therefore, the upper cervical seven vertebrae from the backbone is a distance of 9.87 *cun*.

"These are the measurements of the bones of the average man, which allow the establishment of whether the major channels are long or short. This may be used to visualize the major channels in the human body, to see if one is floating or solid, bright and large with much blood, or thin and sinking with much qi."

Notes

1. *Chi*, the Chinese foot equals ten *cun*.
2. The great bones are from eyebrow to inion to eyebrow.

3. I believe this to be the measurement from the corner of the eye to the seventh cervical vertebra, the Support Bone.

4. Here it means the protrusion of the occipital bone.

5. Kiln Path (Governing Vessel 13).

15. THE FIFTY REGULATORS

Huang Di said, "I wish to hear about the fifty regulators. What are they?"

Qi Bo replied, "Heaven revolves around the twenty-eight constellations. A constellational unit is divided into thirty-six divisions. Man's qi travels in one revolutionary cycle, one thousand and eight divisions, while the sun moves through the twenty-eight constellations. For man, the major channels on top and bottom, to left and right, to front and back, total twenty-eight channels.[1]

"The water clock drippings are divided into one hundred quarters in accordance with divisions of day and night. Consequently, for man, for each exhalation, there is a repeating movement in the channels, wherein the qi travels three *cun*. For each inhalation, there is also a repetitive movement in the channels, and the qi travels three *cun*. For one complete breath there is a travelling motion of the qi of six *cun*.[2] In ten breaths, the qi travels six *chi*, the sun travels two divisions. In two hundred and seventy breaths, the qi travels one hundred and sixty-two *chi*. The qi travels, crosses and penetrates in the center within one revolution through the body. The dripping water measures two quarter intervals, the sun moves twenty-five divisions. In five hundred and forty breaths, the qi makes two revolutions through the body. The dripping water measures four quarter intervals, the sun moves forty divisions. In two thousand seven hundred breaths, the qi makes ten revolutions through the body. The dripping water measures twenty quarter intervals. The sun travels five constellations and twenty divisions. In thirteen thousand five hundred breaths, the qi travels the fifty regulators, fifty revolutions through the body. Water dripping measures one hundred quarter intervals. The sun travels twenty-eight constellations. With this, the water clock is exhausted, and the channels are complete, so it is said to cross and to penetrate the travel one full count. Consequently fifty revolutions is a completion, and is a long life completely from heaven and earth. Within the total movement is eight hundred and ten times ten *chi*."

Notes

1. Twelve major channels times two, for being bilateral, equal twenty-four. In addition, the Conception Vessel, the Governing Vessel, and the Anklebone Mobility Channels, which are bilateral, equal twenty-eight.

2. One complete breath is one exhalation and inhalation.

16. THE NOURISHING QI

Huang Di said, "The way of the nourishing qi is the treasure of the Inner Valley. The valley qi enters the stomach, then transmits to the lungs, flows to fill up the center, covers and spreads to the externals. The seminal essence propagates and travels in the tunnels of the channels. The nourishing never completes, it ends and then returns to the beginning. This is spoken of as the contract of heaven and earth. The qi goes from the Major Yin, the lung, to come out and flow into the Arm Bright Yang, which then ascends to travel and to flow into the Leg Bright Yang. Then the qi travels down to reach the upper surface of the foot and flows to the gap of the big toe to join the Major Yin. Up it travels to go through the buttocks to the spleen and flows to the center of the heart, which goes with the Arm Minor Yin. It comes out at the armpit, descends the arm, and flows to the little finger to join the Arm Major Yang. It then ascends to move and to ride the armpit to come out in the inner cheekbone and flows to the inner point of the eye, mounts to the top of the head, descends to the nape of the neck, and joins with the Leg Major Yang which follows the backbone and goes down to the buttocks and continues to flow down to the tip of the little toe. Then the qi goes to the sole of the foot to flow in the Leg Minor Yin and travels up to flow into the kidney. From the kidney, it flows to the exterior of the heart and spreads in the middle of the breast to follow the Pericardium Channel, which comes out at the armpit, descends the arm, and comes out between the two tendons. Then it enters the middle of the palm and comes out at the tip of the middle finger. The qi then turns around and flows to the tip of the ring finger to join the Arm Minor Yang. Up it travels to flow into the middle of the sternum and spread into the Triple Heater. It goes from the Triple Heater and flows to the gallbladder, to come out at the ribs and flow to the Leg Minor Yang. It descends, travels until it reaches the top of the foot, then turns on the foot to flow to the gap of the big toe, where it joins the Leg Shrinking Yin. It travels up to reach the liver, goes through the liver, and ascends and flows to the lungs. There it goes up to the throat, enters the cavities of the cheekbones and forehead and the apertures of the Nourishing Doors (nasal passages). A branch separates to ascend to the forehead, goes to the top of the head, descends to the middle at the nape of the neck, then follows the spine to enter the coccyx. This is the Governing Vessel. A road goes to the yin organs, then goes up, passes through the middle of the pubic hair to enter the middle of the navel, continues up through the abdomen, enters the Broken Dish, then descends to flow to the center of the lungs, and returns to come out in the Major Yin.

"These are the travels of the nourishing qi and its constant flow and counterflow."

17. THE LIMITS OF THE CHANNELS

Huang Di said, "I wish to hear about the limits of the channels."

Qi Bo replied, "The hands have six yang channels which go from the hands to the head. Each is five *chi* in length.[1] Five times six is a total of thirty *chi*. The hands have six yin channels which go from the hands to the middle of the chest. Each is three *chi* five *cun* in length. Three times six is eighteen *chi*. Five *cun* times six is three *chi*, which combined equals twenty-one *chi*.

"The feet have six yang channels which go from the feet up to the head. Each is eight *chi*. Six times eight is forty-eight *chi*. The feet have six yin channels which go from the feet to the middle of the chest. Each is six *chi* five *cun*. Six times six is thirty-six *chi*. Five *cun* times six is three *chi*, which, combined, equals thirty-nine *chi*.

"The Anklebone Channels go from the foot to the eye. Each is seven *chi* five *cun*. Two times seven is fourteen *chi*. Two times five *cun* is one *chi*, which combined, equals fifteen *chi*.

"The Governing Vessel and the Conception Vessel each is four *chi* five *cun*. Two times four is eight *chi*. Two times five *cun* is one *chi*, which combined, equals nine *chi*. The total of the combinations equals one hundred sixty-two *chi*. This is the great channel and tunnel for the qi. The major channels make the foundation. The branches are horizontal and make the *luo* channels. These channels divide and make tiny channels, which when abundant with blood, quickly drain them. When the qi is abundant, disperse; when hollow, drink medicines in order to tonify.

"The five viscera internally constantly pass through and ascend to the seven orifices. Thus, the lung qi penetrates into the nose. The lung in balance allows the nose to savor smells and fragrances. The heart in balance allows the tongue to savor the five flavors. The liver qi penetrates the eyes. The liver in balance allows the eyes to distinguish the five colors. The spleen qi penetrates into the mouth. The spleen in balance allows the mouth to savor the five valleys. The kidney qi penetrates into the ears. The kidney in balance allows the ears to hear the five tones.

"The five viscera not in balance cause the seven orifices to be impassable. The six bowels not in balance cause a detaining, which will make swellings. Consequently, when the evil qi rests in the bowels, it results in the yang channels being unbalanced. The yang channels being unbalanced causes the qi to detain. The qi detained results in the yang qi being abundant. The yang qi excessively abundant results in the yin not prospering. The yin channels not prospering result in the blood being detained. The blood detained results in the yin qi being abundant. The yin qi excessively abundant results in the yang qi not being able to nourish and prosper. Therefore, these are spoken of as barriers. The yang qi excessively abundant results in the yin qi being unable to nourish and prosper. Therefore, these are spoken of as limits. Yin and yang both abundant and neither being able to prosper is therefore called barriers and limits. Barriers and limits mean one does not receive full term of life so there is death."

Huang Di said, "The Anklebone Channels, how do they begin and how do they stop? What qi nourishes and prospers their waters?"

Qi Bo replied, "The Yin Anklebone Channel separates from the Minor Yin and begins behind Blazing Valley, goes up to the top of the medial anklebone, then goes straight up to the yin surface of the leg and enters the yin part of the body.[2] It continues up into the inside of the breast to enter the Broken Dish, goes up and comes out in front of the Man's Receptor point. It enters the cheekbones, subordinates the inner corner of the eye, and joins with the Major Yang, Bladder Channel, and the Yang Anklebone Channel and travels up. When the qi moves mutually and together, it will result in nourishing the eyes. When the qi does not prosper, it will result in the eyes not closing."

Huang Di said, "When the qi moves uniquely in the five viscera but does not nourish the six bowels, what then?"

Qi Bo replied, "Qi can never be not moving. It is like water flowing, like the sun and moon travelling without rest. Consequently, the yin channels nourish the viscera, the yang channels nourish the bowels. Like a ball without corners, without knowledge of its starting point, the qi finishes and returns to the beginning. The qi flows and spreads. Internally it irrigates the viscera and bowels, externally it moistens the body between the skin and flesh."

Huang Di said, "The Anklebone Channels have a yin and a yang. How do you measure these when including them in the total length of the channels?"

Qi Bo said, "The male measure includes the yang. The female measure includes the yin at the point of measuring the channels. The *luo* channels are not to be measured or included."

Notes

1. *Chi* is a unit of measurement of length in China. In modern times it equals 1/3 meter. It is also called a Chinese foot. It equals 10 *cun* or 100 *fen*.

2. In modern descriptions it starts at the Shining Sea point (Kidney 6).

18. THE BIRTH AND ASSEMBLING OF THE
NOURISHING QI AND PROTECTIVE QI

Huang Di questioned Qi Bo, saying, "How does man receive qi? How do yin and yang meet? Which qi nourishes? Which qi protects? How does nourishing qi follow birth? How and where does the protective qi assemble? The dissimilar qi of the aged and the strong, the different positions of yin and yang, I would like to hear of these and how they meet."

Qi Bo replied, "Man receives qi from the valleys. The valleys enter into the stomach and qi is then transmitted into the lungs. Then the five viscera and the six bowels all receive qi. The clear qi is the nourishing qi; the muddy qi is the protective qi. The nourishing qi is located in the middle of the channels; the protective qi is located outside of the channels. The nourishing qi circulates without stop through the fifty revolutions, then repeats this great assembling. Yin and yang are mutually strung together like a ball without corners. The protective qi travels in the yin for twenty-five stages, and travels in the yang for twenty-five stages which are the divisions of day and night. Therefore, when the qi reaches the yang it begins, when it reaches the yin it stops. So it is said that at midday the yang is heavily yang, while at midnight the yin is heavily yin. Consequently, the Major Yin controls the inside, and the Major Yang controls the outside, and each moves twenty-five stages, divided between day and night.[1]

"At midnight is the abundant yin; after midnight, yin decreases. At dawn, yin is exhausted and yang receives the qi. At midday is the abundant yang, but as the sun goes west, yang decreases. As the sun sets, the yang is exhausted and yin receives the qi. At midnight occurs the great assembly, and the multitudes all sleep. This is proclaimed the closing of yin. At dawn, yin is depleted, and yang receives the qi. This goes without completion, for heaven and earth are bound together."

Huang Di said, "Old men do not close their eyes at night. What manner of qi sends this force? Youngsters do not close their eyes during day time. What manner of qi sends this force?"

Qi Bo replied, "The strong have abundant qi and blood. Their muscles and flesh are smooth. The qi penetrates its way, the nourishing and protective qi move and do not lose their constancy. Thus, the seminal essence is there during the day, and sleeps during the night. The aged have decreased qi and blood, for their muscles and flesh wither and the qi passage is rough. When the five viscera's qi is unbalanced, their nourishing qi is lessened and their protective qi is cut internally. Thus, there is no seminal essence during the day, and no rest at night.

Huang Di said, "I wish to hear about the movement of the nourishing and protective qi, all about how and where their paths lead."

Qi Bo replied, "The nourishing qi comes out in the middle heater, the protective qi comes out in the lower heater."

Huang Di said, "I would like to hear about the Triple Heater and that which comes out."

Qi Bo replied, "The upper heater comes out in the upper mouth of the stomach, with the throat as an upper pass through to the diaphragm, where it extends and spreads to the middle of the chest, travels to the armpit, and follows the branches of the Major Yin as it travels. It turns to reach the Bright Yang, ascends to the tongue, then descends the Leg Bright Yang. It is consistent in nourishing all, in travelling the twenty-five stages of yang, and also in travelling the twenty-five stages of yin, which complete one revolution. Therefore there are fifty stages and a return to the great assembly of the Arm Major Yin."

Huang Di said, "When man has eaten the hot food and drink, they descend to the stomach and the qi is unsettled, and so sweat comes out. Perhaps it comes out in the face, or in the back, or in half the body. It does not follow the way of the protective qi in coming out. Why is that?"

Qi Bo said, "When the exterior is injured by the wind, the interior is opened at the pores, the hair is steamed, and the body fluids leak from the interior. The protective qi travels, but is blocked and cannot obtain and follow its path. The qi is fierce, slippery, and urgent. It sees openings and comes out, because it cannot obtain and follow its path. Thus, this is called a leaking funnel."

Huang Di said, "I wish to hear about the middle heater and that which comes out."

Qi Bo replied, "The middle heater is also together with the middle of the stomach. It comes out behind the upper heater. This is what receives the qi, secretes the dregs, and steams the body fluids. It transforms the fine essence. It goes up and flows into the Lung Channel, then transforms and makes blood in accord with serving the growth of the body. But there is nothing costly in this. Therefore, this qi alone is obtained and travels in the tunnels of the channels. This is called nourishing qi."

Huang Di said, "There is blood and there is qi, different names yet the same species. What can be said about this?"

Qi Bo replied, "The nourishing qi and the protective qi are the essences of the valley qi. There is blood and spirit qi. For blood and qi, there are different names for similar species. Thus, when blood is exhausted, there is no sweat. When sweat is exhausted, there is no blood. Therefore, man can have two types of death, by yin or yang, but not two births.

Huang Di said, "I wish to hear about the lower heater and that which comes out."

Qi Bo replied, "The lower heater separates around the intestine, then flows to the bladder, where it seeps and enters. Therefore the water and food constantly dwell together in the middle of the stomach, some of which become dregs, and all descend into the large intestine and complete the lower heater. When all this descends, the process of seepage takes place. The sap separates from the dregs to follow the lower heater, some of the sap seeps into the bladder."

Huang Di said, "When man drinks wine, the wine also enters the stomach, and the valleys are not heated, the urine begins to descend alone. Why is this?"

Qi Bo replied, "When wine heats the valleys and the body fluids, its qi is fierce and clearing. Therefore, when it enters after food, the former food and body fluids will flow out."

Huang Di said, "Excellent, I have heard it said that the upper heater is like vapors, the middle heater like bubbles, and the lower heater like sluices."

Note

1. Major yin is a poetic reference to the moon. Major yang is for the sun. The water clock's fifty periods of time are divided equally between light and dark.

19. THE QI OF THE FOUR SEASONS

Huang Di requested of Qi Bo, saying, "The qi of the four seasons, each has a different form. The hundred diseases' beginnings, they all have that from which they grow. Moxibustion and acupuncture have their Dao. What are the certainties?"

Qi Bo replied, "The qi of the four seasons, each has its position. Moxibustion and acupuncture's way are to obtain qi at the acupuncture holes. Therefore, in the spring treat the channels, the blood channels, and the divisions in between the flesh.[1] When the disease is extreme, needle deeply; when moderate, needle shallowly. In summer, treat the abundant channels and the tiny *luo* channels. Treat the divisions in between the flesh. Stop the needle just under the skin. In autumn, treat the *shu* stream points on the channels. When evil qi is located in the bowels, treat the *he* confluence or sea points. In winter, treat the *jing* well points and the *ying* spring points. One must needle deeply and detain.

"If there are warm fevers and lack of sweat, it can be treated with fifty-nine possible acupuncture sites. When wind and water swell the skin, there are fifty-seven possibilities for the needle. Treat the skin when the *luo* channels have blood. Treat until the disease is exhausted.

"When there is diarrhea, tonify the three yin as they ascend at Three Yin Junction. Tonify Yin Mound Spring, and detain all the needles for a long time. When there is warm activity, then stop.

"When there are cramped muscles in the yang, treat the yang. When there are cramped muscles in the yin, treat the yin. For all these, heated needling can be used.

"For edema, first treat the point three *cun* below the Round Valley, Wind Market. Use the sword needle to needle. When finished, needle with a tubular needle and insert. Enter repeatedly so that it will drain the edema until the area is solid. When the edema goes slowly, it will cause annoyance and melancholy. When it goes quickly, it will cause peace and quiet. Needle every other day until the edema is exhausted, then stop.

"Drink medicines for obstructions.[2] Properly needle according to the season, following the drinking. To take the medicine properly, drink it without eating food. To dine properly, do not take the medicine. Do not eat the food which would be injurious for a total of one hundred thirty-five days.[3]

"For chronic rheumatism which does not go away, and chronic coldness, treat both by using Three Distances. When the bones are like

93

wooden stems, or the middle of the intestines is not easy, treat with the Three Distances point. If abundant, disperse; if hollow, tonify.

"For swellings caused by wind, needle above the site of the swelling. After this needling is complete, then use the sharp needle to needle the site and press with the hand to push out this evil qi. When the swelling is exhausted, then stop. Be constant in eating the proper food. Do not eat strange food.

"When the center of the abdomen rumbles frequently, the qi is ascending and rushing into the chest. When for a long time it is not possible to settle a panting of breath, the evil qi is located in the large intestine. Needle Throat of the Umbilicus, the Great Hollow Upper Passage and Three Distances.

"From the small intestine, there is control of the marshes, testes, and a passage to the loins and backbone. Then it goes up on a road to the heart. When evil qi is located in the small intestine, the connection to the marshes and testes, is tied. Also, there are ties as it subordinates the backbone and goes through the liver, lungs, and the *luo* channel of the heart. When the evil qi is abundant, it results in a deficiency and a counterflow which rises and rushes through intestines and stomach. It scorches the liver and spreads in the vitals, where it is connected to the navel. Therefore, treat Vital Origin to scatter it. Needle the Lung Channel of the Major Yin and tonify. Treat the Liver Channel of the Shrinking Yin in accord with lowering its energy. Treat the Great Hollow Lower Passage to get rid of excess. To harmonize, press and massage that qi which is excessive in the channels.

"When there is frequent vomiting, and the vomiting has a bitter taste, and the breaths are very long, and the heart center is shaking and shaking, and one has the fear of being apprehended, the evil qi is in the gallbladder. There is a rebellious counterflow in the stomach. The gallbladder leaks body fluids, which causes a bitter taste in the mouth. The stomach qi being in counterflow causes the bitter vomit; therefore, it is called vomiting from the gallbladder. Treat the Three Distances point when the lower stomach qi is in counterflow. Needle the Minor Yang's blood *luo* channels in using them to block and to decrease the counterflow and rebellion in the gallbladder. Harmonize the hollow and the solid in order to put away the evil.

"When drink and food do not descend, the diaphragm is blocked and cannot be penetrated, the evil is located in the ducts of the stomach. When it is in the upper duct, needle to restrain the qi in counterflow and to make it descend. When it is in the lower duct, needle to scatter and to make the evil qi go away.

"When the abdomen is painful and swollen, and there is difficulty in urination, the evil qi is located in the Triple Heater. For this tie-up, treat the Great Luo point of the Major Yang, Yielding Yang. Inspect the *luo* channels of the Shrinking Yin, the Small Luo Channel connections, and the blood. If the swelling goes up to the ducts of the stomach, treat Three Distances.

"Inspect the patient's color. Examine this to see if it is in accord with the idea of the energies scattering or returning. Inspect the color of the eyes and use it to know whether the disease remains or is gone. For each individual body, listen for movement or stillness, take the pulse at the Qi Mouth at the wrist, and at Man's Receptor on the neck to investigate the pulses. If the pulse is solid and abundant and slippery, disease improves day by day. If the pulse is weak, disease will worsen. If all the channels are solid, the disease will be finished in three days. The Qi Mouth is the master of yin; the Man's Receptor pulse is the master of yang."

Notes

1. The "divisions in between the flesh" is the active locus of the acupuncture point where the needle point and qi energy meet.
2. This means difficult urination and constipation.
3. This seems to imply a knowledge of allergic foods.

SCROLL FIVE
20. THE FIVE EVILS

"When the evil qi is located in the lungs, it causes disease and pain in the skin, with chills and fever. There is panting from the ascending qi, sweating, and coughing, which moves the shoulders and back. Treat the point on the lateral side of the chest[1] and also one of the five viscera parts on the back at the third vertebra and to the side.[2] Use the hand to press down quickly, then quickly and promptly needle. Treat the middle of the Broken Dish to disperse the evil qi.

"When the evil qi is located in the liver, it causes pains in the middle and on the sides of the ribs. There is cold in the center. Evil blood is located on the inside. When walking, frequently there are spasms of the joints, and at that time a swelling of the feet. Treat Walking In Between, which will induce the qi to descend from the ribs. Tonify Three Distances in order to warm the middle of the stomach. Treat the blood in the *luo* channels to disperse the evil blood. Treat a point on the Ear Clear Channel in order to do away with the spasms.[3]

"When the evil qi is located in the spleen and stomach, it results in disease. The muscles and flesh are painful. When there is an excess of yang qi and the yin qi is insufficient, there is heat in the middle and frequent hunger. When the yang qi is insufficient and there is an excess of yin qi, the middle is cold, the intestines rumble, and the abdomen is painful. When yin and yang both are in excess or when both are insufficient, it causes cold or heat. For all this, harmonize Three Distances.

"When the evil qi is located in the kidneys, it will cause disease. The bones will be painful, and there will be rheumatism of the yin. For rheumatism of the yin, pressing with the hand may not localize the pain, for the abdomen swells, the loins are painful, bowel movements are difficult, the shoulder, back, and neck are painful, and there is occasional dizziness. Treat Gushing Spring, and Kun Lun Mountain. Inspect the blood and treat by drawing from the *luo* channels, if necessary.

"When the evil qi is located in the heart, it causes disease. There are pains in the heart. It is a time of frequent grief, dizziness, and falling. Inspect to see if there is an excess or insufficiency. Harmonize at the acupuncture points."

Notes

1. The lateral side of the chest refers to the Cloud Door (Lung 2).
2. This refers to the Lung point (Bladder 13).
3. The Ear Clear Channel refers to the Convulsions Channel point (Triple Heater 18).

21. COLD AND HOT DISEASES

"When the skin has chills and fever it means that one cannot stay seated. The hair is scorched. The nose is dried like salted meat. There is no sweating. Treat the *luo* channel of the third yang, the Major Yang to tonify the Arm Major Yin.

"When the muscles have chills and fever, it means muscular pain, scorched hair, dry lips and no sweat. Treat the lower part of the third yang to drain the blood and tonify the Leg Major Yin in order to promote sweating. When the bones have chills and fever, it is a disease where there is no balance. Sweat flows without stop. The tips of the teeth are not rotten. Treat the *luo* channel of the Minor Yin on the medial side of the leg at Big Bell. When the teeth are completely rotten, it means death with no cure. In the case of bone deficiencies, treatment is the same.

"When there is rheumatism of the bones, there is malfunction and pain of all the joints. Sweat flows. There is anxiety of the heart. Treat the three yin channels, and tonify.

"When the body is wounded with much bleeding and attacked by the cold wind, it is as if there was a fall from a height. The four limbs are remiss and flaccid and without control. This is called the body being feeble and exhausted. Treat the junction of the three connecting channels on the abdomen below the umbilicus. The junction of the three connecting channels comprises the Stomach Channel of the Bright Yang, the Spleen Channel of the Major Yin on the Conception Vessel three *cun* below the navel, at Gate of Origin.

"When there is rheumatism from counterflow, the rebellious qi goes up in counterflow to the abdomen. Treat the *luo* points on the yin and yang channels. Examine to master the disease. Disperse the yang channels and tonify the yin channels.

"At the side of the neck there is a moving pulse, the Man's Receptor pulse. This point is on the Stomach Channel of the Leg Bright Yang in front of the muscles which enclose the neck on the side. Behind these enclosing muscles are the Large Intestine Channel of the Arm Bright Yang and a point called Supporting Chimney. The next channel on the neck is the Leg Minor Yang Channel at Celestial Shutters.[1] Next is the Bladder Channel of the Leg Major Yang at the point called Celestial Pillar. Below the armpit is a moving pulse on the Lung Channel of the Major Yin on the upper arm. The point is called Celestial Mansion.

"When the yang is rebellious and in counterflow, the head is painful.

The chest is full and is unable to draw a breath. Treat Man's Receptor. When there is an abrupt loss of speech, the qi hardens. Treat Supporting Chimney, and draw blood from the base of the tongue. When there is an abrupt loss of hearing, the qi becomes covered and blocked, and the ears and eyes lose their brightness. Treat Celestial Shutters. When there are spasms, convulsions, and dizziness, and the feet are unable to bear the body, treat Celestial Pillar. When there is an abrupt thirst and fever, the interior is rebellious and in counterflow causing the liver and lungs to strike at each other. Blood overflows from the nose and mouth. Treat Celestial Mansion and the Celestial Shutters along with five positions.[2]

"The Arm Bright Yang has an entrance to the cheekbones where the teeth and jaw turn. The point is called Great Welcome. It can be used to treat the lower teeth and gums. When there is a cold illness of the arm, tonify, but if it is not a cold illness, disperse. The Leg Major Yang has an entrance into the turn of the cheek and the teeth at Minor Corner. It may be used to treat the upper teeth and gums in the area of the nose and front cheekbones if the channel is full. Right at the time of the disease, fullness requires dispersion. If hollow, it requires tonification. One method says to treat the points to the outside of the nostrils.

"The Leg Bright Yang has clasps along the side of the head, and from the nose has an entrance into the face. This point is called Skull Suspension. It subordinates the mouth, and then goes toward and enters the connections to the root of the eye. Examine to see if there is a problem, and treat. Decrease if there is an excess, increase if there is a deficiency; that is, reverse the extreme.

"The Leg Major Yang has a penetration at the nape of the neck which enters into the brain. This primarily subordinates the root of the eye and is called the connection of the eye. When the head and eye are bitterly painful, treat in the middle region of the neck between two muscles.[3] This penetration enters the brain at the separation of the Yin Anklebone Channel and the Yang Anklebone Channel, for yin and yang intersect mutually, so that yang enters yin and yin comes out of yang with a crossing at the medial corner of the eye. When the yang qi is full, it causes the eyes to glare and remain open. When the yin qi is full, it causes the eyes to close.

"When there is fever and a deficiency, treat the Leg Major Yin and Minor Yang. Detain all the needles. If there are chills and a deficiency, treat the Leg Bright Yang and the Minor Yin in the area of the foot. Detain all the needles.

"When the tongue is slack and saliva drips out with feelings of annoyance and depression, treat the Leg Minor Yin. When there is shaking from cold and noise like 'sa-sa' from a drumming of the jaws, no perspiration, a swollen abdomen, annoyance, and anxiety, treat the Arm Major Yin. Needle hollowness, needle as if it has gone away. Needle solidity, needle as if it has arrived.

"In spring, treat the *luo* channels. In summer, treat the division of the body between skin and flesh. In autumn, treat the Qi Mouths.[4] In winter, treat the *shu* points on the channels. In each of the four seasons, treat to promote balance. The *luo* channels control the skin. The divisions of the body between the skin and flesh control the muscles and flesh. The Qi Mouths control the muscle channels. The *shu* points on the channels control bones and marrow.

"The five viscera have five places where they are manifest on the body. The Crouching Rabbit is one at the top of the thigh. On the legs, the calf is two. The back along the Governing Vessel is three. The five viscera locus points on the back is four. The nape of the neck is five. When there are ulcerous growths at these five locations, it means death.

"When disease begins in the hand and arm, begin by treating the Arm Bright Yang and the Major Yin to provoke sweating. When disease begins in the head, first treat the Major Yang at the nape of the neck to cause sweating. When disease begins in the foot and leg, first treat the Leg Bright Yang to provoke sweating. The Arm Major Yin can cause sweating. The Leg Bright Yang can cause sweating. Consequently, treating the yin to cause sweating to an extreme will stop it in the yang. Treating the yang to cause sweating to an extreme will stop it in the yin.

"All acupuncture wounds, so when disease is attacked and does not go away, it causes the seminal essence to leak out.[5] On the other hand, if it is not attacked and made to depart, it will result in a denseness of qi. When the seminal essence leaks out, it will cause the disease to worsen and renew. A denseness of qi will cause the birth of ulcerations."

Notes

1. Should read "Arm" Minor Yang, since the Triple Heater Channel is the Arm Minor Yang not the Leg Minor Yang.

2. The Celestial Shutters in the middle and the four points around it and may have been a form associated with the Wu Xing, that is, the Five Dynamic Elements.

3. This possibly refers to the Jade Pillow points.

4. Qi Mouths are equal to acupuncture points at their openings. Thus, most possibly, shallow levels of the acupuncture points.

5. "All acupuncture wounds," this phrase tells all: that acupuncture incites a body reaction in hope of redressing and rebalancing the equlibilium of qi and blood. In addition there is a double layer of meaning in the use of *zhong* which in this paragraph means "to attack" but more commonly means "to center."

22. MADNESS AND INSANITY

"The lateral corner of the eye makes a break in the face and the sharp point of the eye. On the medial side adjacent to the nose is the medial corner of the eye. The upper eyelid is with the lateral corner. The lower eyelid is with the medial corner.

"At the very beginning of madness, the symptoms are first a lack of joy, the head is heavy and painful. When the eyes are raised up, they are red. Actions are extreme and there is anxiety of the heart and mind. Inspect the middle of the eyebrows. Treat the Arm Major Yang, Bright Yang and Major Yin. When the blood color changes, then stop.[1]

"When madness begins its work, it twists the mouth. There are cries, gasps, and panting with a fearful throbbing of the heart. Inspect and treat the Arm Bright Yang and Major Yang. If the left is strong, attack the right. If the right is strong, attack the left. When the blood color changes, stop.

"When madness begins its workings, there is first a rebellious stiffness, then it causes pain in the backbone. Examine and treat the Leg Major Yang, Bright Yang, Major Yin, and the Arm Major Yang. When the blood color changes, stop.

"To cure madness, determine its dwelling place. Examine the patient to see which point and which channel should be treated. To reach the illness, inspect; if there is an excess, then drain by bleeding. Place the blood in a bottle or gourd. When it is time to reach the illness again, drain until the blood moves spontaneously. If it does not move, cauterize the extreme bone with twenty moxa cones. The extreme bone is the coccyx.

"When madness reaches the cheekbones, jaws, and teeth, the acupuncture points which relate to them, as well as the divisions of the flesh and the dwellings of the bones, are all full. There is sweating, annoyance, and anxiety. If there is vomiting with a plenitude of foamy saliva, and the qi descends and leaks; there is no cure.

"When madness is in the muscles, the body rolls up with great convulsions and spasms. Needle the major channel at the nape of the neck at Big Shuttle. If there is vomiting with much foamy saliva and the qi descends and leaks, there is no cure.

"When there is a madness of the channels, the body feels as if it is cruelly beaten. The channels on the four limbs are all swollen. If the pulse is not full, cauterize the Major Yang at the pinch of the nape of the neck. Cauterize the Waistband Channel points which are located at the waist and points which are three *cun* away. Cauterize the divisions of the flesh at the *shu* points. If there is vomiting with a plenitude of foamy saliva and the qi descends and leaks, there is no cure.

"When madness quickly becomes like insanity, it is death; no cure.

"When insanity first appears, the self first is grief-stricken; joy is forgotten; there is bitter anger. There is frequent fear, which leads to grief and wasting away. Treat the Arm Major Yin and Bright Yang. Use bleeding treatments until the blood changes, and then stop. Also treat the Leg Major Yin and Bright Yang.

"When insanity begins and issues forth, there is little sleeping and no hunger. There is glorification of the self as being the most virtuous, the most knowledgeable, honorable, and respected. Goodness is cursed and criticized. Day and night there is no rest. Treat the Arm Bright Yang, Major Yang, Major Yin, and the Minor Yin below the tongue at Angular Spring, and the Arm Minor Yin. If examination shows the illness is severe, treat all the above points. If not severe, select points which will release the illness.

"When there is insanity of speech, it is accompanied by fright, frequent laughter, addiction to singing and music, reckless ambling without cease leading to greater fears. Treat the Arm Bright Yang, Major Yang, and Major Yin.

"Insanity has the symptoms of the eyes looking aimlessly, the ears hearing without sense, and frequent sighs. That which gives birth to this is the scarcity of qi. Treat the Arm Major Yang, Major Yin, and Bright Yang. Also use the Leg Major Yin and points on both sides of the head which relate to the problem.

"When it is insanity of overeating, the symptoms are frequent visions of ghosts and spirits, and frequent laughter which has no external sound, leading to excessive joy. Treat the Leg Major Yin, Major Yang, Bright Yang; afterwards, treat the Arm Major Yin, Major Yang, and Bright Yang.

"When insanity is newly arisen and there are no corresponding symptoms to the above, first treat Bending Spring both left and right where there is a moving pulse. If the *luo* channels around the point are full, and one can see blood, then draw blood to finish the illness quickly. If it does not finish, then use the rules of the treatment involving twenty cones of moxa at the coccyx.

"When there is a rebellious wind, the accompanying problems are an abrupt swelling of the four limbs, and the body is bathed in a sweat and shivers with sound of 'xi' at the time as if cold. Lack of nourishment will cause anxiety. Overeating will cause frequent transformations. Treat the Arm Major Yin and its complement of outside and inside, that is the

Arm Bright Yang. Also treat the Leg Minor Yin and Bright Yang Channels. If the flesh is cold, use the spring points. If the bones are cold, use the well and river points.

"When deficiency and rebellion make disease, the feet become cruelly cold, the chest feels as if it were stretched, and the intestines feel pain as if a knife were cutting them. There is annoyance and an inability to eat. The pulses large or small are all rough. If the body is warm, treat the Leg Minor Yin, if cold, treat the Leg Bright Yang. If cold, tonify; if warm, disperse.

"When deficiency and rebellion make the abdomen swell and become full with rumbling, and the chest is congested and breathing is difficult, treat the ribs below the diaphragm on both sides. If there is coughing, move the hand on the *shu* points on the back. If there is a response, massage by quickly slapping the positions.

"When the innards are obstructed and there is difficulty in urination, needle the Leg Minor Yin and Major Yang. Use the long needle at the coccyx point.

"When the qi is rebellious and in counterflow, treat the Leg Major Yin, Bright Yang and Shrinking Yin. When extreme, treat the Minor Yin and Bright Yang. Agitate the channels. When there is a scarcity of qi and the body is bathed in sweat and the speech is with the sound of 'xi-xi', and the bones are diseased and the body heavy, there will be flaccidity and an inability to move. Tonify the Leg Minor Yin.

"Short qi means the breath is short and without regularity. Move and work to haul the qi out. Tonify the Leg Minor Yin and draw blood from the *luo* channels."

Note

1. The blood color refers to a change in the redness of the eye and possibly the complexion of the face.

"When the side of the body is withered, it is nonfunctioning and painful. Words are not changed and the will is not disturbed, for the disease is located in the divisions of the flesh and in between the skin and flesh. Treat with the big needle. Tonify the insufficiency and disperse the excess. Use repeated treatments.

"When paralysis is the disease, the body is without pain but the four limbs are not receptive. When thoughts are disordered but not extreme, and the patients' words still have a little sense, the disease can be controlled. If it is extreme and results in an inability to speak, the disease cannot be controlled. The disease when it first begins is in the yang. Then it turns around and enters the yin. So, first treat the yang and afterwards treat the yin. Treat the yang with a floating superficial insertion.

"When a hot disease is three days old, and the Qi Mouth is quiet but the Man's Receptor pulse is rough and impatient, treat all the yang. Use the method of the fifty-nine points. Disperse the hot so that the patient sweats. On the other hand, solidify the yin in accordance with tonifying an insufficiency. When the body is extremely hot, but both yin and yang are quiet, do not needle. When one can use acupuncture, needle quickly. For, even without sweating, there can be dispersion. Also, the theory prohibiting needling is so because it would allow death to attack.

"When a hot disease has lasted seven or eight days and the Pulse Mouths are agitated and breaths are short, quickly needle so that sweating will occur in the patient.[1] Shallowly needle the point on the thumb, Minor Shang.

"When a hot disease has lasted seven or eight days and the pulses are weak and small and there is blood in the urine while the mouth is dry, in a day and a half there will be death. If the pulse is very irregular, death will occur in one day.

"When a hot disease is complete, and sweating has been achieved but the pulses are still rough with the panting of breath and the fever has returned, do not needle the skin. If the asthmatic panting worsens, it means death.

"When a hot disease has lasted seven or eight days and the pulses are rough, but not scattered or plentiful, and after the third midday there is sweating, then another three days of no sweating, on the fourth day death will occur. If there is no perspiration, one cannot needle between the skin and flesh.

"When a hot disease begins and the skin is painful, the nostrils are obstructed, and the face full, treat the skin. Use the number one needle, the chisel or engraver's needle, and the fifty-nine points. If the nose has a millet-like rash, treat by way of the skin and lungs. If relief is not obtained, treat according to fire and its correspondent, the heart.

"When a hot disease begins and the body is first rough and unsteady with fever, there will be annoyance and distress, and dryness of lips, mouth and throat. Treat the skin. Use the number one, the chisel or engravers needle, and the fifty-nine points. If the skin is swollen and mouth dry with chills and sweating, treat the channels of the heart. If relief is not obtained, treat water and its correspondent, the kidney.

"For a hot disease with a dry throat, much drinking, frequent fear, inability to arise from lying down, treat the skin and flesh. Use the number six, the round and sharp needle, and the fifty-nine points. If the corners of the eyes have a green color, treat the flesh which is resonant to the spleen. If relief is not obtained, treat wood and its correspondent, the liver.

"For a hot disease with green face, a painful brain, agitations of hands and feet, treat the acupuncture points of the muscles. Use the number four lance needle for the rebellious four extremities. If the muscles are lame and the eyes soaking, treat the muscles which are resonant to the liver. If relief is not obtained, treat metal and its correspondent, the lungs.

"For a hot disease with frequent frights, convulsions, and madness, treat the blood channels. Use the number four lance needle. Quickly disperse when there is an excess. When there is insanity and a loss of hair, treat the blood and the heart. If relief is not obtained, treat water and its correspondent, the kidney.

"For a hot disease with the body heavy and the bones painful, the ears deaf and eyes often closed, treat the bones. Use the number four lance needle and the fifty-nine points. Needle the bones. If the disease has the symptoms of not eating, gnashing of teeth, and a greenish colored ear, treat the bones by way of the kidneys. If relief is not obtained, treat earth and its correspondent, the spleen.

"When there is a hot disease but no definitive location for pain, but there is deafness, a dry mouth, and an inability for the self to be receptive, then the yang is heated to an extreme, and the yin side is chilled. This means there is fever in the marrow. It means death, no cure.

"When there is a hot disease, the head is painful at the temporal bones, the eyes twitch, the channels are painful, and there are frequent nosebleeds, it is a perverse hot disease. Use the number three key needle. Examine to see if there is an excess or insufficiency, cold or hot, or piles.

"When there is a hot disease and the whole body feels heavy, and the center of the intestines is hot, treat by using the number four lance needle at the *shu* river points as well as those points on the cracks of the toes. Treat the qi of the stomach channel to obtain the qi.

"When it is a hot disease and the pinch around the navel has spasms and pain, and the chest and ribs are full, treat Gushing Spring, and Yin Mound Spring. Treat using the number four lance needle. Also needle the base of the throat at Angular Spring.

"When there is a hot disease and sweat has come out, then the pulses are smooth because of the sweating. Treat the points: Fish Border, Major Abyss, Great Capital, and Pure White. If dispersion is used, it will cause the heat to depart. If tonification is used, it will cause sweating. If there is excessive sweating, treat the upper boundary channel of the medial ankle, Three Yin Junction to stop it.

"After a hot disease is finished and sweating has been achieved, but the pulses are still rough and full, this means the yin channels are in extremis, then death. But, if the patient sweats and the pulses are quiet, then life.

"In a hot disease, the pulses are full and rough but there is no sweating; this means the yang channels are in extremis, then death. Yet, if the channels are full and rough and a tranquil sweating can be obtained, then life.

"Hot diseases with negative indications for acupuncture total nine. The first: no sweating, the great cheekbones turn red, dry vomiting, this means death. The second: diarrhea with the abdomen extremely extended, this means death. The third: the eyes cannot see clearly, fever cannot be abated, this means death. The fourth: for old people or infants, there is fever and the abdomen is extended, this means death. The fifth: no sweating, vomiting and a discharge of blood, this means death. The sixth: ulcerations at the base of the tongue, fever cannot be abated, this means death. The seventh: coughing with bleeding from the nose, no sweating, or when there is sweating it does not include the feet, this means death. The eighth: fever in the marrow means death. The ninth: fever and convulsions mean death, when the loins are crooked and bent with convulsions, and the teeth locked so there cannot be speech. These are the nine where acupuncture is not indicated.

"Which are the acupuncture points spoken of as the fifty-nine?[2] On both hands, on the exterior and interior surfaces, there are three making

107

a total of twelve points. Each of the gaps between the five fingers has one, for a total of eight points. The points on the feet are similar to those on the hands. On the head, going in one *cun* at a time from the border of the hair are three divisions to each side, for a total of six points. Again entering from the hairline at three *cun* to the side are five points to make a total ten points. To the front and to the back of the ear each position is two, and below the mouth is one. In the center at the nape of the neck is one, for a total of six points. On the apex of the head is one, Hundred Meetings. At the gathering of the skull is one, Skull Gathering. Beyond the Posterior Summit is one. Wind Mansion is one. Angular Spring is one. Wind Pond is two. Celestial Pillar is two.

"When the qi overflows in the chest, it makes a panting breath. Treat the Leg Major Yin at the tip of the big toe. Go from the toenail the thickness of a leek leaf. If cold, detain the needle. If hot, use a rapid insertion. When the qi descends, then stop.

"When there is a hernia of the heart with cruel pain, treat the Leg Major Yin and Shrinking Yin. Also needle to bleed the blood *luo* channels.

"When the throat is paralyzed, the tongue rolled up, the mouth is dry, the heart annoyed, pains in the heart, pain on the medial surface of the arm, and the arm cannot be raised to the level of the head, treat the tip of the ring finger below the fingernail; go the thickness of a leek leaf from the corner of the cuticle.

"If the center of the eye is red and painful and it began at the medial corner of the eye, treat the Yin Anklebone Channel.

"If wind convulsions bend and twist the body, first treat the Leg Major Yang at the center of the crease of the knee and draw blood from the blood *luo* channels. If the middle heater is cold, treat Three Distances.

"When there is no urination, treat the yin channels of the anklebone, namely the Minor Yin and Shrinking Yin Channels, at the Three Hairs point above the toenail, that is, the Big Stump, and draw blood from the blood *luo* channels.

"A boy who has a hernia which appears like a disease of intestinal worms, and a girl who has an internal blockage, have in their bodies symptoms of an untying of the loins and backbone; there is no desire for food or drink. First treat Gushing Spring. Draw blood. Examine to see if the medial ankle above the anklebone has *luo* channels which are full; if so, drain until blood is seen."

Notes

1. Pulse Mouths are the locii on the wrist where the pulses can be felt.

2. Sixty-three are mentioned.

24. PERVERSE DISEASES

"For perverse headaches, swellings which begin in the face, and anxiety of the heart, treat the Leg Bright Yang and Major Yin.[1]

"For perverse headaches, pains in the channels of the head, grief in the heart and frequent tears, examine to see if the moving pulses on the head are full or not. Use the needle to draw blood and then harmonize the Leg Shrinking Yin.

"For perverse headaches which are persistent, heavy and painful, disperse the five points that move to the top of the head as well as the five along the routes.[2] But first treat the Arm Minor Yin, and afterwards treat the Leg Minor Yin.

"For perverse headaches and absent-mindedness, pressing with the hand has no results. Treat the head and face on their left and right active channels. Afterwards, treat the Leg Major Yin.

"For perverse headaches with pain beginning at the nape of the neck, and resonant pain in the loins and backbone, first treat Celestial Pillar and afterwards the Leg Major Yang.

"For perverse headaches which are extremely painful, and the channels to the front and behind the ear throb with heat, disperse and draw blood. Afterwards, treat the Leg Minor Yang.

"For veritable headache with extreme pain, when the brain is exhausted by pain, and the hands and feet are frigid to the joints, it means death, no cure.

"Those headaches which occur from blows or falls which cause the sick blood to remain inside cannot be treated by acupuncture. With injury of the flesh, where the pain does not cease, one can treat by local needling, but not by using distant points.

"Headaches which are not affected by acupuncture come from the illness of great rheumatism. If they are treated daily, one can effect a minor change, but not an end of the problem.

"When half of the head is cold and painful, begin by treating the Arm Minor Yang and Bright Yang. Afterwards, treat the Leg Minor Yang and Bright Yang.

"When there are perverse pains in the heart together with a pain in the back, with frequent spasms which are like a motion of butting from behind the heart, and which can deform the back into a hump, this heart pain is related to the kidneys. Begin by treating Level Bone, and Kun Lun Mountain. If there arise fits which do not stop, then treat Blazing Valley.

"When there are perverse pains in the heart, swelling in the abdomen, fullness in the chest with especially extreme pain in the heart, this heart pain is related to the stomach. Treat Great Capital and Pure White.

"When there are perverse pains in the heart which feel like a sharp awl piercing the heart, and the heart is extremely painful, this heart pain is related to the spleen. Treat Blazing Valley and Major Stream.

"When there are perverse pains in the heart with a grayish pale complexion as if dead, and inability to breathe deeply during the day, this heart pain is related to the liver. Treat Walking In Between and Great Rushing.

"When there are perverse pains in the heart, a lying down as if locked in a room, the heart is moderately painful, activity and work are painful to an extreme, and the color is unchanged, this heart pain is related to the lungs. Treat Fish Border and Major Abyss.

"When there is veritable pain in the heart and the hands and feet are chilled to the joints, the heart is in extreme pain. If this starts in the morning, there will be death in the evening; if it starts in the evening, there will be death in the morning.

"Acupuncture cannot be used if there are pains in the heart and the middle has accumulations and fullness. One cannot treat the acupuncture points in this case.

"When the middle of the intestines has worms and there is a disease of the bowels caused by scaly creatures and intestinal worms, it cannot be treated by using the small needles. The heart of the intestines is painful and nauseous, and there are swellings and accumulations that come and go, move up or down, and pain which at times rests or stops. Also, the abdomen is feverish, there is frequent thirst, and saliva comes out, all because of scaly creatures and intestinal worms. Use the hand to gather together and maintain strong pressure in order to stop movement, then use the big needle, leave it in, and support it for a long time. When the worms and creatures do not move, then withdraw the needle. If the heart and abdomen are painful with nausea, the creatures are in the middle and top.

"For deafness with no hearing, treat the middle of the ear at Listening Palace. For noises in the ear, treat Ear Door, at the pulse to the front of the ear. If there is earache, if there is pus in the ear and it looks as if the ear has dried earwax so the ear is without hearing, do not needle. Again, if there is deafness, treat the ring finger above the fingernail where it makes a junction with the flesh at Capillary Gate. First treat the hand. Afterwards, treat the foot at Cavity of Yin. For

111

noises in the ear, treat the middle finger above the fingernail at the Middle Capillary. For the left, treat the right; for the right, treat the left. First treat the hands, then treat the feet at Big Stump.

"If the legs and thighs cannot be raised, have the patient lie on his side to treat the middle of the joining pivot at Ball Joint. Use the round and sharp needle for acupuncture at this location. Do not use the big needle.

"For disease of discharging blood, treat Bending Spring.

"When wind rheumatism is dripping with debauchery, the disease cannot be finished. It feels as if the feet are walking on ice. There are times when it feels like being in the soup. The thighs and legs feel as if dripping with debauchery. The heart is anxious, the head is painful. At times there is vomiting. At times there is congestion. When dizziness ends, there is sweating, but for a long time, the eyes are dizzy. There is grief in accord with frequent fear. There is a shortness of breath, no joy; less than three years will pass before death."

Notes

1. An archaic word, *jue*, which etymologically represented the difficulty and loss of breath as one climbed up a steep slope, is used in the title and throughout this chapter. Technically, in medicine, it came to mean diseases which arose because the qi was in counterflow to its usual direction. Thus, I have used the word "perverse" to indicate this meaning. In addition, *jue* also means "deficiency" which is not related to this chapter.

2. The five points to the top of the head on the Governing Vessel are Upper Star, Skull Gathering, Anterior Summit, Hundred Meetings and Posterior Summit. The five along the Bladder Channel are Five Places, Receiving Light, Penetrating Heaven, Connect and Withdraw, and Jade Pillow. The five on the Gallbladder Channel are Above the Tears, Eye Window, True Management, Receiving Spirit, and Brain Hollow.

25. DISEASES AND ROOTS

"First disease, and afterwards rebellion and counterflow, cure its roots.

"First rebellion and counterflow, and afterwards disease, cure its roots.

"First cold, and afterwards the beginning of disease, cure its roots.

"First disease, and afterwards the beginning of cold, cure its roots.

"First heat, and afterwards the beginning of disease, cure its roots.

"First diarrhea, and afterwards the beginning of other disease, cure its roots.

"One must harmonize appropriately to cure each specific disease.

"First disease, and then the middle congested, cure its branches.

"First disease and then diarrhea, cure its roots.

"First the middle congested and then anxiety of heart, cure its roots.

"When there are guest qi, when there are similar qi, and the great and small easing of nature are smooth, cure their branches.[1]

"When the great and small easings of nature are too easy, cure their roots.

"Disease begins and there is an excess for the roots and branches. First cure its roots, afterwards cure its branches.

"Disease begins and there is an insufficiency for its branches and roots. First cure the branches, afterwards cure its roots.

"Respectfully and in detail, please examine thoroughly for severity. Use these ideas and harmonize.

"When moderate treat both roots and branches.

"When extreme use special actions.

"First the small and great easings of nature are not smooth.

"And afterwards there is a beginning of other disease, cure its roots."

Note

1. This refers to stool and urine.

"When there is a perverse disease with pain which goes along both sides of the backbone to reach the top of head, and the head nods with heaviness, the eyes are blurred, and loins and spine are stiff and rigid, treat the Leg Major Yang at the point in the middle of the crease of the knee. Use the blood *luo* channels.

"When there is a perverse disease with congestion in the chest, facial swelling, the lips wet and dribbling with saliva, abruptly speech becomes difficult, and if it is extreme, one cannot speak at all, then treat the Leg Bright Yang.

"When perverse qi travels to the throat and there is an inability to speak, the hands and feet are cold, and there is constipation, then treat the Leg Minor Yin.

"When there is a perverse disease and the abdomen is drumming and grumbling, there is much cold qi, or the center of the abdomen is awash with sound, and bowel movements and urination are difficult, treat the Leg Major Yin.

"When the throat is dry and the mouth hot and feeling like glue, treat the Leg Minor Yin.

"When there is pain in the knee, treat Calf's Nose. Use the round and sharp needle every other day for treatment. With this needle with a body as big as a tuft of hair, needle the knee without doubts.

"When there is rheumatism of the throat and an inability to make speech, treat the Leg Bright Yang. If one can speak, treat the Arm Bright Yang.

"When fever attacks every other day but no thirst, treat the Leg Bright Yang.[1] When fever attacks every day and there is thirst, treat the Arm Bright Yang.

"When there are pains in the teeth but no fear of cold drinks, treat the Leg Bright Yang. On the other hand, if there is fear of cold drinks, treat the Arm Bright Yang.

"When there is deafness, but no pain, treat the Leg Minor Yang. For deafness with pain, treat the Arm Bright Yang.

"When a nosebleed does not stop and the blood is flowing, treat the Leg Major Yang. To clot the blood flow, treat the Arm Major Yang. If it does not stop, treat the point below the wristbone, the Wrist Bone point. If it still does not stop, needle the middle of the crease of the knee to draw blood.

"When the lower back is painful, and the pain goes up, and the body is cold, treat the Leg Major Yang and Bright Yang. If the pain goes up, and the body is hot at that location, treat the Leg Shrinking Yin. If one cannot bend over or raise up, treat the Leg Minor Yang. If the center is hot, and there is panting, treat the Leg Minor Yin and the blood *luo* channels at the middle of the crease of the knee.

"When there is frequent anger, and no desire for food, and speech is less and less, needle the Leg Major Yin. If there is anger with many words, needle the Leg Minor Yang.

"When the lower part of the face is painful, needle the Arm Bright Yang and draw blood from full channels on the lower part of the face.

"When the nape of the neck is painful and the neck cannot bend over or raise up, needle the Leg Major Yang. If it cannot move from side to side, needle the Arm Major Yang.

"When the abdomen is full and large, and this fullness travels up to the stomach and reaches the heart, and the body trembles alternately between chills and fever, and there is difficulty in urination, treat the Leg Shrinking Yin.

"When the abdomen is congested with constipation, the abdomen swells greatly and involves the chest and throat, and there is breathing and panting with a 'ke-ke' noise, treat the Leg Minor Yin.

"When the abdomen is congested and food does not transform, and the abdomen is awash with noise, and one cannot move the bowels, treat the Leg Major Yin.

"When there are pains in the heart which induce pains in the loins and backbone, and a desire to vomit, treat the Leg Minor Yin.

"When the heart is painful, the abdomen swollen and stopped up with constipation, treat the Leg Major Yin.

"When the heart is painful and causes back pain so that one cannot breathe, needle the Leg Minor Yin. If it does not stop, treat the Arm Minor Yang.

"When pains in the heart induce congestion in the abdomen and pains both up and down are without a fixed location, and bowel movements and urination are difficult, needle the Leg Shrinking Yin.

"When the heart is painful and one breathes only short breaths which cause an insufficiency of qi, treat the Arm Major Yang.

"When there is heart pain, needle the point at the ninth vertebra, Contracted Muscle, and massage. When the needling is finished, massage to finish the pain at this location. If it does not finish, use points up and down and around to obtain the cessation of the pain.

"When the lower part of the face is painful, needle the Leg Bright Yang where it bends around Jaw Carriage and there is a pulse. Draw blood to finish the pain at this location. If the pain does not cease, massage Man's Receptor on the channel until the pain stops.

"When the qi in counterflow goes up, needle the sinks.[2]

"When the abdomen is painful, needle Celestial Pivot both left and right of the navel. When the needling is finished, massage. Establish that it is finished. If not finished, needle Qi Rushing. When the needling is finished, massage until it is established that the pain has stopped.

"When there is a perverse paralysis, the four extremities feel bound up and depressed. To release quickly, treat twice a day. If there is no sensation, treat for ten days without cease to ensure that it ends. When the disease ends, stop.

"For hiccups, use grass to stimulate the nose to cause sneezing. When the sneezing is finished, do not breathe, then quickly breathe in to lead the qi down. Great fright also can stop hiccups."

Notes

1. Fever probably refers to malaria.

2. Points on the middle of the chest which extend to the pulse on the lower part of the chest.

27. CIRCULATORY RHEUMATISM

Huang Di questioned Qi Bo, "When circulatory rheumatism is in the body, it shifts up and down and moves its abode following the channels. Top and bottom, left and right, all respond to each other. Among all this, why is there no vacuity appearing? I wish to hear about its pain. Is the evil located in the middle of the blood channels? Or will it be located among the divisions of the flesh? What causes this pain that shifts if it cannot be reached beneath the needle? In the periods of accumulated pain one does not give a decisive cure, yet the pain ceases and stops. What are the principles of this? I would hear of its causes."

Qi Bo replied, "This is rheumatism in general, not circulatory rheumatism."

Huang Di said, "I would like to hear of rheumatism in general."

Qi Bo replied, "Each of these is located in its dwelling. At times it arises, at times it stops. It can change its dwelling or change its beginnings. If it appears on the right, there is a reflection on the left. If it appears on the left, there is a reflection on the right, but it is not able to encircle. At times it appears, and at times it rests."

Huang Di said, "Excellent! What is the method of acupuncture for this?"

Qi Bo replied, "For this disease, the pain, although it ceases and stops, must be needled at its dwelling; if not, it will return and start again."

Huang Di said, "Excellent! I would like to hear about circulatory rheumatism."

Qi Bo replied, "Circulatory rheumatism is located in the middle of the blood channels. It follows the channels as they go up and follows the channels as they go down, but is not able to go left and right, so each disease has those points which are its own."

Huang Di said, "What acupuncture can be done?"

Qi Bo replied, "When the pain goes up and down, first needle those on the bottom and close to the pain. Afterwards, needle those on top to resolve it. When pain goes down and up, first needle those on the top to penetrate the pain. Afterwards needle those on the bottom to resolve it."

Huang Di said, "Excellent! How does this pain begin? What is its origin to give it this specific name?"

Qi Bo replied, "The wind which is a cold and humid energy when it is a guest in the exterior and among divisions of the flesh, oppresses and binds to make the body foam. When this foam gets cold, it results in accumulation. Accumulation causes the arrangement in the divisions of flesh to separate and to crack. These separations and cracks cause pain. Pain causes the spirit to concentrate. The spirit concentrating causes heat. Heat causes the pain to be released. The pain released causes a perverse counterflow of qi. This perverse counterflow causes another rheumatism to arise. When it arises, it exists."

Huang Di said, "Excellent! I have received completely these theories, for this disease, when on the inside, is not located in the viscera, and on the outside does not arise in the skin, but dwells uniquely among the divisions of the flesh. The genuine qi is unable to circulate, so it is named the circulatory rheumatism.

"In order to needle rheumatism one must begin to bind and to follow the lower six channels. Inspect to see if they are hollow or solid, and if the great *luo* blood connections are blocked. If the disease is hollow and the channels are depressed and vacant, harmonize by ironing it out and penetrating with moxa and tonification. When there are spasms and rigidity, turn it around and induce it to move."

Huang Di said, "Excellent! I have completely received these ideas, and also the information about them. That is, the nine needles and the smooth flow of their principles, and the twelve major channels yin and yang, and disease."

28. QUESTIONS ON THE ORAL TEACHING

Huang Di was relaxing in his room when he ordered his attendants both left and right to leave, and asked Qi Bo, saying, "I have heard all about the nine needles and the channels, as well as discussions about yin and yang, the smooth flow and rebellious counterflow of qi, and finally in conclusion about the six channels. I now wish to obtain all understanding of questions on the oral teaching."

Qi Bo left his seat, repeatedly bowed, and said, "How felicitous is this question about what these first teachers transmitted orally."

Huang Di said, "I would hear of these oral transmissions."

Qi Bo replied, "They concern the hundred diseases, their beginning and birth. All are given birth by wind, rain, cold and heat, yin and yang, joy and anger, drink and food, dwellings and position, great fright and sudden fear. They cause the blood and qi to divide and to separate, yin and yang to break and to suffer, the major channels to labor under a perverse energy and to be cut off, the routes of the channels to be blocked, yin and yang to be mutually rebellious, the protective qi to be delayed and detained, the collateral channels to be hollow and vacant, blood and qi to be disordered, and constancy to be lost. These discussions cannot be found in the ancient classics but, if you please, this is the Dao, the way of their laws."

Huang Di said, "When a man yawns, what qi is responsible?"

Qi Bo replied, "The protective qi and the sun travel in the yang during the day. At midnight, the travel is in the yin, for yin controls the night. At night, man lies down to sleep. Yang controls the upper parts. Yin controls the lower parts. Consequently, yin qi accumulates in the lower parts because the yang qi is not completely exhausted; the yang is led to rise while the yin is led to descend. When yin and yang stretch each other, it results in numerous yawns. When the yang qi is exhausted and the yin qi is full, it causes the eyes to close. When the yin qi is exhausted, and the yang qi is full, it causes one to wake up from sleep. For problems concerning yawning, disperse the Leg Minor Yin and tonify the Leg Major Yang."

Huang Di said, "When man belches, what qi is responsible for this?"

Qi Bo said, "The valley qi enters into the stomach. The stomach qi flows up into the lungs. This has the consequence of making cold qi and fresh valley qi both turn around and enter the stomach. The fresh qi causes a mutual rebellion. The genuine qi and evil qi attack each other. This causes the qi to be doubly and mutually in rebellion and in counterflow. It returns to come out from the stomach, which results in belching. Tonify the Arm Major Yin and disperse the Leg Minor Yin."

Huang Di said, "When man sighs deeply, what qi is responsible for this?"

Qi Bo said, "In this instance the yin qi is abundant and the yang qi is hollow. The yin qi is quick. The yang qi is slow. When the yin qi is abundant, and the yang qi is tied up, the consequences are deep sighs. Tonify the Leg Major Yang, disperse the Leg Minor Yin."

Huang Di said, "When man is shaking with cold, what qi is responsible for this?"

Qi Bo said, "When cold qi is a guest in the skin, the yin qi is abundant, and the yang qi is hollow. Consequently, there is shaking from the cold, and cold shivers. Tonify all the yang."

Huang Di said, "When man burps, what qi is responsible for it?"

Qi Bo said, "When cold qi is a guest in the stomach, a perverse and rebellious qi goes down and up and scatters. It returns to come out in the stomach thus making burps. Tonify the Leg Major Yin and Bright Yang. One doctrine says to tonify the root of the eyebrow at Drilling Bamboo."

Huang Di said, "When man sneezes, what qi is responsible?"

Qi Bo said, "The yang qi is harmonious and profits, but it overflows in the heart to come out in the nose. This causes sneezing. Tonify the Leg Major Yang to benefit the root of the eyebrow. One doctrine says needle at the top of the eyebrow."

Huang Di said, "When man's body hangs down, what qi is responsible?"

Qi Bo said, "When the stomach is not firm, it causes all the channels to be hollow. If all the channels are hollow, it causes the muscle channels to be flaccid and indolent. When the muscle channels are flaccid and indolent, the result is that the yin uses a person's strength; when he is walking the qi cannot return, so it causes the body to hang down. Treat the locations from which this originates, and tonify it between the divisions of the flesh."

Huang Di said, "When man is sad with tears and a runny nose, what qi is responsible?"

Qi Bo said, "The heart is the master of the five viscera and six bowels; the eye is the ancestral channel where they all assemble.[1] The ascending body fluid roads go to the mouth and nose, which are doors and openings for qi. Consequently, grief and sorrow, worry and sadness can agitate the heart. When the heart is agitated, it causes the five viscera and six bowels all to swing. Swinging results in vibration of the ancestral channel. When the ancestral channel moves, it results in the body liquids opening their roads. When the roads of the body fluids are open, then tears and a runny nose result. The body fluids pour the essences into the moist body cavities and orifices. Consequently, the body fluids ascending on the path to the openings result in tears. But if these tears do not stop, it can cause the body fluids to exhaust. The body fluids, when exhausted, cause a situation in which these essences cannot be poured. If the essences cannot be poured, it results in the eye being without sight. Consequently, this is called seizing the essence. Tonify Celestial Pillar on the channel along the pinch of the neck."

Huang Di said, "When man has great sighs, what qi is responsible?"

Qi Bo said, "Grief and thought can cause the heart to be tight and anxious. When the heart is tight and anxious, it results in the qi path being restrained. This restraint results in an impedance. Consequently, these great sighs are in order to stretch and let out the qi. Tonify the Arm Minor Yin, the Pericardium, and the Leg Minor Yang, and detain the needle."

Huang Di said, "When man drips saliva, what qi is responsible?"

Qi Bo said, "Drink and food all enter the stomach. When there is heat in the middle of the stomach, it causes the agitation of worms. When worms are agitated, it causes the stomach to slow. When the stomach slows, it causes the Angular Spring to open, which causes saliva to drip down. Tonify the Leg Minor Yin."

Huang Di said, "When man has noises in the middle of the ear, what qi is responsible?"

Qi Bo said, "The ear is a location where the ancestral channels accumulate. Consequently, when the middle of the stomach is empty, it causes the ancestral channels to be hollow. Hollowness results in a downward flow. The channels become exhausted, causing noises in the ear. Tonify the Guest and Master point. Tonify also the point beyond the fingernail where it joins the flesh on the thumb, the Minor Shang point."

Huang Di said, "When a man bites his own tongue, what qi is responsible?"

Qi Bo said, "When there is a perverse rebellious energy which travels upward, the qi of all the channels is reached and affected. The Minor Yin qi, when reached, results in biting one's tongue. The Minor Yang, when reached, results in biting one's cheek. The Bright Yang when reached, causes biting one's lips. Examine to see which channels control the problems, then tonify.

"The sum of the above is twelve evil diseases. Each and every one of these evils travels to the cavities and orifices, which causes evil to reside in a specific location. When these make insufficiencies, it causes the rising qi to be insufficient; the brain is not full, the ear suffers from tinnitus, the head suffers and leans over, the eyes are dizzy. When the middle qi is insufficient, the wastes of the body abnormally change, the intestines suffer and make noises. An insufficiency of the lower qi causes a disease of weakness and perverse flow, which depresses the heart. Tonify below the lateral anklebone.[2] Detain the needle."

Huang Di said, "How can these be cured?"

Qi Bo said, "The kidneys control yawning; treat the Leg Minor Yin. The lungs control belching; treat the Arm Major Yin, or the Leg Minor Yin. For sighs, yin and yang are tied; therefore tonify the Leg Major Yang and disperse the Leg Minor Yin. When there is shaking with cold, tonify all the yang. For burps tonify the Major Yin and Bright Yang. For sneezes, tonify the Leg Major Yang at the root of the eyebrow. When a man's body leans down, use the location where it is manifest and tonify it between the divisions of the flesh. For tears, tonify Celestial Pillar on the channel at the pinch of the neck. These pinches are divided by the middle of the head. For great sighs, tonify the Arm Minor Yin, the Pericardium and the Leg Minor Yang, and detain. For dripping saliva, tonify the Leg Minor Yin. For tinnitus, tonify Guest and Master and the point on the thumb beyond the nail where it meets the flesh. When one bites one's own tongue, examine to see what controls the problem, then tonify. When the eyes are dizzy and the head leans down, tonify the point below the lateral anklebone, and detain. For weakness and a perverse disease when the heart is depressed, needle Major Pivot two *cun* beyond the crack of the big toe and detain, or needle the point below the lateral anklebone, and detain."

Notes

1. I assume the ancestral channels are the channels with which one can communicate with history and ancestors through sight and hearing.
2. The Kun Lun Mountain points.

29. TEACHING AND TRANSMITTING

Huang Di said, "I have heard that the first teachers had encyclopedic hearts and minds, but did not compose standard literature. I wish to hear what was in the storehouses of their minds in order to act, first to cure the people, and second to cure the body, and how to let the Hundred Families be without disease. We must harmonize and relate high and low. Virtue must seep below and flow. Little children must be without grief. We must transmit this to future generations without there being a limit to time. I would hear how this may be obtained."

Qi Bo said, "How far reaching is this question, for to cure the people is to cure the self. To cure that is to cure this. To cure the small is to cure the great. To cure the state is to cure the household. When we are without rebellion, then we are able to cure, for when things are smooth and flowing, they are complete. To flow smoothly is not unique to the yin and yang channels. Discuss how qi can be in counterflow or smooth flowing. The Hundred Families and the general population all desire to flow smoothly in their wills."

Huang Di said, "What is to flow smoothly?"

Qi Bo said, "Enter a country and question the customs. Enter a household and question the taboos. Go up to the court and question the proprieties. When examining a sick man, question what is advantageous."

Huang Di said, "What is advantageous to a sick man?"

Qi Bo said, "When the center is fevered and melting, it is advantageous to cool it. If cold subordinates the center, it is advantageous to warm it. When the middle of the stomach is hot, it causes a melting of the valley qi. This person's heart feels suspended and has frequent hunger. When the skin above the navel is hot, the middle of the intestines is hot, and will cause stools which are yellowish like porridge. When the skin below the navel is cold, the middle of the stomach is cold, and will cause swelling of the abdomen. When the middle of the intestines is cold it will result in noises in the intestines and diarrhea. When the middle of the stomach is cold and the middle of the intestines is hot, it will result in swelling together with diarrhea. If the middle of the stomach is hot and the middle of the intestines is cold, it will result in pangs of hunger, but the abdomen will be painful and swollen."

Huang Di said, "If the stomach desires cold drinks, but the intestines desire hot drinks, and both are in mutual rebellion, what can be advantageous in this situation? Moreover, what will control kings, dukes, and other aristocrats who eat blood? Unbridled lusts follow the desires of frivolous men who are not able to stop. Prohibitions cause rebellion of their will, and leniency will add to their disease. To cure, how can one begin?"

Qi Bo said, "Man's desire is neither for sickness nor for death, but for joy and life. Announce the uses of these adversities. Speak about what is in accord with virtue. Instruct on what is in accord with that which is advantageous. Open that which is in accord with that which is suffering, for even though the person is not on the way of the Dao, how can one not listen?"

Huang Di said, "What is the cure?"

Qi Bo said, "In spring and summer, first cure the branches, and afterwards cure the roots. In autumn and winter, first cure the roots, and afterward cure the branches."

Huang Di said, "What can be advantageous when there is a mutual rebellion?"

Qi Bo said, "These are advantageous: food and drink and clothes must be desirable and suitable to cold or warmth, so that winter's cold will not be miserably cold, and summer's heat will not cause profuse sweating. For food and drink, hot does not mean charring; cold does not mean dark and dank. Cold and warmth, when suitable and moderate, cause the qi to be strong and supportive; thus the evil qi will not reach you."

Huang Di said, "In the chapter of "The Body and the Viscera", it mentions accordance with the physical body, its branches, sections, joints, and flesh, and distinguishes whether the five viscera and six bowels are small or large. Now if kings, dukes, and aristocrats, and even the king who is holding court in the governing position ask the question, who can place his hand to examine and afterwards have a reply?"

Qi Bo said, "The human body has branches and joints, and the viscera and bowels are hidden, but the areas in the face which should be examined carefully are not hidden."

Huang Di said, "The qi of the five viscera can be examined in the face. I would like to complete my knowledge of this and how this is in accord with the knowledge of the limbs and sections. What is done?"

Qi Bo said, "For the five viscera and six bowels, the lungs make a covering lid at the height of the square of the shoulder and the hollow of the throat. These may be seen and surveyed from the exterior."

Huang Di said, "Excellent!"

Qi Bo said, "Of the five viscera and six bowels, the heart is the master. The Broken Dish makes the road to the skeletal bone at the tip of the shoulder. Examine and survey this in relation to the tip of the sternum, the xiphoid process, to see if it is excessive."

Huang Di said, "Excellent!"

Qi Bo said, "The liver controls and commands. It is the emissary and surveyor of the outside. When one desires to know if the liver is firm and solid, examine to see if the eyes are small or large."

Huang Di said, "Excellent!"

Qi Bo said, "The spleen is master of the body's protection. It is the emissary and receiver of provisions and grain. Inspect the lips and tongue for health or disease and to forecast good luck or misfortune."

Huang Di said, "Excellent!"

Qi Bo said, "The kidneys control the externals. They are the emissary of distant hearing. Inspect the ears for health or disease which may be used to know the kidney's nature."

Huang Di said "Excellent! Now I would like to hear about the survey of the six bowels."

Qi Bo said, "Of the six bowels, the stomach is the sea. When there is a wide frame, a large neck and a strong chest, it reflects the capacity for the five valley qi. If the tunnels of the nose are long, it is in accord with the survey of the large intestine. If the lips are thick and the Center of Man, the philtrum, is long, they are in accord with the survey of the small intestine. If the lower eyelid is large, the gallbladder is extensive. If the nostrils are to the outside, the bladder will leak urine. If the pillar of the nose arises in the very center, the Triple Heater will then be in agreement.

"This is the survey of the six bowels. From top to bottom are three divisions and classes. If they and the viscera are balanced, it means excellence."

30. THE PARTITIONS OF QI

Huang Di said, "I have heard that man has seminal essence, qi, body fluids, saliva, blood, and pulses. I take it that there is one qi, but it can be distinguished into six names and types. I do not understand why."

Qi Bo said, "The spirits, male and female, mutually contend, join, and complete the physical form. This is the first constant at the conception of a human being, and is spoken of as the seminal essence."

Huang Di asked, "What is meant by qi?"

Qi Bo said, "The upper heater opens and goes forth displaying the flavors of the five valleys.[1] It is like vapor from the skin. It flows through the body to nourish the hair, like mist and dew. This is spoken of as qi."

Huang Di asked, "What is meant by body fluids?"

Qi Bo said, "Between the skin and the flesh there arises a leakage, sweat like river headwaters from the earth. This is spoken of as body fluids."

Huang Di asked, "What is meant by saliva?"

Qi Bo said, "When food enters the valleys and the qi becomes full, it nourishes and flows to the bones. The bones subordinate bending and stretching. The seepage nourishes and benefits the brain and marrow. The skin is enriched and nourished. This is spoken of as saliva."

Huang Di asked, "What is meant by blood?"

Qi Bo said, "The central heater receives qi and grasps the gravy from food to transform and change it to red. This is spoken of as blood."

Huang Di asked, "What is meant by pulses?"

Qi Bo said, "The clogging and hindering of the nourishing qi, which cannot be avoided. This is spoken of as pulses."

Huang Di said, "The six types of qi can be excessive or insufficient. The qi can be abundant or sparse. The brain and marrow can be hollow or solid. The blood and pulses can be clear or muddy. How do you know this?"

Qi Bo said, "If the seminal essence is stripped, the ears become deaf. If the qi is stripped, the eyes are not clear. If the body fluids are stripped, the pores open and sweat pours out in great amounts. If the saliva is stripped because the bones subordinate bending and stretching, there is a diminishing of these abilities. The colors die young, the brain and marrow melt. The legs become tired, and the ears multiply noises. If the blood is stripped, the color whitens. It is like death due to lack of nourishment. The pulses become vacant and hollow. These are the observations."

Huang Di said, "How can the six qi be rich or poor?"

Qi Bo said, "Each of the six qi has its place of control. However, their being rich or poor, well or ill, is dependent on constant control by the five valleys in the stomach, which makes the great sea."

Note

1. The five flavors of the five valleys are sour, bitter, sweet, spicy and salty.

31. THE INTESTINES AND STOMACH

Huang Di asked Bo Gao, "I wish to hear how the six bowels transmit the valley qi and about the size of the intestines and stomach, whether they are small or large, long or short, as well as if what they receive from the valley qi is plentiful or sparse."

Bo Gao said, "Please excuse this lengthy speech. Here are the dimensions the valley qi follow as they exit and enter and whether they are shallow or deep, far or near, long or short. The lips to the teeth is a length of nine *fen*. The width of the mouth is two and one-half *cun*. From the teeth back to the meeting of the pharynx is a depth of three and one-half *cun*. The mouth has a capacity in volume of five *ge*. The tongue has a weight of ten *liang*, a length of seven *cun*, a width of two and one-half *cun*.[1] The door of the pharynx weighs ten *liang*; its width is one and one-half *cun*. To the stomach is one *chi* six *cun*. The stomach goes roundabout, curves and bends and stretches. Its length is two *chi* six *cun*. Its circumference is one *chi*, five *cun*. Its straight diameter is five *cun*. Its circumference is one *chi* five *cun*. Its straight diameter is five *cun*. Its capacity is three *dou* and five *shen*.[2]

The back of the small intestine is adjacent to the backbone to the left. It turns repeatedly, and in increments, it flows into its lower part, the turning intestine, which externally is adjacent to the top of the navel. Then it turns, returns, and spirals with sixteen curves. Its circumference is two and one-half *cun*. Its diameter is eight *fen* and one-third. Its length is thirty-two *chi*. The turning intestine at the point of the navel circles to the left, turns like a coiled unit in its additions as it descends. The turns, returns, and spirals make sixteen curves. Its circumference is four *cun*. Its diameter one *cun* and one-third. Its length is twenty-one *chi*.

The wide or horizontal intestine propagates near the backbone and receives from the turning intestine. It circles to the left and unites with the backbone, going up and down. Comparatively, its circumference is eight *cun*. Its diameter is two and two-thirds *cun*. Its length is two *chi* eight *cun*. The intestines and stomach, from beginning to end, have a length of sixty feet four *cun* and four *fen*. The turns, curves, and spirals make thirty-two curves."

Notes

1. *Liang*: unit of weight. Sixteen *liang* make one *jing*. One Chinese *jing* equals one-half of a kilogram.

2. *Ge, shen, dou*: According to an ancient Chinese system of measurement, ten *ge* make one *shen*, and ten *shen* make one *dou*. One *shen* is equal to 31.6 cubic inches. The size of one *dou* has varied slightly in Chinese history, but it is approximately equal to 316 cubic inches, similar to an English peck.

32. THE BALANCED MAN AND STARVATION

Huang Di said, "I wish to hear about man when he does not eat. That after seven days, death results. Why?"

Bo Gao said, "Your Highness, if you please, I will speak of the causes. The stomach's circumference is one *chi* five *cun*, its diameter is five *cun*, its length is two *chi* six *cun*. The width of its distention and capacity as it receives from water and grains is three *dou* and five *shen*.[1] It is the center for grains and it can consistently hold two *dou*. Water with the volume of one *dou* five *shen* will fill it up.

"When the upper heater leaks qi, this flux will extract the essence. This can make a violent trembling and a slippery quickness in the qi. The lower heater has a descending seepage to all the intestines.

"The small intestine has a circumference of two and one-half *cun*. Its diameter is eight and one-third *fen*, its length thirty-two *chi*. Its capacity as it receives the grains is two *dou* and four *shen*, as well as six *shen* and three and two-thirds *ge* of water. The turning intestine has a circumference of four *cun*. Its diameter is one and one-third *cun*. Its length is twenty-one *chi*. It can receive from the grains one *dou*, and its capacity in water in addition is seven and one-half *shen*.

"The wide or horizontal intestine has a circumference of eight *cun*. Its diameter is two and two-thirds *cun*. Its length is two *chi* eight *cun*. It can receive from the grains nine *shen* and three and one-eighth *ge*.

"The length of intestines and stomach is a total of fifty-eight *chi* four *cun*. Their capacity in receiving from the water and grains is nine *dou* and two *shen* and one and two-thirds *ge*. The intestines and stomach can therefore receive this measure from the water and grains.

"The balanced man thus will not be like this. The full stomach causes the intestines to empty. The full intestines cause the stomach to empty. This cycle of empty and full causes the qi to move up and down, which settles and pacifies the five viscera. The blood, veins, and arteries will be harmonized and smooth. The seminal essence and spirit will be housed. Therefore, the spirit comes from the seminal essence and qi of the water and grains. Consequently, the center of the intestines and stomach can at that point hold from these grains two *dou*, and of water, one *dou* five *shen*. Thus, the balanced man twice a day can eliminate two *shen* and one-half. For one entire day, five *shen*. In seven days, five times seven, or three *dou* and five *shen*, which means the amount detained from water and grains is completely drained. Consequently, the balanced man who does not eat or drink for seven days will die, for the water, grain, seminal essence, qi, body fluids, and saliva will be totally exhausted."

Note

1. See notes at the end of chapter 31 for discussion of ancient Chinese measurement.

33. AN ESSAY ON THE SEAS

Huang Di asked Qi Bo, saying, "I have heard about the laws of acupuncture according to the sages, what the sages spoke about cannot be separated from the nourishing, protective, blood and qi. The twelve major channels internally resonate with the bowels and viscera and externally connect the limbs and joints. For the sages, how were these in resonance with the four seas?"

Qi Bo replied, "Man also has four seas and twelve river-like channels. Rivers all flow to the sea. There are seas to the east, west, south and north. Thus it is said for seas."

Huang Di said, "What in man corresponds to this?"

Qi Bo said, "Man has the sea of marrow, the sea of blood, the sea of qi, and the sea of the water and grains, for a total of four which correspond to the four seas."

Huang Di said, "How far reaching! The sages were in resonance with man, heaven, earth, and the four seas. I would like to hear about the correspondence."

Qi Bo said, "You must first understand clearly yin and yang, external and internal, the locations of nourishing acupuncture points, and the definition of the four seas."

Huang Di said, "What are their definitions?"

Qi Bo said, "The stomach is the Sea of Water and Grains. It transports up to the acupuncture point of Qi Rushing and it descends and reaches Three Distances. The Penetrating Vessel, is the Sea of the Twelve Channels. It transports up to Big Shuttle and going down it comes out at the Great Hollow points, both Upper and Lower Passage. The center of breathing is the Sea of Qi. It transports up to the pillar bone both above Mute Door and below Big Vertebra. To the front it is located at Man's Receptor. The brain is the Sea of Marrow. It transports up to be positioned at the cover of the head, Hundred Meetings and lower down at Wind Mansion."

Huang Di said, "The sum of the four seas, what profits? What injures? What makes for growth? What makes for defeat?"

Qi Bo said, "To obtain the smooth flow is growth. To obtain the rebellious counterflow is defeat. To understand harmony is profitable. Not to understand harmony is injurious."

Huang Di said, "How can the four seas be in rebellious counterflow or in smooth flow?"

Qi Bo said, "When the Sea of Qi is in excess, qi overflows in the middle of the chest. The breath is listless and the face red. When the

Sea of Qi is insufficient, it results in the qi being too sparse and insufficient to make speech. When the Sea of Blood is in excess it causes constant thought; the body is large and puffy. There is no knowledge that it is disease. When the Sea of Blood is insufficient, there is also constant thought; the body is small and diminished. There is no knowledge that it is disease. When the Sea of Water and Grains is in excess, it causes fullness of the abdomen. The Sea of Water and Grains being insufficient, it results in hunger but not receiving food. When the Sea of Marrow is in excess, it results in a facile strength and much power; the self exceeds its limits. When the Sea of Marrow is insufficient, it results in the revolving of the brain, noises in the ear, weakness of the legs, dizziness with spots, and the eyes without vision. There is a languid idleness with desire to lay down calmly.

"Huang Di said, "I have completed the hearing of rebellious counterflow and smooth flow, but what is to harmonize?"

Qi Bo said, "Investigate by manipulation of the acupuncture points which relate to the four seas, and harmonize the hollow and solid. But do not violate and injure the body. To obtain a return to smoothness, one must defeat the rebellious."

Huang Di said, "Excellent!"

34. FIVE REBELLIONS

Huang Di said, "There are twelve major channels which can be separated according to the five dynamic elements, or divided according to the four seasons. How can their harmony be lost through rebellion? How can their harmony be gained through a cure?"

Qi Bo said, "The five dynamic elements have their order. The four seasons have their division. When flowing together smoothly, it causes a cure. When flowing against each other in disorder, it causes a rebellion."

Huang Di said, "What is meant to flow together smoothly?"

Qi Bo said, "The major channels are twelve. They are resonant to the twelve months. The twelve months are divided into the four seasons. The four seasons are spring, autumn, winter, and summer. Each climatic qi is different. When the nourishing and protective qi follow yin and yang together completely in harmony, the clear and the muddy do not offend each other, and this results in flowing smoothly and a cure."

Huang Di said, "What are counterflow and rebellion?"

Qi Bo said, "The clear qi is located in the yin, while the muddy qi is located in the yang. If the nourishing qi flows smoothly in the veins and arteries, but the protective qi travels in a disorderly counterflow, the clear and muddy qi offend each other, and there is rebellion in the chest. This is spoken of as a great depression. A consequence of the qi rebelling in the heart is anxiety of the heart and deep sighs, a bowed head which is quiet and prostrate. If there is rebellion in the lungs, it results in a bending down and looking up with gasping and panting. Press with the hand to make an exhalation. If there is rebellion in the intestines and stomach, there are sudden disorders. If there is rebellion in the arms and legs, it causes the four limbs to be weak and deficient. If there is rebellion in the head, it causes a perverse counterflow, the head becomes heavy and dizzy and the person may fall down."

Huang Di said, "For the five rebellions, what is the way of acupuncture?"

Qi Bo said, "There is the road that comes and there is the road that goes. Examine to know which road is spoken of as the treasures of the body."

Huang Di said, "Excellent! I wish to know about these roads."

Qi Bo said, "When the rebellious qi is located in the heart, treat the Arm Minor Yin, Heart Channel at its control, the stream *shu* point. If the rebellious qi is located in the lungs, treat the Arm Major Yin at the spring *shu* point and the Leg Minor Yin at the stream *shu* point. If the rebellious qi is located in the intestines and stomach, treat the Leg Major Yin and Bright Yang. If it does not decline, treat Three Distances. If the qi is located in the head, treat Celestial Pillar and Big Shuttle. If it is not acknowledged, treat the Leg Major Yang spring *shu* and stream *shu* points. If the rebellious qi is located in the arms and legs, treat by first drawing blood from the blood veins. Afterwards, treat the Bright Yang and Minor Yang's spring *shu* and stream *shu* points."

Huang Di said, "How does one tonify or disperse?"

Qi Bo said, "To enter slowly and to withdraw slowly is called to seize the qi. When tonification and dispersion are not distinct it is called similar essentials. This is when there is neither excess nor insufficiency, but the rebellious qi are in counterflow against each other."

Huang Di said, "How promising is this way of Dao! How enlightened is this discussion! Please compose it on jade tablets and call it, 'To Cure Rebellions.'"

35. AN ESSAY ON SWELLINGS

Huang Di said, "What Inch Mouth pulses at the wrist correspond to swellings?"

Qi Bo said, "For swellings the pulses are large, firm, and rough."

Huang Di said, "How does one apply the knowledge of viscera and bowels to swellings?"

Qi Bo said, "Yin are the viscera. Yang are the bowels."

Huang Di said, "That qi which causes swellings in man is an evil which is positioned in the middle of the blood veins. How does it penetrate the viscera and bowels?"

Qi Bo said, "There are the sum of the resting places, that is, the blood veins, viscera, and bowels which, even without swellings, are the locations."

Huang Di said, "I wish to hear about these locations for swellings."

Qi Bo said, "Generally swellings are located to the exterior of the viscera and bowels. They push aside the viscera and bowels which expands the chest walls and swells the skin. This is called swellings."

Huang Di said, "The viscera and bowels are located inside the foundation of the chest, ribs and abdomen, like stored hidden tools within the space of a box. They each have a name corresponding to location and different names even if in the same area. Each of these territories is in the middle. Each of their qi is different. I wish to hear the reasons for this.
Since the theory is still not explained. I will listen again."

Qi Bo said, "The chest and abdomen form the outer walls for the viscera and bowels. At the center of breathing, under the sternum, the heart controls the territory of the palace. The stomach is the major granary. The throat and small intestine transmit and send. The stomach has five openings, like the inner gates and doors in a village. The points Angular Spring and Beautiful Jade are the path of body fluids and saliva. Each of the five viscera and six bowels therefore has its boundaries. Each of their diseases also has its particular form and appearance. The nourishing qi follows the channels. The protective qi, when rebellious and in counterflow, swells the channels. The protective qi and the channels follow the divisions of the flesh in making swellings of the skin. To control, use Three Distances and disperse, or an adjacent point and disperse; if near, lower once, if far, lower thrice.[1] Without a question of hollow or solid, the technique is to drain and disperse the location."

Huang Di said, "I would like to hear about the forms of swellings."

Qi Bo said, "When the heart is swollen and anxious, there is shortness of breath. Sleep is not restful. When the lungs are swollen there is a hollow congestion with panting and coughing. When the liver is swollen the area of lower ribs is congested and pain is induced in the abdomen. When the spleen is swollen there is frequent belching and the four limbs are lax and leaden, the body is heavy and unable to wear clothes. Sleep is not tranquil. When the kidneys are swollen, the abdomen is congested and induces the back to be flaccid. The loins and buttocks are painful. For swellings of the six bowels: when the stomach is swollen, the abdomen is congested and the stomach channels are painful. The nose smells burning stenches, and there is difficulty in eating and with bowel movements. When the large intestine is swollen, the intestines rumble with the pain of their being awash. They are severely affected by the cold of a winter's day, causing diarrhea of the evening meal because it does not transform. When the small intestine is swollen, the abdomen is distended, which induces the loins to be painful. When the bladder is swollen, the qi of the abdomen is blocked. When the Triple Heater is swollen, the qi overflows into the middle of the skin. There is lightness, weakness and instability. When the gallbladder is swollen, the area below the ribs is painful and swollen. The center of the mouth is bitter and there are frequent sighs.

"For all of these swellings the path is one: to understand clearly the rebellious counterflow and the smooth flow. Each acupuncture treatment should be without loss. For to drain and disperse hollowness, or to tonify solidity, will drive away the spirit from his house. It will result in evil and the loss of the primary qi. The genuine qi cannot be established; this dense stupidity injures and is spoken of as causing a premature end to life. To tonify hollowness, however, and to drain and disperse solidity will allow the spirit to return to this house and to be established himself for a long time in the orifices. This is said to be an excellence of technique."

Huang Di said, "How do swellings arise? What are the origins?"

Qi Bo said, "The protective qi in the body circulates along with the veins and channels to follow the divisions of the flesh. Its movements can be rebellious or smooth. Yin and yang have their mutual motions in obtaining harmony with the heavens. The five viscera alternate their beginnings; the four seasons follow the same principles. The five valley qi transform.

"When there is a perverse deficient qi positioned on the bottom, the nourishing and protective qi will be detained and stopped. Cold qi in rebellious counterflow will arise, and the genuine and evil qi will attack each other. The two qi will be transmitted together and joined will make swellings."

Huang Di said, "Excellent. But how do you resolve these delusions?"

Qi Bo said, "Join to the genuine qi. When the three are joined, the genuine qi is obtained."[2]

Huang Di said, "Excellent."

Huang Di questioned Qi Bo, "This discussion on swellings says there is no question of hollowness or solidity. The technique is to disperse quickly; if adjacent, one descent of the needle; if far, three descents of the needle. What if there are three and they do not improve the problem? What is it that they pass by?"

Qi Bo replied, "These words are about a sinkhole in the flesh and vitals that are in the center of the qi hole. When the needle is not centered in the qi hole, it causes the qi to be internally blocked. If the needle is not in this sinkhole of the vitals, it will cause the qi to stop moving, and the evil qi will ascend, pass over, and attack the flesh, causing the protective qi to be in mutual rebellion, and yin and yang to be mutually pursued. So, in the case of swellings at that point, dispersing does not disperse, and the qi consequently does not descend and is not treated. If after treatments, there is no improvement, one must repeat the methods until the qi descends, then stop. If it does not descend, repeat and begin again. For even with ten thousand to complete, how can there be danger? When there is swelling, one must investigate the channels, veins, and lips. At the points, disperse if it must be dispersed, and tonify if it must be tonified. Like a drum responding to the drumstick, how can the illness not be beaten?"

Notes

1. Manipulation in this instance can mean depth of insertion or the number of needle thrusts.

2. "The three" refer to heaven, man, and earth.

36. THE FIVE SWELLINGS, THE FERRYING OF SECRETIONS AND THEIR DIVISIONS

Huang Di asked of Qi Bo, saying, "The water and grains enter the mouth. They transport to the intestines and stomach. Their secretions may be separated into five. When the weather is cold and clothes thin, they become urine and qi. When the weather is hot and clothes thick, they become sweat. The qi of grief and lament becomes tears. When the middle is hot and the stomach is slow, they become saliva.

"When evil qi is internally rebellious and in counterflow, it results in the qi being blocked and obstructed so that it cannot move. If it does not move, it causes swelling from water. I know of these things, but do not know why they originate and begin. I would like to hear of their way."

Qi Bo said, "The water and grains all enter the mouth. Their flavors are five. Each flows to its sea. In the ferrying of secretions, each travels its own path. Thus the qi as it comes out from Triple Heater warms the muscles and flesh, flows to the skin, and makes a moistening. When it flows but is not active, it makes secretions. When there is summer's hot climate and one's clothes are thick, it causes the pores to open and sweat to come out. When cold is detained between the divisions of the flesh, there is an accumulation of foam which results in pain. When cold weather causes the pores to be blocked, the qi becomes sodden and does not move. Water descends to be detained in the bladder, and becomes urine and qi.

"Of the five viscera and six bowels, the heart is the master. The ears do the hearing. The eyes do the observing. The lungs work as manager. The liver commands. The spleen protects. The kidneys control the externals. Therefore, when the ferrying of the secretions of the five viscera and six bowels all rise and seep into eyes, the heart is grieved, and the qi results in the heart being tight and anxious. The heart being tight and anxious, the lungs are raised up. As the lungs are raised up, the secretions flow upwards. The heart is connected to the lungs and cannot be constantly elevated, so when the heart qi goes up suddenly then down suddenly it causes coughing and tears.

"When the middle is hot, it causes the stomach to melt the grains. Melting the grains causes worms to work up and down. When the intestines and stomach are full, it causes the stomach to slow. If the stomach slows, it results in the qi being rebellious and in counterflow so that saliva is spit out.

139

"The ferrying of secretions from the five grains harmonize and join in making the marrow. Internally they seep into the bone cavities to augment and fill up the brain and spinal column. While in descent, it flows to the yin area of the thighs.

"When yin and yang are not in harmony, the secretions are conveyed and flow down into the yin. The spinal fluid secretions are all reduced with the descent. If this descent trespasses certain limits, it results in hollowness. Hollowness causes pain in the loins and back, and disease of the legs. When the yin-yang path of the qi is impenetrable, the four seas become blocked and obstructed. The Triple Heater does not drain. The ferrying of secretions transforms not. The water and grains advance and move to the middle of the intestines and stomach, and separate in the turning intestine, and are detained in the lower heater. There is no seepage into the bladder, this causes the lower heater to swell. Water overflows which causes water swelling.

"This is the ferrying of secretions into five, and their rebellious counterflow and smooth flow."

37. THE FIVE EXAMINATIONS AND
THE FIVE EMISSARIES

Huang Di questioned Qi Bo, "I have heard that there are in acupuncture theory five senses and five examinations which are used to see the five qi. The five qi are the emissions of the five viscera, and may be likened to the five seasons which make a set. I wish to hear about these five emissions and where and how they appear."

Qi Bo said, "The five senses may manifest the five viscera."

Huang Di said, "I wish to hear how these come out and appear, and how these can be made constants."

Qi Bo said, "The pulses come out in the Pulse Mouth. The colors may be seen in the Bright Hall of the nose. The five colors change as they come out and are in correspondence with the five seasons. Each has its constant. Where the qi of the channels enters the viscera is the appropriate point to control the inside."

Huang Di said, "Excellent. The five colors uniquely are separated at the Bright Hall of the nose, how?"

Qi Bo said, "The five senses are complete and distinct. When the separation at the court (the forehead) is wide, it establishes the Bright Hall of the nose and the Bright Hall is extensive and large. Look at the fence and the cover to see if the squares of the dividing walls are high and firm or if they lead to a hanging down of the outer room of the ear.[1] When the five colors are controlled, there is peace which is ample, extensive and large. This means a long life that can continue for a hundred years.

"Examine these things. The use of acupuncture must be complete, like the being of man. So when the blood and qi are in excess, or the muscles and flesh are firm and reaching, then use the needle properly."

Huang Di said, "I would like to hear about the five sensory organs."

Qi Bo said, "For the nose, the lungs are the internal organ. For the eyes, the liver is the organ. For the mouth and lips, the spleen is the organ. For the tongue, the heart is the organ. For the ears, the kidneys are the organ."

Huang Di said, "Concerning these organs what can be expected?"

Qi Bo said, "Think of what is symptomatic of the five viscera. Therefore, when the lungs are ill, there is panting breath, which stretches the nose. When the liver is ill, the corners of the eyes are green. When the spleen is ill, the lips are yellow. When the heart is ill, the tongue is rolled short, and the cheeks are red. When the kidneys are ill, the forehead and cheeks are blackish."

Huang Di said, "When the five pulses appear tranquil, and the five colors are seen to be tranquil, what danger is there in this constancy of color?"

Qi Bo said, "When the five senses are not distinct and the separation at the court is not wide, and the Bright Hall of the nose is small; and if the fence and cover are not prominent, and there is a depression in the walls, and beneath the walls is no foundation and the hanging corner of the ear turns out, this being so, although there is tranquility, there is constant danger of added illness."

Huang Di said, "The five colors as seen in the Bright Hall of the nose may be used to inspect the qi of the five viscera. Left and right, high or low, where is each appearance?"

Qi Bo said, "Each of the bowels and viscera which are located in the middle has its orderly habitat. Left or right, up or down, each goes to its boundaries."

Note

1. The "fence and the cover" is the appearance at the side of the forehead and the opening of the ear. The "squares of the dividing wall" is the skeletal structure of the face.

38. REBELLIOUS OR SMOOTH, FAT OR LEAN

Huang Di asked Qi Bo, "I have heard that with the way of acupuncture practiced by the sages, many could comprehend its entirety. The correspondences of this way of the sages are as if lost, and accordingly we do not have the foundations. What were the questions, studies, and skills of the sages? How did they conduct an examination and investigate matter, and what arose in their hearts and minds?"

Qi Bo said, "The way of the sages, Dao, was in tune with the heavens above, in tune with the earth below, and centrally in tune with human affairs. They must have had brilliant rules to make use of beginnings, ends and measurements. Their rules had the pattern and arrangement of their signatures, so how could they be transmitted to later generations? Consequently, craftsmen cannot abandon *chi* and *cun* when thinking of short and long. They cannot let go of blackened string to make wood level. Workmen cannot give up the compass to make a circle, or abandon the carpenter's square to make right angles. But knowledge is useful to establish the spontaneous self amongst the multitude.[1] Easy to use and to teach for the rebellious counterflow and smooth flow are constants."

Huang Di said, "I have heard about this spontaneous self. What is it?"

Qi Bo said, "It is comparable to a deep breakout of water. Without the use of effective strength, the water can completely drain out. So follow and excavate to the break and rushing water so that the channel can be penetrated. This is like saying the qi is smooth or rough, the blood is clear or muddy, and the movements are rebellious or smooth."

Huang Di said, "I would like to hear about man being white or black, fat or thin, small or long, and how each has its destiny."

Qi Bo said, "When the year is disposed to being fertile and great, blood and qi flow in abundance. The skin is leathery, firm and strong. These facts must be added in accord with the evil qi, so that the needle should go deep and be detained, like the method for fat men. When the shoulders across the armpits and neck are extensive, the flesh is thin and the skin thick with a black color, the lips thick and hanging down, and the blood black and muddy, the qi will be rough and slow. These men are greedy and grasping. Needle this type deep, and detain often, to augment his destiny."

Huang Di said, "How does one needle a thin man?"

Qi Bo said, "For a thin man, the skin is thin and the color slight, the flesh is frugal and sparse, lips are thin and speech light. His blood is clear and qi slippery. It is easy to injure the blood and easy to damage the qi. Needle these people shallowly and quickly."

Huang Di said, "How does one needle a common man?"

Qi Bo said, "Examine whether he is white or black and how each may be harmonized. If he is regular and honest and sincere, then blood and qi will be tuned and harmonized. Needle all without loss of the constants or destiny."

Huang Di said, "How does one use acupuncture for the strong commoner with true bones?"

Qi Bo said, "Acupuncture for the strong commoner with true bones, firm flesh, and slow joints must be inspected and examined. These heavy men cause the qi to be rough and the blood muddy. Acupuncture in these cases should be deep and detained, and often, to augment his destiny. Strength causes the qi to be slippery and the blood clear. Needle this shallowly and quickly."

Huang Di said, "How is acupuncture done on children?"

Qi Bo said, "Children, since their flesh is fragile, their blood sparse, and qi weak, should be needled with the fine needle. Shallowly needle, then quickly withdraw the needle. During a day it may be repeated."

Huang Di said, "What is meant by a deep breakout of water?"

Qi Bo said, "When the blood is clear and the qi is slippery, to drain quickly and disperse will exhaust the qi."[2]

Huang Di said, "To follow and excavate to the break and rushing water, what does that mean?"

Qi Bo said, "When the blood is muddy and the qi rough, quickly disperse so that the channels become passable."

Huang Di said, "What makes the movement of the veins and channels rebellious or smooth?"

Qi Bo said, "The three yin channels of the arm follow the viscera to the hand. The three yang of the arm go from the hand to the head. The three yang of the leg go from the head to the foot. The three yin of the leg go from the foot to the abdomen."

Huang Di said, "Does the Minor Yin Channel move down by itself?"

Qi Bo said, "That is not so, for the Chong Penetrating Channel is the sea for the five viscera and six bowels, and to which the five viscera and bowels all transmit. As it goes up, it comes out in the throat and cheekbones and seeps into all the yang and pours the seminal essence into all. As it descends, it flows to the great *luo* point of the Minor Yin, Big Bell. It comes out at Qi Rushing then follows the yin, the medial side of the thigh to enter the middle of the crease of the knee. Then it bends in moving to the lateral side of the shin bone to the posterior of medial ankle where it belongs and separates. A branch descends together with the Minor Yin Channel and seeps into the three yin. A branch to the front bends and moves to come out at the foot and descends following the instep to enter the crack of the big toe. Then it seeps to all the *luo* connecting channels and flows to the muscles and flesh. Consequently when the separate *luo* connection is tied up, it results in the upper part of the foot not moving. Not moving results in a perverse deficiency. This results in coldness."

Huang Di said, "How do you use this intellegence?"

Qi Bo said, "Use these words to lead and intimately examine them. They do not have to move, but afterwards they will and can illuminate the movements of rebellion or smoothness."

Huang Di said, "How distressing! The sage's way of Dao, bright as sun and moon, as fine as a hair. But for those who are not sages, how can we take the way of Dao?"

Notes

1. Zi Ran is "the spontaneous self." It is the self which has begun to blaze and burn, one whose energy and heat are different from the multitude.

2. The text reads "muddy qi" and is probably an error.

39. AN ESSAY ON THE BLOOD'S LUO CHANNELS

Huang Di said, "I wish to hear about those different evils which are not located in the channels."

Qi Bo said, "Those diseases are in the blood *luo* channels."

Huang Di said, "How do you needle the blood *luo* channels when someone is struck down by fainting, and why? If the blood comes shooting out, what then? If the blood is a little black and muddy, what then? If the blood comes out clear, but half looks like sap, what then? If upon withdrawing the needle there is swelling, what does this mean? If the blood coming out is plentiful or sparse, and the color of the face turns greenish gray, what does this mean? If upon withdrawing the needle, the color of the face does not change, but there are palpitations and depression, what does this mean? If there is much blood, but no moving or shaking, what then? I would like to hear the reasons for the above."

Qi Bo said, "If the qi in the channel is abundant, but the blood is hollow, needling will result in stripping the qi. Stripping the qi will cause fainting.

"When blood and qi are both abundant and the yin qi is plentiful, the blood will be slippery so that needling will cause it to shoot out. When the yang qi collects and accumulates and has been detained for a long time, do not drain. This blood is black and muddy and thus will not shoot out.

"Freshly drunk liquids and body fluids seep into the *luo* channels, but do not join or harmonize in the blood. Consequently, when blood is drawn, the saps of the body fluids are separate. He who has not recently drunk liquids, yet his body has water, if this has been retained for a long time can cause swellings.

"The yin qi accumulates in the yang and follows the *luo* channels. Therefore, needle so that the blood does not come out and the qi goes ahead and causes swelling.

"The yin and yang qi when recently merged are not harmoniously tuned. The results of draining will be mutual stripping of yin and yang so that the external and internal will be mutually separate, and the consequences are a stripping of the color so they appear greenish grey.

"When much bleeding takes place with needling, but the color does not change and there are palpitations and depression, it is because needling the *luo* channel causes the channel to empty. A hollow channel subordinates the yin. If the yin is overcome, it results in palpitations and depression.

"When yin and yang are received together and join to make rheumatism, this will make the internals flow to the major channels and the externals flow into the *luo* channels. In this case yin and yang are both in excess although much blood comes out. It is not possible to make a state of hollowness."

Huang Di said, "How can you observe this?"

Qi Bo said, "The blood's veins, arteries, and channels, when full, firm, and extensive are red. When they are up or down without a constant location, they may be small like a needle or large like a tendon. The result of draining even ten thousand times will not cause one loss. The loss of even one is contrary to curing, but each must be appropriate to its limits."

Huang Di said, "The needle enters and the flesh tightens, why?"

Qi Bo said, "Hot qi follows the needle and results in heating the needle. The heat causes the flesh to tighten on the needle resulting in firmness."

40. YIN AND YANG, CLEAR AND MUDDY

Huang Di said, "I have heard that the twelve major channels have correspondences to the twelve rivers, that each of the five colors is different, and that clear and muddy are not the same. Yet man's blood and qi are as one, what are the correspondences?"

Qi Bo said, "If man's blood and qi are as one, so men under heaven are as one, how is it sickness can have disorders?"

Huang Di said, "I am asking about one man, not asking about everyone under heaven."

Qi Bo said, "For one man may have disordered qi, while the multitudes under heaven also may have disordered men. These in conjunction make one."

Huang Di said, "I wish to hear about man's qi being clear or muddy."

Qi Bo said, "That qi which is received from food is muddy. That qi which is received from the atmosphere is clear. Clear flows to the yin organs. Muddy flows to the yang organs. Muddy then clear arises to come out in the throat. Clear then muddy results in lower movements. When clear and muddy are in mutual opposition it is called disordered qi."

Huang Di said, "Yin clear and yang muddy, yet muddy has clear and clear has muddy; how do you separate the clear and the muddy?"

Qi Bo said, "When the qi has a great separation, the clear flows up into the lungs. The muddy travels down into the stomach. The clear qi of the stomach arises to come out in the mouth. The muddy qi of the lungs flows down into the channels and accumulates internally in the seas."

Huang Di said, "All yang organs are muddy. Which yang organ is the most muddy?"

Qi Bo said, "The Arm Major Yang is unique in receiving the muddy qi of the yang. The Arm Major Yin is unique in receiving the clear qi of the yin. This clear qi arises up and travels to the apertures and orifices. This muddy qi descends and moves to all the channels. All yin is completely clear. The Leg Major Yin alone receives the muddy qi."

Huang Di said, "What cures are there?"

Qi Bo said, "Clear means its qi is slippery. Muddy means its qi is rough. These are constants. Consequently, needle yin deeply, and detain. Needle yang shallowly and rapidly. When clear and muddy are mutually opposed, use the proper number to harmonize."

SCROLL SEVEN
41. YIN AND YANG AND THEIR CONNECTIONS
TO THE SUN AND MOON

Huang Di said, "I hear that heaven is yang, earth is yin. The sun is yang, the moon is yin. How are these joined in man?"

Qi Bo said, "Above the waist is heaven. Below the waist is earth. For heaven is yang and earth is yin. Therefore, the twelve major channels of the leg make a correspondence to the twelve months. The moon begins in water. Consequently, that which is below is yin. The ten fingers of the hand make a correspondence to the ten days of the Chinese week. The sun controls fire. Consequently, that which is above is yang."

Huang Di said, "How do they join in the channels?"

Qi Bo said, "Of the twelve earthly branches:[1]

Yin and the first month gives birth to yang and controls the Left Leg Minor Yang Channel.

"Wei and the sixth month control the Right Leg Minor Yang.

"Mao and the second month control the Left Leg Major Yang.

"Wu and the fifth month control the Right Leg Major Yang.

"Chen and the third month control the Left Leg Bright Yang.

"Si and the fourth month control the Right Leg Bright Yang. The two yang, major and minor, join to their front; therefore, it is called the Bright Yang.

"Shen and the seventh month give birth to yin and control the Right Leg Minor Yin.

"Chou and the twelfth month control the Left Leg Minor Yin.

"You and the eighth month control the Right Leg Major Yin.

"Zi and the eleventh month control the Left Leg Major Yin.

"Xu and the ninth month control the Right Leg Shrinking Yin.

"Hai and the tenth month control the Left Leg Shrinking Yin. The two yin, major and minor, intersect and exhaust, therefore it is called the Shrinking Yin.

"Of the ten celestial stems:[2]

"Jia controls the Left Arm Minor Yang.

"Ji controls the Right Arm Minor Yang.

"Yi controls the Left Arm Major Yang.

"Wu controls the Right Arm Major Yang.

"Bing controls the Left Arm Bright Yang.

"Ding controls the Right Arm Bright Yang.

"The two fires combine resulting in the Bright Yang.

"Geng controls the Right Arm Minor Yin.
"Gui controls the Left Arm Minor Yin.
"Xin controls the Right Arm Major Yin.
"Ren controls the Left Arm Major Yin.

"Thus the leg's yang, from the yin includes the minor yang, and the leg's yin, from the yin, includes the major yin. The arm's yang, from the yang, includes the major yang, and the arm's yin, from the yang, includes the minor yin. Above the waist is yang. Below the waist is yin.

"These are manifest in the five viscera. The heart at the center of yang proceeding to Major Yang. The lungs at the center of yin proceeding to Minor Yin. The liver at the center of yin proceeding to Minor Yang. The spleen at the center of yin proceeding to the Extreme Yin. The kidneys at the center of yin proceeding to the Major Yin."

Huang Di said, "What use is this in therapy?"

Qi Bo said, "In the first, second, and third months, man's qi is positioned to the left. Do not needle the yang of the left leg. In the fourth, fifth, and sixth months, man's qi is positioned on the right. Do not needle the yang of the right leg. In the seventh, eighth, and ninth months, man's qi is on the right. Do not needle the yin of the right leg. In the tenth, eleventh, and twelfth months, man's qi is on the left. Do not needle the yin of the left leg."

Huang Di said, "For the five dynamic elements, the eastern quarter has resonance with the celestial stems, Jia, Yi. In addition, wood is the emperor in spring. Spring has the color of green, which controls the liver. The liver is the Leg Shrinking Yin Channel. This in accord with Jia and the Left Arm Minor Yang. Why was this not used in the tally?"[3]

Qi Bo said, "Heaven and earth and yin and yang are not without the four seasons or five dynamic elements in their successive motions. Moreover, yin and yang may have names without physical appearance. Consequently, the arithmetic and tally makes ten, which separated makes a hundred, which divided makes a thousand, which enlarged makes ten thousand. This is the axiom."

Notes

1. Various calendric notations were used by the ancient Chinese to create a system for counting with names rather than numbers. This was especially useful in the creation of cycles - the primary one of sixty which

incorporated a sliding rotation of the twelve earthly branches and ten celestial stems.

See appendix B for further discussion of the twelve earthly branches and ten celestial stems.

2. The ten celestial stems, like the above, were notations for numerical change. Each stem corresponds to the name of a day in the ancient Chinese week of ten days.

3. The Triple Heater Channel is in the numerical sequence of six instead of five. Before the Wu Xing, the five dynamic elements, there may well have been a system based on the number six.

42. THE PROPAGATION OF DISEASE

Huang Di said, "I have received the theory of the nine needles from the sages and a secret survey of the methods. Thus these will lead to the conduct of the movement of qi, by massage, moxibustion, ironing out, needling, fire needling or drinking medicines. If one method alone can protect, why use all of them?"

Qi Bo said, "All the methods are for all people but one cannot be moved by all."

Huang Di said, "This is what is meant by protecting one without loss for all the myriad beings. These things I have already heard, the attributes of yin and yang, the principles of hollow and solid, the inclination to shift into the excessive, and subsequently, what can cure. Now I would like to hear about the changes and transformations of disease. How debauchery propagates, cuts off and spoils so there is no cure. How can I hear about this?"

Qi Bo said, "These questions are of vital importance. Like the Dao, how bright it is when they are like the sun waking up. How distressing it is when they are like the night with closed eyes. If possible one should wear the Dao as clothes. The spirit completes, and all will fit. All should be taken willingly. Then the spirit will be obtained naturally. The birth of the spirit is the basic principle. So compose these items on silk and bamboo so that they are not only transmitted to sons and grandsons."

Huang Di said, "What is meant by the sun waking up?"

Qi Bo said, "Brightness in yin and yang is like doubts being unravelled, like waking up from being drunk."

Huang Di said, "What is meant by the night with closed eyes?"

Qi Bo said, "It is muteness, that is, without sound. It is a desert that is without shape. Shear the hair to reveal the base. If the primary qi excessively pours out, the debauched evil will flow and amplify. The blood channels will propagate the flow and great evil qi will enter the viscera. The abdomen will become painful and the lower parts debauched. All these can cause death. If this does not happen, it means life."

Huang Di said, "What is it when the great evil qi enters the viscera?"

Qi Bo said, "If disease first appears in the heart, with one day it possesses the lungs, three days the liver, five days the spleen, and three days more not completed, death in winter at midnight, in summer at noon.

"If disease first appears in the lung, three days and it possesses the liver, another day the spleen, in five days the stomach. Before ten days are completed, death in winter at sunset, or in summer at sunrise.

"If disease first appears in the liver, three days and it possesses the spleen, in five days the stomach, three days more the kidneys, and before three more days are completed, death in winter at sunset, or in summer at early morning.

"If disease first appears in the spleen, in one day it possesses the stomach, in two days the kidneys, in three days the buttocks and bladder. Ten days not completed, death in winter when man is fixed in sleep, or in summer after a quiet evening meal.

"If disease first appears in the stomach, in five days it possesses the kidneys. In three days more the buttocks and bladder; in five days more up to the heart; and before two days more are completed, death in winter at midnight, or in summer at sunset.

"If disease first appears in the kidneys, in three days it possesses the buttocks and bladder. Three days more up to the heart, again three days and it possesses the small intestine. Three days more not completed, death in winter at daybreak, or in summer late at sunset.

"If disease first appears in the bladder, in five days it possesses the kidneys, one day more the small intestine, yet another day the heart. Before two more days are completed, death in winter at cock crow, or in summer before sunset.

"All diseases are in accord with the arrangement of mutual propagation.[1] Like reality, all have a period before death when acupuncture cannot be done. But when it is in between one viscera and the second, third or fourth viscera, then acupuncture can be done."

Note

1. For commentary on mutual propagation, see appendix A.

43. THE DEBAUCHED EVIL AND
THE DEVELOPMENT OF DREAMS

Huang Di said, "I have heard that the debauched qi swirls and flows, how is that?"

Qi Bo said, "The primary evil travels from the outside and raids the inside without having a fixed abode. It disorients and debauches the viscera, and by not obtaining a fixed dwelling, it travels together with the nourishing and protective qi and flies about with the animal spirit and human soul and sends dreams constantly to man so his sleep cannot be peaceful. If the qi debauches the bowels, it results in an excess in the externals and an insufficiency in the innards. If the qi debauches the viscera, it results in an excess in the innards and an insufficiency in the externals."

Huang Di said, "What forms do excess and insufficiency take?"

Qi Bo said, "If the yin qi is abundant, it causes dreams of fording great waters and fear and fright. If the yang qi is abundant it causes dreams of great fires and roasting sacrificial beasts. When yin and yang are both abundant it causes dreams of mutual killing. If the top of the body is full it causes dreams of flying. If the lower part of the body is full it causes dreams of falling. Extreme hunger causes dreams of seizing things. Extreme fullness causes dreams of walking. Abundant liver qi causes dreams of anger. Abundant lung qi causes dreams of anxiety and fear, weeping or silent tears, and flying about. Abundant heart qi causes dreams of easy laughter, fear and awe. The spleen qi abundant causes dreams of songs and happiness. The body is heavy and unable to rise. Abundant kidney qi causes dreams of the loins and the spine being loose and unconnected. For all the above twelve abundances, disperse to fix and finish.

"When a perverse and deficient qi is a guest in the heart, it results in dreams of seeing mounds and mountains, smoke and fire. As a guest in the lungs, it results in dreams of flying about, seeing extraordinary creatures of gold and iron. As a guest in the liver, it results in dreams of mountains, forests, trees and wood. As a guest in the spleen, it results in dreams of mounds and hillocks and large swamps, ruined houses, wind and rain. As a guest in the kidneys, it results in dreams of weeping and whirlpools and dwelling in water. As a guest in the bladder it results in dreams of wandering. As a guest in the stomach, it results in dreams of drink and food. As a guest in the large intestine it results in dreams of fields and wild lands. As a guest in the small intestine, it results in dreams of crowds in cities and rushing highways. As a guest in the gallbladder, it results in dreams of quarrels, lawsuits, and self-inflicted wounds. As a guest in the yin organs, it results in dreams of sexual intercourse. As a guest in the neck, it results in dreams of beheading. As a guest in the legs, it results in dreams of walking but being unable to move forward and dwelling in deep vaults, cellars, and gardens. As a guest in the elbow and arm, it results in dreams of propriety, regulations, worshiping, and rising. As a guest in the bladder and rectum, it results in dreams of urination and bowel movements. All above fifteen deficiencies may be reached by tonification to fix and to finish."

44. THE SMOOTH FLOWING QI DIVIDES ONE DAY INTO FOUR SEASONS

Huang Di said, "The hundred diseases have that which gives them beginning and birth. Each must arise from dryness or humidity, winter's cold or summer's heat, wind or rain, yin or yang, joy or anger, drink or food, in a place or dwelling. The evil qi joins the body and makes an appearance. When it is received by the viscera, then it has a name. I understand these things positively. But as for the hundred diseases, why are they so often clever in the morning, quiet in daytime, increased in the evening, and extreme at night?"

Qi Bo said, "It is the qi sent by the four seasons."

Huang Di said, "I would like to hear about the qi of the four seasons."

Qi Bo said, "Spring gives birth. Summer grows. Autumn harvests. Winter stores. This is the constant of the qi. Man also responds to this so that one day can be divided into four seasons. Dawn thus is spring. Midday is summer. Sunset is autumn. Midnight is winter. Dawn causes man's qi to begin life. The disease qi diminishes and it causes the morning's lucidity. At midday man's qi grows and can overcome the evil so it causes quietude. Evening causes man's qi to begin to lessen while the evil qi begins to grow, resulting in an increase. At midnight man's qi has entered the storehouses and the evil qi is alone dwelling in the body in general, which results in a worsening."

Huang Di said, "How can these time cycles be disoriented?"

Qi Bo said, "When a person is not in resonance with the qi of the four seasons, each viscera suffers its disease. When a person begins to be dissonant to the seasons, one must make an accord so that the viscera's qi is not overcome by the season and worsened. When the viscera's qi is in accordance with the seasons, harmony begins."

Huang Di said, "What are the cures?"

Qi Bo said, "Flow smoothly with heaven's seasons and disease will be limited. Smooth flowing is the good doctor's technique. Unruly and counterflowing is the coarse doctor's practice."

Huang Di said, "Excellent! I have heard acupuncture has five transformations, which are in accord with control of the five *shu* points. I would like to hear the explanation."

Qi Bo said, "Man has five viscera. The five viscera have five transformations. The five transformations have five *shu* transporting points. Consequently, there are five times five or twenty-five *shu* points which are in resonance with the five seasons."

Huang Di said, "I would like to hear about the five transformations."

Qi Bo said, "The liver is a male viscera: its color is green, its time is spring, its tone is *jiao*, its taste is sour, its days are Jia and Yi. The heart is a male viscera: its color is red, its time is summer, its days are Bing and Ding, its tone is *zhan*, its taste is bitter. The spleen is a female viscera: its color is yellow, its time is the long summer, its days are Wu and Ji, its tone is *gung*, its taste is sweet. The lungs are female viscera: their color is white, their tone is *shang*, their time is autumn, their days are Ceng and Xin, their taste is pungent. The kidneys are female viscera, their color is black, their season is winter, their days are Ren and Guei, their tone is *yu*, their taste is salty. These make the five transformations."

Huang Di said, "What are the controls of the five *shu* points?"

Qi Bo said, "The viscera, or storehouses, control winter's qi. For winter, needle the well *shu* point. Colors control the spring qi. For spring, needle the spring *shu* point. Time periods control summer. For summer, needle the stream *shu* points. The tones control the long summer. For the long summer, needle the confluence *shu* points. These are spoken of as the five transformations controlling the five *shu* points."

Huang Di said, "When all of the source points are tranquil and tuned, they reach the six acupuncture points of the six yang channels."

Qi Bo said, "The source points do not correspond to the five seasons, but take their harmonies from the channels so it responds to this count, which makes six times six is thirty-six points."

Huang Di said, "What are the meanings of: the viscera control winter, time periods control summer, tones control the long summer, tastes control autumn, colors control spring? I would like to hear the reasons."

Qi Bo said, "When disease is located in the viscera, treat the well *shu* points. When disease changes in color, treat the spring *shu* points. When disease is extreme intermittently, treat the stream *shu* points. When disease changes in tone, treat the *jing* river points. When the channels are full with blood, disease is located in the stomach. For when drink and food are not partitioned, it will result in this disease. Treat with the confluence *shu* points, for it is said the flavors control the confluence points. This is what is meant by the five transformations."

157

45. EXTERNAL MEASUREMENTS

Huang Di said, "I have heard about the nine needles and the nine essays. I personally have been receptive to these harmonics and I am inclined to these ideas. For the nine needles, begin with one and end with nine, yet this does not necessarily obtain the reality of the Dao. For the nine needles, can small be without an interior, can big be without an exterior? How can there be depth below the nadir, or a cover to the apex? Can there be haziness and obscurity without extremes? Can there be a current or flow without a pivot? I know there are harmonics between the Dao of heaven and the affairs of men and the transformations of the four seasons, yet I would hear about the finest detail and minutiae of these mixtures. How can this chaos be bound into the one unity?"

Qi Bo said, "How illustrious are your questions. Not only for the Dao of a single needle, also the ways to control the state."

Huang Di said, "I wish to hear about the Dao of acupuncture, not about the affairs of state!"

Qi Bo said, "To control the state means to be with the Dao. Without the Dao, how could small and big, deep and shallow, mix and combine to make one unity?"

Huang Di said, "I would like to hear all about this."

Qi Bo said, "The sun resonates with the moon, the water with mirrors, the drum with drumming sounds. For the sun and moon are bright and do not lose their shadows, water and mirrors reflect and do not lose their images, drums and drumming sounds resonate in time to their sounds. Moving and shaking causes an additional resonance. To obtain this is to get to the heart of the matter."

Huang Di said, "How embarrassingly difficult. Bright and shining, this brilliance cannot be covered up. Why it cannot be covered up is because yin and yang cannot be lost. Make a complete examination and feel the pulse to understand. Seek and you will receive, like clear still water and bright mirrors which do not lose their images. If the five tones are not distinct, the five colors not bright, the five viscera are like unsettled waves, for it must be that the internal and external are mutually supportive. Like the drum resonating to the drumstick, the drumming sounds resonating to tunes, the shadow reflects the physical appearance. Consequently, the distant administers the external and measures the internal. This is spoken of as the pivot of yin and yang, which covers heaven and earth. Please store them in the spiritual fragrant chambers without spoilage or leaking."[1]

Note

1. The spiritual fragrant chamber is the king's library.

46. THE FIVE TRANSFORMATIONS

Huang Di questioned Shao Yu, saying, "I have heard of the hundred diseases' beginning periods, that they must start in wind or rain, winter's cold or summer's heat, and following the fine hairs, enter into the foundations between skin and flesh. Either they return and repeat or detain and stop. Either they make wind swellings with sweating or a melting from overwork. Either they make chills and fever, or detain with rheumatism, or accumulate. Each evil qi debauches and flows. They are numerous and beyond counting. I would like to hear about the causes. How are diseases subject to similar times when they are this disease or that disease? Does heaven give birth to wind disease for each man? How do diseases differ?"

Shao Yu said, "When heaven gives birth to wind, it is not because of a hundred secret natures. These actions and workings are equal, just, and straight. To violate will mean disease, to evade will mean no danger. When wind does not disturb man, yet there is disease, then he himself is the violator."

Huang Di said, "Each time there is an encounter with the wind, at the same time there is disease. Yet the diseases each are different. I would like to hear about the causes."

Shao Yu said, "How excellent are these questions! If you please, an analogy may be made with a craftsman. A craftsman sharpens his axe and blade, whets his knife, peels and cuts his material into pieces. Wood is yin and yang. Moreover it is strong or fragile. When strong it cannot be penetrated. When fragile it can lose its skin. When reaching joints or nodes, the axe and blade can be broken. Each piece of wood has strong and fragile parts which are different. Strong results in hardness. Fragile is easily injured. Moreover the structure of the wood is dissimilar. The skin can be thick or thin, the sap may be plentiful or sparse, for each is different. Wood's insects and flowers begin with the birth of leaves. When encountering spring frost and strong winds, it causes the flowers to fall and the leaves to wither. Long exposure and great drought results in weak wood and thin skin. In the branches and twigs the sap is sparse and the leaves withered. A long period of darkness and debauchery of rain will result in thin skin and much sap. The skin decays and oozes. When there are sudden arisings of violent winds, it results in both strong and fragile wood having broken branches and injury to the tops. When there is autumn frost and quick winds it results in both strong and fragile wood having their roots shaken and leaves withered. All of this is five. Each has that which injures. How can man avoid these?"

Huang Di said, "Man resonates with wood, but how?"

Shao Yu replied, "Of those things which injure wood, all injure the branches. The branches, whether strong or fragile, if firm will not be injured. When man often has disease, it may also originate in his bones and joints, or skin, or the foundation between skin and flesh when they are not firm and solid. The evil takes residence there and is the cause of these frequent diseases."

Huang Di said, "When man often has disease of wind, and perverse sweat pours out, what are the symptoms?"

Shao Yu replied, "The flesh is without firmness. The foundation between skin and flesh is sparse. These result in vulnerability to wind disease."

Huang Di said, "What are the reasons and the symptoms of the flesh not being firm?"

Shao Yu replied, "When the flesh at the major joints is not firm, the foundations are not properly separated. These foundations are coarse and thick. Thick foundations will not convey to the skin, causing the foundations and pores of the skin to be sparse. This is said to be chaos."

Huang Di said, "When man often has the disease of melting from overwork, what are the symptoms?"

Shao Yu replied, "The five viscera all are weak and febrile, then there is often the disease of melting from overwork."

Huang Di said, "What is in accord with the knowledge that the five viscera are weak and febrile?"

Shao Yu replied, "When the viscera are weak and febrile, the qi is hard and strong. Hard and strong causes much anger, while weakness is easily injured."

Huang Di said, "What are the symptoms of weak and febrile viscera and hard and strong qi?"

Shao Yu replied, "These men have thin skin, their eyes are firm and solid and deep. Their upper eyebrow, the long streamer, is straight and raised, the heart is hard. This hardness causes much anger. Anger causes the qi to flow upwards in rebellion and accumulate in the chest. Blood and qi are in counterflow and detained. The skin swells and the flow is to the muscles. The blood pulses do not move but change into fever. Fever results in a melting and fatigue of overwork. This is what meant by this type of man being violent and hard, yet the muscles and flesh are weak."

161

Huang Di said, "When man often has the disease of chills and fever, what are the symptoms?"

Shao Yu replied, "The bones being small and the flesh weak are symptoms of often having the disease of chills and fever."

Huang Di said, "What are these symptoms, where the bones are small or large, and the flesh is firm or weak? Is this not in accord with one color?"

Shao Yu replied, "The cheekbones are the root of the bones. When the cheekbones are large, it means the bones are large. When the cheekbones are small, it means the bones are small. When the skin is thin, the flesh is lacking at the joints, so the shoulder and upper arm are weak and soft. The color of earth (the chin) is a positive danger if it is not the same color as heaven (the forehead). When they are muddy and each is different with these signs, after this, the arm thins and the marrow lessens, causing disease of chills and fever to be frequent."

Huang Di said, "What are the symptoms of a man who has constant rheumatism?"

Shao Yu replied, "The man whose foundations are coarse and whose flesh is not firm has frequent rheumatism."

Huang Di said, "Why does rheumatism have a high or low dwelling?"

Shao Yu replied, "To know high or low, each disease must be examined for its location."

Huang Di said, "When man often has disease of accumulation in the intestines, what are the symptoms?"

Shao Yu replied, "The skin is thin and without gloss. The flesh is not firm and is slippery and marshy. Things like this cause ills of the intestines and stomach. These ills cause the evil qi to detain and stop so the accumulation injures the area between the spleen and stomach. The cold and the warm are out of order, the evil qi reaches in slightly, stores, increases, detains, and stops, so that a great accumulation begins."

Huang Di said, "I have heard about the appearances of disease, and that is already known. Now I desire to hear about the seasons."

Shao Yu replied, "First establish the year in accord with knowledge of its seasons. When the time cycle is high, it causes a beginning. When the time cycle is low, it causes peril, although it does not sink lower at that point of the year when there is a rushing penetration, disease will begin. This is spoken of as the original appearance and birth of disease. This is the record of the five transformations."

47. THE BODY AND THE VISCERA

Huang Di questioned Qi Bo, saying, "Man has blood, qi, seminal essence, and spirit which nourish life and complete the nature of life's destiny. The major channels are those where movement of blood and qi nourishes yin and yang, moistens the muscles and bones, and benefit the gates and joints. The protective qi is that which warms the divisions of the flesh, flows to the skin, fertilizes the foundation between the flesh and skin, and administers the gates and covers. Will and thought can manage the seminal essence and spirit, can hold in the animal spirits and human soul, can adapt to cold and warmth, and can harmonize joy and anger. Thus when blood harmonizes, the major channels flow and move. The nourishing qi repeatedly penetrates the yin and yang. The muscles and bones become good and strong. The gates and joints are clear and benefit. When the protective qi harmonizes, then the divisions of the flesh relax and benefit. The skin is in tune and is tender. The foundation between flesh and skin is dense. When will and thought are in harmony, then the seminal essence and spirit can focus and be true, the animal spirit and human soul do not scatter, regrets and anger do not begin. The five viscera do not receive evil. When cold and warmth harmonize, then the six bowels transform the valley energy, wind rheumatism has no effect, the major channels penetrate and benefit, the limbs and joints obtain tranquility. These men are constantly peaceful. The five viscera store the seminal essence, spirit, blood, qi, animal spirit, and human soul. The six bowels transform water and food and move the body fluids. These men receive from heaven, without stupidity, which knowledge and wisdom do not resemble, without leaning against one another. They have and possess, each to the utmost, the benefit of heaven, longevity, and are without evil and can avoid disease. A hundred years with no weakening. Although they encounter wind and rain, sudden cold and great summer heat, they cannot be injured. There are others who use screens to cover up the inner room. They are without anxiety and fear even when they are not spared by disease. Why is this? I would like to hear the reasons?"

Qi Bo replied, "How embarrassingly difficult are these questions. The five viscera, because they correspond to heaven and earth, are subsidiary to yin and yang, moved by the four seasons, and metamorphosed by the five divisions.[1] The five viscera are small or large, high or low, firm or fragile, correct and upright, or to the side and inclined. The six bowels also are large or small, long or short, thick or thin, knotted or straight, slow or quick. For all of these twenty-five changes, each is different, for good or for ill, whether fortunate or unfortunate. If you please, these are the rules.

"The heart being small results in tranquility that external evil is unable to injure. However, it is easily injured because of worry. The heart being large is not injured by worry, but is easily injured by external evil. When the heart is high, it causes congestion in the middle of the lungs, palpitations and frequent forgetfulness, and difficulty in opening a conversation. When the heart is low, it results in the organ being more to the outside so that it is easily injured by cold, and easily frightened by words. When the heart is firm, the organ is tranquil and maintains strength. When the heart is weak, it results in frequent disease from fatigue and overwork with fever in the center. When the heart is correct and upright, it results in harmony and profit and is difficult to injure. When the heart is to the side and inclined, its management and support are not unified so that it cannot administer.

"The lungs being small results in a small intake of water so there are no diseases of gasping or inhalation. The lungs being large results in much drinking, so there often are diseases like rheumatism of the chest, rheumatism of the throat, and qi in counterflow. When the lungs are high it results in ascending qi, so the shoulder is involved in breathing and coughing. When the lungs are low, they sit on the cardiac orifice and are oppressed. The lower ribs are frequently painful. When the lungs are firm, it results in no disease of coughing from ascending qi. When the lungs are weak, it results in a withering disease, fatigue from overwork, and they are easily injured. When the lungs are correct and upright, it results in harmony and profit, and they are difficult to injure. When the lungs are leaning to the side, it results in the side of the chest being painful.

"The liver being small results in the organ being tranquil and no disease in the lower ribs. The liver being large causes and compels the stomach to oppress the throat and larynx. This oppression causes suffering in the middle of the diaphragm and moreover, the lower ribs are painful. When the liver is high, it elevates the cardiac orifice. The ribs are annoyed and breathing strenuous. When the liver is low, it causes and compels the stomach and the area of the lower ribs to be hollow. The area of the lower ribs being hollow makes it easily receptive to evil. When the liver is firm, it results in the organ being tranquil and difficult to injure. When the liver is weak, it results in frequent disease of fatigue and overwork, and is easily injured. When the liver is correct and upright, it results in harmony and profit and it is difficult to injure. When the liver leans to the side it causes the lower ribs to be painful.

"The spleen being small results in the organ being tranquil. It is difficult to injure by external evil. The spleen being large results in suffering from an accumulation of pain in the area of the ribs. There is an inability to walk quickly. When the spleen is high, it causes the area of the ribs to induce pain in the lowest rib. When the spleen is low, it descends and imposes on the large intestine which causes this viscera to suffer and to receive evil. When the spleen is firm, the viscera are tranquil and difficult to injure. When the spleen is fragile, it causes frequent illness from fatigue and overwork, and is easily injured. When the spleen is correct and upright, it results in harmony and profit and is difficult to injure. When the spleen leans to the side, there is frequent congestion and swelling.

"The kidneys being small results in the organ being tranquil and difficult to injure. The kidneys being big causes frequent disease with painful loins, and not being able to bend forward or backward. They are easily injured by external evil. The kidneys being high results in suffering from the back and the buttocks being painful, and one cannot bend forward or backward. When the kidneys are low, it causes the pain in the loins and sacral area. One cannot bend forward or backward and there is a fox (hernia). When the kidneys are firm, one does not suffer from loin and back pain. When the kidneys are weak, it results in the frequent disease of fatigue from overwork and they are easily injured. When the kidneys are correct and upright, it results in harmony and profit and they are difficult to injure. When the kidneys lean to the side, it causes suffering and pain in the loins and sacral area.

"All of these above are the twenty-five transformations which in man can cause suffering and disease."

Huang Di said, "What is in accord with the above knowledge?"

Qi Bo said, "A red color and small lines on the skin when the heart is small, thick creases or lines when the heart is large. When there is barely a breastbone, the heart is high. When the breastbone is short and raised, the heart is low. When the breastbone is long, the heart is low and firm. When the breastbone is weak, small and thin, the heart is weak. When the breastbone is straight, low, and not raised, the heart is correct and upright. The breastbone leaning to one corner means the heart is leaning to the side.

"A white color and small lines mean the lungs are small. Thick lines mean the lungs are large. A square shoulder, a prominent chest and a deep throat means the lungs are high. When the closure of the armpits and the ribs is extensive, the lungs are low. Good and thick shoulders and back means the lungs are firm. If the shoulders and back are thin, the lungs are weak. When back and chest are thick, the lungs are correct and upright. If the ribs are lean and sparse, the lungs are leaning to the side.

"A green color and small lines mean the liver is small; thick lines, the liver is large. A wide chest and prominent ribs mean the liver is high. If the box of the ribs is like a rabbit that is hidden, the liver is low. When the chest and ribs are good, the liver is firm. When the rib bones are fragile, the liver is weak. When the chest and abdomen are good and mutually receptive, the liver is correct and upright. If the rib bones are raised to the side, the liver is leaning to the side.

"A yellow color and small lines mean the spleen is small. Thick lines mean the spleen is large. Raised and exposed lips mean the spleen is high. Low and relaxed lips mean the spleen is low. When the lips are firm, the spleen is firm. When the lips are large, but not firm, the spleen is weak. When the lips are raised to the side, the spleen is leaning to the side.

"A black color and small lines mean the kidneys are small; thick lines, the kidneys are large. When the ears are high, the kidneys are high. When there is a depression behind the ears, the kidneys are low. The ears firm mean the kidneys are firm. When the ears are thin and not firm, the kidneys are weak. When the ears are good and dwell to the front of the teeth's carriage, the kidneys are correct and upright. If the ears are leaning and high, the kidneys are leaning to the side. For all of these transformations, support will cause peace; diminishing will cause illness."

Huang Di said, "Excellent. Yet those are not my questions. I would like to hear about how man has or does not have disease, how he reaches to complete the life span indicated by heaven, even though there are deep fears and great apprehensions, or a fearful and cautious will. Cannot fear diminish this span? Cannot extreme cold and great heat injure the life span? For there is no separation between the screens and covers and the interior of a room. Also, even though there is no fear and apprehension and terror, yet one cannot avoid disease. Why? I would like to hear about the causes."

Qi Bo said, "If you please, I will speak about the causes when evil is resident in the five viscera and six bowels. When the five viscera all are small and the disease is small, the heart will suffer from heat and there is great sorrow and worry. When the five viscera all are large, there will be a slowness in affairs and difficulty in causing worry. When the five viscera all are high, there is fondness to arrange and to elevate actions to heights. When the five viscera all are low, there is a fondness in a person to bend low. When the viscera all are firm, there is no disease. When the viscera all are weak, there is no separation from disease. When the five viscera all are correct, harmony and profit are obtained in man's heart and mind. When the five viscera all are leaning to the side, there is evil in the heart and mind and a tendency to criminality. This man cannot be made balanced; he has no consistency in his words and speech."

Huang Di said, "I would like to hear the resonance of six bowels."

Qi Bo replied, "The lungs are in tune with the large intestine. The large intestine resonates with the skin. The heart is in tune with the small intestine. The small intestine resonates with the blood channels. The liver is in tune with the gallbladder. The gallbladder is in tune with the muscles. The spleen is in tune with the stomach. The stomach is in tune with the flesh. The kidneys are in tune with the Triple Heater and bladder. The Triple Heater and bladder resonate with the foundations between flesh and skin, pores, and the fine body hairs."

Huang Di said, "What are the resonances?"

Qi Bo said, "The lungs resonate with the skin. When the skin is thick, the large intestine is thick; when the skin is thin, the large intestine is thin. When skin is slow, and the area of the abdomen is large, the large intestine is large and long. When the skin is anxious, the large intestine is anxious and short. When the skin is slippery, the large intestine is straight, while when the skin and flesh cannot be separated, the large intestine is knotted.

"The heart resonates with the blood channels. When the skin is thick, the channels are thick and the small intestine is thick. When the skin is thin, the channels are thin. When the channels are thin, the small intestine is thin. When the skin is slow, the channels are slow. When the channels are slow, the small intestine is large and long. When the skin is thin and the channels are rushing and small, the small intestine is small and short. When all of the yang channels meander and bend, the small intestine is knotted."

"The spleen resonates with the flesh. When the flesh of the major joints is firm and abundant, the stomach is thick. When the flesh of the major joints is weak, the stomach is thin. When the flesh of the major joints is not appropriate to the body, the stomach is low. When the stomach is low, the lower ducts are restrained and do not benefit. When the flesh of the major joints is not firm, the stomach is slow. When the flesh of the major joints is tied up except for small areas, the stomach is anxious. When the flesh of the major joints is plentiful with small areas tied up, the stomach is knotted. When the stomach is knotted, the upper ducts are restrained and do not benefit.

"The liver resonates with the nails. When the nails are thick and the color yellow, the gallbladder is thick. When the nails are thin and the color red, the gallbladder is thin. When the nails are firm and the color greenish blue, the gallbladder is anxious. When the nails are glossy and the color red, the gallbladder is slow. When the nails are straight and the color white without streaks, the gallbladder is straight. When the nails are sick, and colored black with many streaks, the gallbladder is tied up.

"The kidneys resonate with the bones. When the skin is thick with hidden lines, the Triple Heater and bladder are thick. When the skin is thin with wide lines, the Triple Heater and bladder are thin. When the pores are far apart, the Triple Heater and bladder are slow. When the skin is tense and without the fine body hair, the Triple Heater and bladder are tense. When the hair is beautiful and thick, the Triple Heater and bladder are correct. Scattered fine body hairs mean the Triple Heater and bladder are tied up."

Huang Di said, "Thick, thin, beautiful, or sick, all have their form. I wish to hear about that which is disease."

Qi Bo said, "Examine the external resonances of the body in order to know the body's inner viscera. Thus you will know that which is diseased."

Note

1. The five divisions also means the five joints of time. Spring, summer, long or "Indian" summer, autumn and winter.

48. RESTRICTIONS AND THE MAJOR CHANNELS

Lei Gong questioned Huang Di, saying, "This humble self, to acquire and to receive, will undertake to penetrate the text 'Sixty Chapters on the Nine Needles.'[1] Morning and evening with diligence and willingness I have recently unravelled the knots. For a long time these bamboo documents have been dusty, so honor or ridicule my recitation, I will not put it aside until the theories are completely understood. The 'External Estimates' chapter says, 'Binding chaos makes unity.'[2] I do not understand what this means, for largeness cannot be without an exterior, or smallness without an interior. For the concepts large or small without pivot, or high and low without a limit, how can they be bound? The scholar who has talent and strength perhaps may be thick or thin, but knowledge and consideration are narrow and shallow and cannot achieve the greatest profound depths. An individual wishing strongly to study like my humble self dares to question the rules for I fear this knowledge could be scattered in coming generations, cut off from our sons and grandsons."

Huang Di said, "What excellent questions. These were the first teachers' restrictions. Present sacrificial offerings in the transmission of secrets. Cut the arm and draw blood to seal the contract. For if you wish, why not perform the rituals, fasting and ablutions to study and obtain these secrets?"

Lei Gong bowed again and rose to say, "Pleased am I to hear your commands and so be it." Then he performed the rituals for three days, then politely asked, "May I dare question if this day is Primary Yang, for this humble self desires to suffer the contract."

Then Huang Di and he both entered into the ritual chamber and cut their arms to draw blood. Huang Di personally made the congratulations and said, "This day of the Primary Yang is to draw blood and to transmit laws. For those who dare to turn their back on their word, may their contrariness suffer misfortune!"

Lei Gong bowed again and said, "I have received."

Huang Di then with his left hand grasped his hand and with the right passed on the book, saying, "Caution as caution is. I say to you, for all of acupuncture's principles, the major channels make the beginning, and nourishment is that which acts. Know the person's limits and measurements. When disease is internal, needle the five viscera. When external, needle the six bowels. Investigate and examine the protective qi and the mothers of the hundred diseases. Harmonize the hollow and the solid, so the hollow and solid then will end. Disperse the blood *luo* channels, so that when the blood is exhausted there will be no danger."

Lei Gong said, "All of this I can penetrate, but what is in contract with these rules I do not know."

Huang Di said, "These contracts and rules are like a purse to be tied. When the purse overflows, there is no restriction as a result of the movement and leakage. Rules that are completed without contracts cause the spirit to be without wholeness."

Lei Gong said, "I desire to be an apprentice, but is there no completeness without the contract?"

Huang Di said, "There is no completeness, but knowledge of the contracts are what makes medical technique, and this can be done only by the worldly teacher."

Lei Gong said, "I would like to hear about medical techniques."

Huang Di said, "The pulse at the Inch Mouth controls the center. The pulse at the Man's Receptor point controls the external. Both resonate mutually. Together they go forward and together they come, as if drawn by a string, large and small all in attendance. In spring and summer the Man's Receptor pulse is slightly large. In autumn and winter the Inch Mouth is slightly large. When it is like this, it is called the balanced man.

"When the Man's Receptor pulse is twice as large as the Inch Mouth pulse, disease is located in the Leg Minor Yang Channel. When twice as large and rough, disease is located in the Arm Minor Yang. When the Man's Receptor pulse is three times as large, disease is located in the Leg Major Yang. When three times as large and rough, disease is located in Arm Major Yang. When the Man's Receptor pulse is four times as large, disease is located in the Leg Bright Yang. When four times as large and rough, disease is located in the Arm Bright Yang. Fullness in the pulse causes and makes heat. Hollowness causes and makes cold. Tightness causes and makes pain and rheumatism. Irregular pulses cause and make at times a worsening and at times a moderation. When full, disperse. When hollow, tonify. When tight with pain, treat the divisions of the flesh. When irregular, treat the blood *luo* channels and moreover, drink medicines. When the pulses are sinking and depressed, then use moxibustion. When neither full nor hollow, treat the channels; this is spoken of as needling the channels. When the Man's Receptor pulse is five times as large as the Inch Mouth, and is large and rapid, it is called overflowing yang. Overflowing yang means being locked out. Death, there is no cure. It is necessary to examine by pulse diagnosis the roots and branches, to examine whether the body is cold or hot, and to examine the viscera and bowels for disease.

"When the Inch Mouth pulse is twice as large as the Man's Receptor pulse, disease is located at the Master of the Heart. When the Inch Mouth is three times as large, disease is located at the Leg Minor Yin. When the Inch Mouth is three times as large as and rough, disease is located at the Arm Minor Yin. When the Inch Mouth is four times as large, disease is located at the Arm Major Yin. Fullness of the pulses causes swelling and congestion, coldness in the middle, and food not transforming. Hollow pulses cause the middle to be hot, the feces to appear like dissolved wastes; there is little qi, and a changeable color of urine. Tight pulses cause pain and rheumatism. Irregular pulses result in pain which stops intermittently. When the pulses are full, disperse. When hollow, tonify. When tight, needle first and afterwards use moxibustion. When irregular, treat the blood *luo* channels and afterwards harmonize. When the pulses are sinking and depressed, treat with moxibustion. For sinking and depressed means the blood channel is knotted in the middle; the middle has settled blood. The blood is cold. Consequently, it is appropriate to cauterize. When the pulses are neither full nor hollow, treat the channels. When the Inch Mouth pulse is five times as large as the Man's Receptor pulse, it is called locked in. Locked in and large and rapid means death, no cure. It is necessary to examine and investigate the body's roots and branches for heat and cold, and to examine the viscera and bowels for disease.

"Penetrate the nourishing acupuncture points which transport. Then one can transmit by the great axioms. The great axioms say 'When full, only disperse. When hollow, only tonify. When tight, cauterize and needle and drink medicine. When sinking and depressed, only use moxibustion. When neither full nor hollow, treat the channels.' This is what is meant by curing the channels, to drink medicine. Also it is said, for moxibustion and acupuncture, when the pulses are anxious, then guide with the therapy; the pulses large and weak, then the desire is for peace and quiet. Use strength without laboring."

Notes

1. "Sixty Chapters on the Nine Needles" is probably an ancient text which has been lost.
2. "External Estimates" is probably a lost ancient text.

49. THE FIVE COLORS

Lei Gong asked Huang Di, "How may the five colors each be distinguished at the area of the Bright Foyer? I humbly do not understand what is meant."

Huang Di said, "The Bright Foyer is the nose. The Watch Tower is between the eyebrows. The Court is the forehead. The Fence is the cheek. The Shield refers to the area around the Ear Door. For these places and in between one would desire that they be correct and large, so that from ten paces all the externals can be seen. If they are like this it means long life and one must hit a hundred years."

Lei Gong said, "The five organs may be distinguished how?"

Huang Di said, "When the bone of the Bright Foyer is high and rises, and is balanced and straight, the five viscera are arranged in series in the very center and the six bowels clasp the two sides. On the upper head and face is the Watch Tower and Court. The King's Palace, the heart, is located at the Lower Pivot (between the eyebrows). When the five viscera are tranquil in the body cavity, honest colors result. With disease, color cannot be seen. When the Bright Foyer is moist, glossy, and clear, how may the diseases of the five organs be diagnosed since there are no distinguishable colors?"

Lei Gong said, "The colors indistinguishable? May I hear about this?"

Huang Di said, "The five colors are visible. Each appears at its color location. At the locations of bony depressions, the colors of disease cannot be concealed. If these locations of color may be taken advantage of and united, then even though the disease is severe, there will be no death."

Lei Gong said, "The quality of the five colors, what is it?"

Huang Di said, "Green and black make pain. Yellow and red make heat. White makes cold. This is the meaning of the five qualities."

Lei Gong said, "When disease is increasingly severe, or lessening, what are the colors like?"

Huang Di said, "Locate all disease positions that exist externally and internally. They may be connected with the Pulse Mouth. When the pulses are slippery, small, tight, and sinking, the disease is increasing in severity and the problem is located in the middle. When the pulse of the Man's Receptor point is great, tight, and floating, the disease is increasing in severity and the problem is in the exterior areas. When the Pulse Mouth is floating and slippery, disease will advance during the day. When the Man's Receptor pulse is sinking and slippery, the disease will be lessened during the day. When the Pulse Mouth is slippery and sinking, disease will advance during the day and is in the internal areas. When the Man's Receptor pulse is slippery and full and floating, disease will advance during the day and is in the exterior areas. When the pulse is floating, then sinking at the Man's Receptor pulse, while at the Inch Mouth pulse the qi is small, then large and waiting, this disease is difficult to cure. When disease is located in the viscera and the pulses are sinking and large, it is easily finished; small is a counterflow of qi. When disease is located in the bowels and the pulses are floating and large, this disease is easily finished. When the Man's Receptor pulse is full and firm, the injury is from cold. When the Qi Mouth pulse is full and firm, the injury is from food."

Lei Gong said, "How do the colors say whether disease is severe or moderate?"

Huang Di said, "When the colors are slightly bright, disease is moderate. When the colors are sinking and somber, disease is severe. When the colors are heightened in movement, the disease will increase in severity. When the colors are lowered in movement, like clouds retreating and scattering, the disease can be correctly finished. Each of the five colors has a location for the viscera, with exterior positions and interior positions. When the colors go from the exterior positions and travel to the interior positions, the disease goes from the exterior and travels to the interior. When the colors go from the interior and travel to the exterior, the disease goes from the interior and travels to the exterior.

"When the disease begins in the interior, first cure the yin, afterwards cure the yang. If the therapy is reversed, the disease will increase in severity. When disease begins in the yang, first cure the exterior, afterwards cure the interior. If the therapy is reversed, the disease will increase in severity. When the pulses are slippery and large, then irregular and long, the disease follows the exterior in coming. The disease may be seen in the eyes and the will is affected by the sickness. This is a condition of the yang in conflict; it can be changed and finished."

Lei Gong said, "Humbly I have heard that the wind is the beginning of a hundred diseases, that perverse and rebellious counterflow of qi arises in cold and humidity. How can they be distinguished?"

Huang Di said, "The symptoms are usually at the Central Watchtower at the middle of the eyebrows. When thin and glossy, it is made by the wind. When sunken and muddy, it is made by rheumatism. When the symptoms are positioned at the Ground Point (the chin), it is made by perverse qi. These are the constants. Each is in accord with the color which relates to its disease."

Lei Gong said, "The person who is without disease but suddenly dies; what is known about this?"

Huang Di said, "A great qi enters into the viscera and bowels, so even though there is no disease, suddenly there is death."

Lei Gong said, "When there is disease, a little healing, and suddenly there is death, what is known about this?"

Huang Di said, "When a red color comes out on the cheekbones as large as a thumb, disease, although a little healed, will lead to sudden death. When a black color comes out at the Court in the middle of the forehead, and it is as large as a thumb, even though there is not necessarily disease, there will be sudden death."

Lei Gong bowed again and said, "How wonderful. Is there a fixed date for death?"

Huang Di said, "An examination of colors will tell the time."

Lei Gong said, "Amazing. I would like to hear about all of this."

Huang Di said, "The Court in the middle of the forehead relates to the head and face. Above the Watchtower relates to the throat. The Central Watchtower is the lungs. The Lower Pivot which is between the eyes relates to the heart. Straight below, the bridge of the nose relates to the liver. To the left of the liver location is the gallbladder. Lower on the nose is the spleen. Squared and above is the stomach.[1] Right in the middle below the cheekbones is the large intestine. Clasping the large intestine position on the face from the sides are the kidneys. At the point of the kidneys is the navel. Above the King of the Face, the tip of the nose, on the cheekbones is the small intestine. Below the King of the Face, on a level with the philtrum, on the sides, are the locations of the bladder and reproductive organs. The cheekbones relate to the shoulder. Behind the cheekbones relates to the upper arm. Below the position of the upper arm is the hand. The inner corner of the eye and above relates to the breasts and nipples. Holding the Cords and above (the margin of the ear) relates to the back. Following the teeth carriage (the mandible) and below relates to the thighs. Right in the middle (below the cheekbones) relates to the knees. Below this position for the knees is the area which relates to the lower leg. Below this point for the lower leg is the area which relates to the foot. The Great Divide (the area to the sides of the mouth) relates to the inner thigh. The Great Bend (on the flesh below the jaw) relates to the knee and knee caps. These are the locations for the five viscera and six bowels, the limbs and articulations. Each has its proper locations. Use the yin to harmonize the yang. Use the yang to harmonize the yin. At the point of understanding clearly the proper locations, ten thousand transformations can be effected and ten thousand will each be to the point. This ability to separate left from right is spoken of as the Great Dao. Man and woman have different positions, and therefore it is said there is yin and yang. Examine and investigate the glossy and somber. This is what is meant by superior technique.

"When the facial colors are sinking and muddy, disease is at the interior. When floating and glossy, disease is at the exterior. Yellow and red are made by the wind. Green and black are made by pain. White is made by cold. Yellow and oily and moist is made by pus. Extremely red is made by blood. Extreme pain is made by spasms. Extreme cold makes it so that the skin is numb.

"Each of the five colors may be seen in its location. Examine to see if it is floating or sinking, to know whether the disease is shallow or deep. Examine to see if it is glossy or somber in accord with the appearance of victory or defeat. Examine to see if it scatters or gathers to know whether the disease is distant or near. Look at the colors up and down, to know the dwelling place of disease. Focus the spirit in the heart and mind to know present and past. Therefore, if one examines the qi not minutely, one cannot know the distinction; subordinate the will so that it does not depart, then understand the new or the past.

"When the colors are clear, the person is not thick with disease. But sinking and somber colors are made by severe ills. When the colors are neither bright nor glossy, the disease is not severe. When the color is scattered and coltish, there is no accumulation. When the disease is scattered but the qi painful, it is an accumulation without completion.

"When the kidneys ride the heart, the heart begins to be diseased. The kidneys will resonate. The colors will reflect all of this.

"When a boy has a diseased color at the King of the Face, the abdomen will be painful. If lower down on the face, the testicles will be painful. When the diseased color is at the circular and straight (the philtrum), the penis is painful. When high (on the philtrum), it is the root; when low, it is the head, and fox hernias will follow.

"When a girl has a diseased color at the King of the Face, the bladder and reproductive organs will be ill. If the color is scattered it is pain. If it is gathering, it is an accumulation. Whether square or round, left or right, each will be like its color and form. If this diseased color goes lower, it relates to the bottom of the body being debauched and having an outflow with a greasy appearance from violent food which is not clean.

175

"For the diagnosis, left is left and right is right. For the colors which relate to the evil which accumulates and scatters without clues, the facial colors are the pointers. These colors: green, black, red, white, and yellow, all are clues to congestion having separate homelands. That homeland which is red in color, it is as large as an elm thistle. Its location is the tip of the nose, called the King of the Face, and there forever. If the diseased color is on the upper point of the nose, that is an indication by the upper orifices of the head. If on the lower point, it is the inclination by the lower orifices to disease. Positions on the left and right have similar rules.

"The colors command the viscera. Green is the liver. Red is the heart. White is the lungs. Yellow is the spleen. Black is the kidneys. The liver is in tune with the muscles. The heart is in tune with the blood channels. The lungs are in tune with the skin. The spleen is in tune with the flesh. The kidneys are in tune with the bones."

Note

1. "Squared and above" means on both sides of the nostrils.

Huang Di questioned Shao Yu, "There are men who walk or stand in similar ways, whether their age is old or young, who are alike, whether their clothes are thick or thin, and whether encountering the violent wind or violent rain, some may but some may not become ill, or perhaps become totally ill or not ill at all. What are the reasons for this?"

Shao Yu said, "How urgent are the emperor's questions?"

Huang Di said, "I wish to hear all."

Shao Yu said, "Spring is the green wind. Summer is the yang wind. Autumn is the cool wind. Winter is the cold wind. This is the total of the winds of the four seasons. Each disease that comes from them has a different form."

Huang Di said, "The winds for the four seasons, what are the men like who are affected and get ill from them?"

Shao Yu said, "The person who is of yellow color, thin-skinned, and weak in flesh cannot compete with the hollow winds of spring. He who is of a white color, thin-skinned, and weak in flesh cannot compete with the hollow winds of summer. He who is of green color, thin-skinned, and weak in flesh cannot compete with the hollow winds of autumn. He who is of red color, thin-skinned, and weak in flesh cannot compete with the hollow winds of winter."

Huang Di said, "Does a person who is of a black color not have disease?"

Shao Yu said, "He who is of black color, whose skin is thick, and flesh firm, is solid and not injured by the winds of the four seasons. But if his skin is thin and the flesh not firm and his color is not of a oneness, the hollow winds of the long summer will reach him with disease. However, if his skin is thick and the muscles and flesh are firm, even though the long summer reaches with its hollow winds, there will be no disease.

"If a person has thick skin with firm muscles and flesh, and he has been affected repeatedly by cold, and both exterior and interior are affected, then there is illness."

Huang Di said, "Excellent."

Huang Di said, "There are persons who can endure pain and others who cannot endure pain, yet it is not a division of courage and timidity. The brave soldier who cannot endure pain, seeing difficulties will advance, seeing pain, will stop. The timid soldier who can endure pain, hearing of difficulties is fearful, yet encountering pain, is not agitated. The brave soldier who can endure pain, seeing difficulties is not frightened, encountering pain, is not agitated. The timid soldier who cannot endure pain, encountering difficulties and pain will roll his eyes and screw up his face. He is so frightened he cannot talk. He loses his breath with fright and the colors of his forehead change and transform. He is neither dead nor alive. I see this positively but do not understand its reasons nor why. I would like to hear the reasons."

Shao Yu said, "A person who can endure pain or not endure pain has skin which is thin or thick, muscles and flesh which are firm or weak and may be divided into slow or quick, but cannot be said to be brave or timid."

Huang Di said, "I would like to hear about the origins of bravery and timidity."

Shao Yu said, "The brave soldier, his eyes are deep and hard. His eyebrows are long, flowing, straight and raised. The Triple Heater is established and extensive. His heart and mind are correct and straight. His liver is large and firm. His gallbladder is full and plentiful. Anger causes the qi to be abundant, the chest to strengthen, the liver qi to be raised, the gallbladder qi to be extended, and the gap between the eyebrows and eyes to be raised. The hair rises and the face becomes green. These are the origins of a brave soldier."

Huang Di said, "I would like to hear about the origins of the timid soldier."

Shao Yu said, "The timid soldier has eyes that are large but do not shrink; yin and yang are mutually lost. The heater's foundations are unsecured. His breastbone is short and small. The liver is stringy and slow. His gallbladder is not full but relaxed. The intestines and stomach are unnaturally straight. There is a hollowness beneath the ribs. Although there may be a proper and great anger, qi is unable to fill the chest, and although the qi of the liver and lungs are raised, the qi is sparse and returns below. Therefore, anger cannot be sustained for a long period. These are the origins of a timid soldier."

Huang Di said, "When the timid soldier has obtained wine and is angry, he does not avoid the brave soldier. What viscera are responsible for this?"

Shao Yu said, "Wine is the essence of the water and grain. It heats the fluids of the valleys. Its qi is fierce and violent. As it enters the middle of the stomach, it causes the stomach to elongate, the qi rises in counterflow, and overflows into the chest. The liver qi floats, the gallbladder qi extends, and at this point in time of drunkenness he is as solid as the brave soldier. When the qi weakens, it will result in later regrets.

"This is of similar appearance in the brave soldier; this not understanding caution and avoidance is called the drunken perverseness."

51. THE BACK SHU ACUPUNCTURE POINTS

Huang Di asked Qi Bo, "I desire to hear about the *shu* acupuncture points of the five viscera which come out on the back."

Qi Bo said, "In the middle of the back are the great *shu* acupuncture points. At the tips of the shuttle bone are the Big Shuttle points. The lung *shu* points are located at the gaps of the third vertebra.[1] The heart *shu* points are located at the gaps of the fifth vertebra.[2] The diaphragm *shu* points are located at the gaps of the seventh vertebra. The liver *shu* points are located at the gaps of the ninth vertebra. The spleen *shu* points are located at the gaps of the eleventh vertebra. The kidney *shu* points are located at the gaps of fourteenth vertebra.[3] All of these points clasp the spine on both sides on lines which are three *cun* apart.[4] Therefore, when there is a desire to examine, place the hand at the point location. It will resonate with pain which is located in the interior. To release, use these *shu* points. Moxibustion can be effective when needling is not effective. When the qi is full, disperse; when hollow, tonify. When using fire to tonify, do not blow on the fire. In a moment it will go out by itself. When using the fire to disperse, quickly blow on the fire to propagate the action of the *Artemisia*, then extinguish the fire."[5]

Notes

1. Due to a copyist error in Chinese, the word for "heat" is used six different times for "vertebra." Since the word occurs each time with a number which corresponds to the correct anatomical position of the acupuncture point refered to, it seems obviously a copyist error. This location is equal to the lower end of the spinous process of the third vertebra.

2. The spinous process of the fifth thoracic vertebra.

3. The second lumbar vertebra.

4. Three *cun* apart is one and one-half *cun* each from the midline of the spine.

5. *Artemisia* is the herb used in making moxa.

52. PROTECTIVE QI

Huang Di said, "The five viscera are the storehouse of the seminal essence, the spirit, the animal spirit, and the human soul. The six bowels are those which receive water and valley qi and act to transform food materials. The body's qi internally penetrates the five viscera and externally circulates in the limbs and articulations. That floating qi which does not follow the channels is the protective qi. The seminal essence qi moves in the channels and is the nourishing qi. When yin and yang follow together, outside and inside are connected together like a sphere without corners. It flows quick and slow like a pulse. How can this have an end? However, these divisions and separations of yin and yang all have branches and roots, hollowness and solidity, and that which is separate from the location. The ability to distinguish yin and yang and the twelve major channels is to know disease and what gives birth to it, by the symptoms of hollowness and solidity where they are located, and the ability to know whether the disease is located high or low. Understanding the six bowels' qi roads is the ability to understand what is released, tied up, contracted, or connected in the gates and doors. The ability to understand hollowness or solidity and what is firm or pliable is to know where to locate tonification or dispersing. The ability to understand the six channels' branches and roots is to act without doubt under heaven."

Qi Bo said, "What achievement! A sage emperor's words! This subject would like to complete the thought and comprehend the speech. The roots of the Leg Major Yang are located above the heel by five *cun*. The branches are located on the two channels to Life Doors. Life Doors are the eyes. The roots of the Leg Minor Yang are located at Cavity of Yin. The branches are located in front of the Window Basket, at Hearing Center. The Window Basket is the ear. The roots of the Leg Minor Yin are located three *cun* in total up and down from the center of the inner anklebone. The branches are located at the kidney *shu* points on the back and below the two channels of the tongue (at Angular Spring). The roots of the Leg Shrinking Yin are located at Walking in Between and the points five *cun* above. The branches are located at the liver *shu* points on the back. The roots of the Leg Bright Yang are located at Tip Exchange and the branches at the Man's Receptor which clasp the neck under the jaw.

"The roots of Leg Major Yin are located four *cun* above Center Seal. The branches are located at the spleen *shu* points on the back and at the base of the tongue.

"The roots of the Arm Major Yang are located behind the outer wristbone. The branches are located one *cun* above Life's Doors. The roots of the Arm Minor Yang are located above the crack between the little finger and the next finger by two *cun*. The branches are located beyond the ear's top corner and below the external corner of the eye. The roots of the Arm Bright Yang are located in the middle of the elbow bone, then it goes up to reach the separation of the yang. The branches are located at the temples where, descending, they join above the pincers (the ears).

"The roots of the Arm Major Yin are located in the center of the Inch Mouth. The branches are located in the inside of the armpits where there is a moving pulse.

"The roots of the Arm Minor Yin are located at the edge of the Sharp Bone on the wrist. The branches are located at the heart *shu* points on the back.

"The roots of the Arm Pericardium Channel are located in the center of the inner arm between two tendons, two *cun* beyond the wrist. The branches are underneath the armpits by three *cun*.

"These are all of the symptoms. When the lower body is hollow, it causes a perverse flow and deficiency. When the lower body is full, it causes heat. When the upper body is hollow, it causes dizziness. When the upper body is full, it causes heat and pain. Therefore, when it is solid, cut off and stop. When hollow, induce the qi to arise.

"If you please, I will speak about the roads of qi. The chest qi has a road. The abdomen qi has a road. The head qi has a road. The leg qi has a road. Thus when qi is located and accumulates in the head, it stops in the brain. When qi is located in the chest, it stops and accumulates at the chest and the *shu* points on the back. When qi is located in the abdomen, it stops and accumulates at the *shu* points on the back, and in the Chong Penetrating Vessel Channel which goes left and right from the navel where there are moving pulses. When the qi is located in the lower leg, it stops and accumulates in the qi road at Supporting Mountain and above and below the ankle. To treat these problems, use the hair-fine needle. It is necessary to first massage the locations for as long a time as there is a resonance in hand. Then needle to give that which can be cured; headaches, dizziness and fainting, pain in the abdomen with the middle congested and cruelly swollen. These problems can be reached and freshly accumulated. Pain which shifts can be easily finished. Accumulations without pain are difficult to cure."

53. A DISCUSSION OF PAIN

Huang Di questioned Shao Yu, "The tendons and bones are strong or fragile. The muscles and flesh are firm or weak. The skin is thick or thin. The foundation between skin and flesh and pores is spaced or tight. Each is different. What do you say about the stone needle and cauterization and pain? The intestines and stomach are thick or thin, firm or weak, and thus not alike. What do you say about these and the poisons of medicine? I would like to hear about this in its entirety."

Shao Yu said, "When a man's bones are strong, tendons light, flesh slow, and skin thick, he can endure pain, the pain of the stone needles as well as the heat of cauterization."

Huang Di said, "How can you know who can endure the fire of cauterization?"

Shao Yu replied, "Additionally if his complexion is black and he has excellent bones, he can endure the fire of cauterization."

Huang Di said, "How do you know who cannot endure the pain of the stone needles?"

Shao Yu said, "Firm flesh but thin skin does not endure the pain of stone probes nor the heat of the fire of cauterization."

Huang Di said, "When man is ill, does injury come in the similar season? Perhaps it is easy to finish. Perhaps it is difficult to finish. What do you say are the reasons?"

Shao Yu said, "If injured in the similar season, the body with much heat is easily cured. If the body has much cold, it is difficult to cure."

Huang Di said, "How can you tell if a person will not be injured by the poisons of medicine?"

Shao Yu said, "If the stomach is thick, the complexion is black, the bones are large, and the body fat, all these will not be injured by the poisons of medicine. Therefore, he who is thin or with a thin stomach, all of these will be injured by the poisons of medicine."

54. THE ALLOTTED YEAR OF A MAN'S LIFE

Huang Di asked Qi Bo, "I would like to hear of man's conception and birth, how qi builds and makes the foundations. What establishes and makes the parapets. What is lost in death. What is obtained in life?"

Qi Bo said, "The mother makes the foundations. The father makes the parapets. Losing the spirit is death. Obtaining the spirit is life."

Huang Di said, "What is the spirit?"

Qi Bo said, "When blood and qi are complete and harmonized, when the nourishing and protective qi are complete and penetrating, when the five viscera are complete and matured, the spirit qi is sheltered in the heart and mind, the animal spirit and human soul complete the organs, then man is complete."

Huang Di said, "Man can live a long time or die young; each man is different. Perhaps there is early death or old age, perhaps there is an abrupt death, perhaps there is long lasting illness, I would like to hear of their Dao."

Qi Bo said, "When the five viscera are firm and strong, the blood channels harmonize and are in tune. The muscles and flesh are relaxed and profitable. The skin creases are tight. The nourishing and protective qi move. There is no loss of the body's constants. Inhalation and exhalation are fine and slow; the qi travels to the boundaries of the body; the six bowels transform the valley qi, the body fluids are arranged and distributed; each is like its primary constant. Because of this there is the ability for a long life."

Huang Di said, "Long life for man means a hundred years until death. What is in accord with reaching that?"

Qi Bo said, "When the envoys and leads of the tunnels are long, when the foundations and the high walls are square, they will be penetrated and harmonized by the nourishing and protective qi.[1] When the three places, forehead, nose and chin, arise from the three neighborhoods and the bones are high and the flesh abundant, there will be a hundred years before the end."

Huang Di said, "The body's qi waxes and wanes until death. Can I hear about this?"

Qi Bo said, "In the tenth year of man's life, the five viscera begin to be fixed, the blood and qi are complete and penetrating, and the body's qi is located below. Consequently, there is excellence in running. At twenty years, blood and qi begin to be abundant, the muscles and flesh have grown up. Consequently, there is excellence in striding swiftly. At thirty years, the five viscera are large and fixed. The muscles and flesh are firm and hard, the blood channels are full and abundant. Consequently, there is excellence in striding. At forty years, the five viscera, six bowels and twelve major channels are all large and abundant because they are balanced and established. The foundation between skin and flesh and the pores begin to be spaced, so that the glory of the countenance begins to descend and scatter. The hair on the temples becomes variegated and white. There is peace and abundance but no swinging. Consequently, there is excellence in sitting. At fifty years, the liver qi begins to decrease, the liver sap begins to thin, the gallbladder sap begins to lessen, the eyes begin to dim. At sixty years, the heart qi begins to decrease, there may be suffering from grief and laments, the blood and qi are indolent and languid. Consequently, there is excellence in lying down. At seventy years, the spleen qi is hollow, the skin withers. At eighty years, the lung qi decreases, the soul separates, causing words to be frequently mistaken. At ninety years, the kidney qi is scorched, the other major channels of the four viscera are empty and hollow. At one hundred years, the five viscera all are hollow, the spirit qi all has gone, the physical appearance and bones are orphaned dwellings. Then man's life is finished."

Huang Di said, "For those not able to complete the long life and die, what is it like?"

Qi Bo said, "In those persons, the five viscera all are infirm, the envoys and the leads are not long, the external holes of the nostrils are extended, the breath pants abruptly and quickly. In addition, the foundations of the face are low and the walls thin, there is little blood in the channels, the flesh is not firm. Time and again there are attacks by cold winds, the blood and qi are hollow, the channels are blocked, the genuine and evil qi attack each other, so the rebellion is mutually induced. Consequently, these attack long life through exhaustion."

Note

1. The envoys and leads of the tunnels are the philtrum, the foundations are the chin, and the high walls are the facial structures.

55. COUNTERFLOW AND SMOOTH FLOWING

Huang Di asked Bo Gao, "I hear that qi can be in counterflow or smooth flowing, that the pulses can be abundant or sparse, and that acupuncture has great regulations. Can I hear about these things?"

Bo Gao said, "Qi may be in counterflow or smooth flowing because it is in resonance with heaven and earth, yin and yang, the four seasons, and five dynamic elements. The pulses may be abundant and sparse because they are symptomatic of blood and qi being hollow or solid and there being an excess or insufficiency. Acupuncture has great regulations, for one must clearly understand disease to know when to perform acupuncture, when it is not the right time for it, and when it should never be done."

Huang Di said, "What are the symptoms?"

Bo Gao said, "The rules of war say do not welcome the roll of drums and do not strike with courtly dignity in battle. The rules of acupuncture say do not needle fever with fire, do not needle flowing sweat, do not needle turbid and disorganized pulses, do not needle the disease when the pulses are paradoxical."

Huang Di said, "What are the symptoms indicating acupuncture?"

Bo Gao said, "The superior technique is to needle when the disease is not yet born. A secondary technique is to needle when it is not yet abundant. Following this is the technique of needling when the disease is already diminished. The lowest technique needles when the disease is in full attack, or when its appearance is abundant or when the disease shows by the pulses being paradoxical.

"Therefore it is said, when the disease is abundant do not presume to needle because it will injure, but needle once it has changed, then there will be great glory. Thus it is said, the superior technique is used to prevent disease not to cure when already diseased. This is the saying."

56. THE FIVE FLAVORS

Huang Di said, "I would like to hear about food and drink that is the valley qi possessing five flavors, how these enter the five viscera and are divided and separated."

Bo Gao said, "The stomach is the sea of the five viscera and six bowels. The water and valley qi all enter the stomach. The five viscera and six bowels all receive their qi from the stomach. Each of the five flavors travels to the place that it favors. The valley qi whose flavor is sour first travels to the liver. The valley flavor bitter first travels to the heart. The valley flavor sweet first travels to the spleen. The valley flavor pungent first travels to the lungs. The valley flavor salty first travels to the kidneys. When the valley qi and body fluids are complete and moving, the nourishing and protective qi penetrate greatly, transform the dregs and dross, then following, this transmits below."[1]

Huang Di said, "How do the nourishing and protective qi move?"

Bo Gao said, "The valley qi begins by entering the stomach. It becomes fine and minute. First it comes out of the stomach to the second heater and seeps into the five viscera, separates, and comes out in two dynamics, the nourishing and the protective ways. The body's great qi gathers, but does not move. It accumulates in the chest and is named the sea of qi. It comes out in the lungs and follows the throat and is the reason exhalations come out, and inhalations go in. For the seminal and essential qi of heaven and earth the Great Mathematical Constant is: to exit is three, to enter is one.[2] Consequently, when valley qi does not enter in half a day, it will result in the body's qi decreasing; in one day, it will result in the body's qi being sparse."

Huang Di said, "The valley qi has flavors. May I hear about them?"

Bo Gao said, "I am pleased to explain some more. For the five valley qi, rice grains are sweet, hemp is sour, large beans are salty, wheat is bitter, yellow rice is pungent. Of the five fruits, jujubes are sweet, plums are sour, chestnuts are salty, almonds are bitter, peaches are pungent. Of the five meats, beef is sweet, dog is sour, pork is salty, mutton is bitter, chicken is pungent. Of the five vegetables, sunflowers are sweet, leeks are sour, beans are salty, shallots are bitter, onions are pungent. Of the five colors, the yellow color is appropriately sweet. The green color is appropriately sour. The black color is appropriately salty. The red color is appropriately bitter. The white color is appropriately pungent. For all these five, each has that which is proper.

"The five proprieties which are mentioned with the five colors are as follows. When the spleen is ill it is appropriate to eat cooked rice, beef, jujubes and mallows. When the heart is ill, it is appropriate to eat wheat, mutton, apricots and shallots. When the kidneys are ill, it is appropriate to eat large beans such as soybean sprouts, pork, chestnuts, and coarse vegetables. When the liver is ill it is appropriate to eat hemp grains, dog meat, plum, and leeks. When the lungs are ill, it is appropriate to eat yellow rice, chicken, peaches, and onions.

"There are five prohibitions. For a disease of the liver, pungent foods are prohibited. For a disease of the heart, salty foods are prohibited. For a disease of the spleen, sour foods are prohibited. For a disease of the kidneys, sweet foods are prohibited. For a disease of the lungs, bitter foods are prohibited.

"The liver's color is green, it is appropriate to eat sweet foods: cooked rice, beef, jujubes, mallows, all of which are sweet. The heart's color is red, it is appropriate to eat sour foods: dog flesh, hemp, plum and leeks, all of which are sour. The spleen's color is yellow, it is appropriate to eat salty foods: large beans, pork, chestnuts, coarse vegetables, all of which are salty. The lungs' color is white, it is appropriate to eat bitter foods: wheat, mutton, apricots, shallots, all of which are bitter. The kidneys' color is black, it is appropriate to eat pungent foods: yellow rice, chicken, peaches and onions, all of which are pungent."[3]

Notes

1. "Dregs and dross" mean urination and defecation.

2. This seems to refer to the Triple Heater. Qi and foods must center the first heater, they are transformed in the second, and exit the body through the third.

3. This last paragraph does not conform neatly into any of the Wu Xing cycles but may be read as:

earth nourishes wood,
wood feeds fire,
water moistens earth,
fire forms metal,
metal generates water.

57. WATER SWELLINGS

Huang Di questioned Qi Bo, "Water makes the skin swell, drum-like swellings, moldy intestines, abdominal masses, and the rock and water disease. How may they be distinguished?"

Qi Bo replied. "When water begins to arise, on the eyelids there will be a slight swelling, which is like the appearance when one has just arisen, the pulses at the neck are active. At this time there is coughing. On the inner thighs and in between it is cold. The leg and shins are swollen. The abdomen enlarges. This means the water swelling is already complete. By using the hand to press at the abdomen, and having the hand go to where it is arising, the shape is like a wrapping of water. These are the symptoms."

Huang Di said, "What are the symptoms of swelling of the skin?"

Qi Bo said, "When there is swelling of the skin, it means that cold qi is a guest in and between the skin. There are sounds like a hollow drum and no firmness. The abdomen enlarges, the entire body swells, the skin thickens. When the hand is pressed on the abdomen, it remains deep and does not rise. The color of the abdomen does not change. These are the symptoms."

Huang Di said, "What does it mean to swell like a drum?"

Qi Bo said, "The abdomen swells, the entire body enlarges, and this enlargement makes the skin swell as well. The color is greenish yellow. The veins of the abdomen are engorged. These are the symptoms."

"What are moldy intestines?"

Qi Bo said, "Cold qi is a guest in the outer intestines, and battles with the protective qi. The qi does not receive nourishment, and because they are tied together, indigestion comes from internal confusion. The sick qi then rises, and sick flesh is born. At the commencement of its birth, it is as large as a chicken's egg. Gradually, it increases its size until it reaches its conclusion with a shape like carrying a child. For a long time, that is with years intervening, if the hand is used to press, it will feel solid, but if it is pushed, it will move. The menstrual period will be in accord with the tides. These are the symptoms."

Huang Di said, "What are the abdominal masses?"

Qi Bo said, "The abdominal masses begin in the middle of the womb. Cold qi is a guest at the mouth of the womb. The mouth of the womb is blocked and obstructed. Qi cannot penetrate. Sick blood should leak but does not leak. The bleeding at times is detained and stops, day by day it will increase in size so that the appearance will be like pregnancy.

The menses do not respond to the tides. All these problems can occur in females. These problems should be treated in the lower part of the body."

Huang Di said, "Swelling of the skin, swelling like a drum, can you needle this evil?"

Qi Bo said, "First drain the swelling of the blood *luo* channels and afterwards harmonize the body's channels and needle to draw blood from its blood *luo* channels."

Huang Di said, "Sir, you say the thieving wind and evil qi injure man, and cause men's diseases. These causes are not separate from the screens which cover it up; they do not come out from the middle of their vacant room; yet suddenly there is disease. This is not inseparable from the thieving wind and evil qi. What are the causes?"

Qi Bo said, "All of these persons have been injured by the humid qi which is stored in the middle of the blood channels, and between the divisions of the flesh, where it has been detained for a long time and does not leave. It is like having a fall. The sick blood remains inside and does not go. Suddenly there is joy and anger without control. Drink and food are not suitable. Cold and warmth are not timely. The pores are blocked, yet if they open they encounter wind and cold, which causes the blood and qi to congeal and tie up, so that the evil qi draws them together to result in cold rheumatism. If the body is heated, there is sweating. Sweating results in the receiving of the wind, and although there is no encounter with the thieving wind and evil qi, there will be the additional evil qi which makes the disease occur."

Huang Di said, "Sir, the causes of which you have spoken, all sick people can know that themselves. But those who have not encountered the evil qi, and have no fear and worry in the mind, they suddenly become sick; what are the reasons for this? Does this only originate with the affairs of ghosts and spirits?"

Qi Bo said, "These also have causes of evil which detain and do not arise. For in the origins of mind, there may be that which is evil or that which may be admirable. When blood and qi rebel internally, both qi battle together. But in the body, that which follows and comes is minute. It appears, but is not seen. It sounds, but is not heard. Consequently, there is resemblance to ghosts and spirits."

Huang Di said, "For these ills, what incantations will finish them?" How can this be done?"

Qi Bo said, "In the beginning, wizards originally knew the hundred diseases and what would overcome them. The ancients knew of the body's diseases, that which followed and that which gave birth to them, so that they could use incantations to finish them."

Huang Di said, "The protective qi detained in the middle of the abdomen drags along, accumulates, and does not move. There it luxuriates and collects and is not fixed in a proper place. This causes congestion in man's limbs, ribs, and the middle of the stomach. There is panting and an unruliness in breathing. What may be used to make it go?"

Bo Gao said, "When qi accumulates in the middle of chest, treat the upper regions of the body. When the qi accumulates in the middle of abdomen, treat the lower regions. When both upper and lower are congested, treat the sides."

Huang Di said, "What should be treated?"

Bo Gao replied, "When qi accumulates in the upper region, disperse the points, Man's Receptor, Celestial Chimney, and Middle of the Throat. When qi accumulates in the lower regions disperse the points, Three Distances, and Qi Road. When both upper and lower are congested, treat both upper and lower and the point one *cun* below the lowest rib. If the disease is severe, treat using the chicken foot method of insertion.

When examination shows the pulses to be big and taut like a bowstring, and anxious, then broken off and not reachable, and the skin of the abdomen is extremely anxious, do not use acupuncture."

Huang Di said, "Excellent."

Huang Di questioned Bo Gao, "What is known about the diseases of skin, flesh, qi, blood, tendons and bones?"

Bo Gao said, "Color arises between the two eyebrows where it is thin and reflective, and is symptomatic of disease located in the skin. The color of the lips, whether green, yellow, red, white, or black tells of disease located in the muscles and flesh. When the nourishing qi appears weak, disease is located in blood and qi. The color of the eyes, whether green, yellow, red, white or black tells of disease in the tendons. The ears, when hot and dry and suffering from dust and dirt, tell of disease of the bones."

Huang Di said, "In what forms do diseases make their appearance?"

Bo Gao said, "The hundred diseases all mutate and change. It is impossible to enumerate all of them. Diseases of the skin have regions; of the flesh have segments and layers; of blood and qi have transporting points; of bones have those points of subordination."

Huang Di said, "I would like to hear about the causes."

Bo Gao said, "For the regions of the skin, the communicating points are on the limbs. For the segments and layers of the flesh, the communicating points are at the gaps and points on the yang division of arms and legs as well as the gaps and points on the Leg Minor Yin region. For the blood and qi, the transporting acupuncture points are on all the *luo* channels. When qi and blood are detained in a place, it results in fullness and a rising. For disease of the tendons when there is no designated region, neither yin nor yang, neither left nor right, use the location where there are symptoms of disease. For bones that are affected, when the hollows of the bones receive fullness, there is fullness in brain and marrow."

Huang Di said, "What are the treatments?"

Bo Gao said, "Since diseases mutate and change and they float and sink or are deep and shallow, there is nothing equal to thorough investigation. Each has its dwelling. When disease is moderate, it is shallow, when extreme, it is deep. When disease is moderate, it is small, when extreme, it is multitudinous. Follow the changes and harmonize the qi. This is called superior technique."

Huang Di questioned Bo Gao, "Man can be fat or thin, large or small, cold or warm, and as regards age, he can live to old age, a robust age, be a minor or a youngster. What are the distinctions?"

Bo Gao replied, "When man has reached fifty years or more he is considered old. Twenty years or more and he is of robust age. Eighteen and above (to twenty) is a minor. Six years and above (to eighteen) are youngsters."

Huang Di said, "What are the standards of fat and thin?"

Bo Gao said, "A person may be fat, oily, or fleshy."

Huang Di said, "How do you separate them?"

Bo Gao said, "If the flesh of the major joints is firm and the skin abundant and overflowing, he is fat. If the flesh at the major joints is not firm and the skin is slow and relaxed, he is oily. If the skin and flesh cannot be separated from each other, he is fleshy."

Huang Di said, "When the body is cold or warm, what is it like?"

Bo Gao said, "For the oily type, the flesh is greasy. When the foundation is coarse, the body is cold; when the foundation is fine, the body is warm. For the fat type, the flesh is firm. When the foundation is fine, the body is warm; when the foundation is coarse, the body is cold."

Huang Di said, "How about fat and thin, large and small?"

Bo Gao said, "For the oily type, qi is plentiful and skin is relaxed. Therefore, he has a relaxed abdomen and hanging fat. For the fleshy type, the volume of body is large. For the fat type, the body is tight and small."

Huang Di said, "How about the amount of qi and blood in these three types?"

Bo Gao said, "For the oily type, there is much qi; a plentitude of qi means heat. Heat means he can endure cold. For the fleshy type, much blood fills the physical body and results in peacefulness. For the fat type, his blood is clear, his qi slippery and sparse. Consequently, he is not able to grow structurally. These are the distinctions between all of these types of men."

Huang Di said, "What do you mean, all of these types of men?"

Bo Gao said, "All of these types of men have a surface which is fleshy, fat, or oily. They cannot be added together, for their blood and qi cannot be mutually plentiful. Therefore, their body form, whether small or large, each individually is appropriate to his own body. So it is said of all these types of men."

Huang Di said, "Excellent. What are the controls?"

Bo Gao said, "First you must distinguish the three body shapes, and whether the blood is plentiful or sparse, whether the qi is clear or turbid, then afterwards harmonize. Cure so that they are not out of their usual order of flow.

"The reality thus is that the oily type of man has a relaxed abdomen which hangs down and is fat. The fleshy type of man has a large appearance top to bottom. The fat type of man, although fat, cannot grow large."

Huang Di said, "I consider the small acupuncture needles to be minute in the general order of things, yet you, sir, have said they are in tune above with heaven, in tune below with earth, and in tune centrally with man. I regard this theory of the needles to be excessive, but I would like to hear your reasons."

Qi Bo said, "What in the general order of things is as large as heaven? Yet large and great, how is the needle compared with the five weapons of war which provide death.[1] Is not the needle an instrument of life? Moreover, man is within the magnetic spells of heaven and earth. How can he not act or not blend within the triad? Cure all the people only by using the needle. So for the needles and the five weapons, which of them is small?"

Huang Di said, "There is disease which at the time of its beginning has unmeasurable joy and anger, food and drink are not controlled, the yin qi is insufficient, the yang qi is excessive, the nourishing qi does not move, and it arises as ulcers and gangrene. Yin and yang are blocked. The two heats, inner and outer, battle each other, so there is a transformation into pus. How can the little needles' abilities treat this?"

Qi Bo said, "The master can only cause changes when the evil has not been detained for a long time. Thus it is like two armies together at one point. Flags and banners can be seen by both sides. The white edges of swords are arrayed in the middle of the wild ground. There is not one day for planning. To make the people obey instructions, warn the knights and foot soldiers not to contend with the shining swords. There is not one day to instruct. It must be treated instantly. To reach when the body has reached the disease of ulcers and gangrene, where pus and blood have accumulated, is not this also far and separate from the Dao? For when ulcers and gangrene emerge, pus and blood complete. This does not follow the issue of heaven, nor follow the emanations of earth. When disease has accumulated a little of that which gives it birth, then the wise man or master can cure it himself before it has form, but the stupid man deals after it has formed."

Huang Di said, "If these diseases have completed their form and appearance and one cannot be granted steps forward, if pus has already completed and one is not granted the sight of it, what can be done?"

Qi Bo said, "When pus is completely formed, only one in ten can survive. Therefore, the wise man does not let it form but clarifies excellent formulas, writes them on the bamboo strips to let the able man follow, and then they are transmitted to future generations without end because the common people cannot make the steps forward."

Huang Di said, "When these diseases already have pus and blood, what steps can be taken afterwards, since there are no instructions on how to use the small needles to control it?"

Qi Bo said, "Use the small to cure the small. Its effect is small. Use the big to cure the big. When there is much injury, which is the case when these diseases have already completed pus and blood, then only the stone probes, the sword needle, and lance needle can treat it."

Huang Di said, "When there is much injury can it be cured in its entirety?"

Qi Bo said, "It is based on counterflowing and smoothflowing."

Huang Di said, "I would like to hear about the counterflowing and smoothflowing."

Qi Bo said, "When there is injury from these diseases, the white of the eye is greenish, the pupil of the eye is small. This is the first rebellion and counterflow. When there is a vomiting of medicines which are taken, this is the second rebellion and counterflow. When the abdomen is painful and there is extreme thirst, this is the third rebellion and counterflow. When the shoulder and the center of the neck are stiff, this is the fourth rebellion and counterflow. When sounds are made like a neighing horse and color is stripped from the face, this is the fifth rebellion and counterflow. Remove these five and make the qi smooth flowing."

Huang Di said, "All diseases have their rebellious counterflow and smoothflow. May I hear about this?"

Qi Bo said, "When the abdomen is swollen, the body is hot, and the pulses large, this is the first rebellion. When the abdomen makes noises and is congested, the four limbs are cold, there is diarrhea, and the pulses are large, this is the second rebellion. When there is bleeding from the nose without stop and the pulses are large, this is the third rebellion. When there is coughing and blood in the urine, the physical body is stripped and the pulses small but with some moving power, this is the fourth rebellion. When there is coughing, the physical body is stripped, the body is hot and the pulses are small and quick, this is the fifth rebellion. When the symptoms are like these, before fifteen days have passed there will be death.

"In addition, when the abdomen is greatly swollen, the four limbs are cold, the physical body is stripped, and there is extreme diarrhea, this is the first rebellion. When the abdomen is swollen, there is blood in the stools, the pulses are large and at times cut off, this is the second rebellion. When there is coughing, blood in the urine, the flesh on the body stripped, the pulses beating slowly, this is the third rebellion. When there is a vomiting of blood, the chest is congested and this pulls the back, the pulses are small and quick, this is the fourth rebellion. When there is coughing and vomiting and the abdomen is swollen and moreover, there is diarrhea of the evening meal and the pulses are cut off, this is the fifth rebellion. When the symptoms are like these, not one time period, that is, not one day, will pass before death. The doctor who does not examine all of this before using the needle is said to oppose a cure."

Huang Di said, "Sir, you have spoken about the needles being extremely great and in accord with heaven and earth. Above, it is numbered with the text of heaven; below, it is measured by the regulations of earth; internally, it distinguishes the five viscera; externally, it follows the six bowels. The major channels have twenty-eight assemblies; in all they have a rotating discipline. But this ability to kill a living man is not the ability to raise the dead. Is there a way to reverse this?"

Qi Bo said, "The ability to kill the living man is not the ability to raise the dead."

Huang Di said, "I hear, because of imperfect virtue, yet I would like to hear about the Dao, and why it does not move in man."

Qi Bo said, "There is the brilliant Dao; it must be so. It is like the edge of a sword which can kill man. It is like drinking wine which causes man to be drunk. Still, without examination, what may be known is undecided."

Huang Di said, "I would like to hear all."

Qi Bo said, "Man is who receives qi from the valley qi. The valley qi is that which flows to the stomach. The stomach is the sea of the body's water, valley qi, qi and blood. The sea is that which produces the clouds of qi which are under heaven. The stomach is that which emits qi and blood into the channels' tunnels. And the tunnels are the great *luo* roads of the five viscera and six bowels. They receive, control and complete."

Huang Di said, "The upper and lower parts of man have what numerology?"

Qi Bo said, "They are received at Five Distances on the Arm Bright Yang. The central road stops there. The five viscera's qi reach there and complete. The five flow there while a viscera's qi can be exhausted from there. Thus five times five is twenty-five and it can be exhausted by this acupuncture point. This is what is spoken of as seizing the

197

celestial qi, and although one is not able to cut off a person's fate and destiny, this can tip over and shorten his long life."

Huang Di said, "I wish to hear about it completely."

Qi Bo said, "Scrutinize the door, then needle. Death may be in the middle house. Penetrate the doors when needling; death may be in the upper foyer."

Huang Di said, "What excellent rules! Bright will be the Dao. Please compose on tablets of jade and make these weighty gems transmit to future generations so they can consider acupuncture and its prohibitions and so command the people so they will not dare to violate these rules!"[2]

Notes

1. The "five weapons" are the bow, spear, lance, sword and halberd.

2. Jade was considered the most precious of gem stones in ancient China, thus to engrave essays on such tablets meant words of great importance.

61. THE FIVE PROHIBITIONS

Huang Di questioned Qi Bo, "I hear acupuncture has five prohibitions. What is meant by five prohibitions?"

Qi Bo said, "Prohibitions means not to be needled."

Huang Di said, "I hear acupuncture has prohibitions called the five deprivations."

Qi Bo said, "It means do not disperse by stripping them."

Huang Di said, "I hear acupuncture has prohibitions called the five trespasses."

Qi Bo said, "It means not trespassing the limits of tonifying or dispersing."

Huang Di said, "I hear acupuncture has five oppositions."

Qi Bo said, "When disease makes the channels and pulses flow against each other, it is named the five oppositions."

Huang Di said, "I hear acupuncture has nine proprieties."

Qi Bo said, "Illustrious is the knowledge in the essay, the 'Nine Needles,' so they are called the nine proprieties."

Huang Di said, "What is meant by the five prohibitions? I would like to hear about when not to needle and its timing."

Qi Bo said, "On the Jia and Yi days, the qi naturally arises, so do not use acupuncture on the head.[1] Do not use the method, to shoot the cover, for the interior of the ear. On the Bing and Ding days, the qi naturally arises, so do not use the method to 'shake the dirt' at the shoulder, throat, and Angular Spring. On the Wu and Ji days, the qi naturally arises in conjunction with the four seasonal quarterly days so do not needle the abdomen and do not use the method to 'remove the claw,' or to drain water.[2] On the Geng and Xin days, the qi naturally arises. Do not needle the gates and articulations at the thighs and knees. On the Ren and Gui days, the qi naturally arises, so do not needle the foot and shins. These are the five prohibitions."

Huang Di said, "What is meant by the five deprivations?"

Qi Bo said, "When there is great hollowness, if the physical body and flesh are already wasted and seized, this is the first deprivation. After a great draining of blood, this is the second deprivation. After an enormous sweating, this is the third deprivation. After great diarrhea, this is the fourth deprivation. After great bleeding, just after childbirth, this is the fifth deprivation. For all of these, do not use the needles to disperse."

Huang Di said, "What is meant by the five oppositions?"

Qi Bo said, "When there is disease and fever, yet the pulses are tranquil, or after sweating is complete, yet the pulses are full and rough, this is the first opposition. When there is disease and diarrhea, yet the pulses are great and flooding, this is the second opposition. Fixed rheumatism without migration, fever in the body and ceased pulse on one side, this is the third opposition. Debauchery and stripping of figure, fever in the body, white complexion like the recently dead, the body is feverish the color of the face is of one who will die young, pallid and white, blackish blood in the stools, and a serious heavy leaking of blood, this is the fourth opposition. When there are chills and fever in a wasted body, yet the pulses are firm with strength, this is the fifth opposition."

Notes

1. See appendix B for discussion of the Ten Celestial Stems and Twelve Earthly Branches.
2. The four seasonal quarterly days are Chen, Xu, Chou, and Wei days.

62. MOVING AND TRANSPORTING

Huang Di said, "Of the twelve major channels, only the Arm Major Yin, Leg Minor Yin, and Leg Bright Yang have movement without stop. Why?"

Qi Bo said, "There is the Bright Stomach Channel. The stomach is the sea of the five viscera and six bowels; its clear qi ascends and flows to the lungs. The lung qi follows the Major Yin in its travels. It travels with the going and coming of breath. Thus, when man makes one inhalation, the channels and pulse echo the movement. For each exhalation the channels and pulse also echo the movement. As long as inhalation and exhalation do not finish, then the echoing movements do not stop."

Huang Di said, "When qi passes by the Inch Mouth, the time unit is ten in the ascending breath, the unit is eight in the descent and yielding. What is the path in following, then returning? Is there no knowledge of its pivot?"

Qi Bo said, "Qi, when it leaves from the viscera suddenly, like arrows shooting from a bow or crossbow, or like water flowing over a bank, ascends into the Fish and thins out. The excessive qi thins and disperses because it is rebellious as it ascends, therefore its movement is diminished."

Huang Di said, "The Leg Bright Yang, what is the origin of its movement?"

Qi Bo said, "The stomach qi ascends and flows to the lungs. This violent qi ascends and rushes to the head, following the throat. It ascends and travels to the cavities and orifices of the head, follows the eye connections, and enters the *luo* channel of the brain, comes out on the temples, and descends to the Guest and Master. Then it follows the carriage of the teeth, joins with the major branch of the Bright Yang, and together they descend to Man's Receptor. This stomach qi separately travels in the Bright Yang. Consequently, yin and yang, upper and lower, all their movements are as one. Therefore, for a yang disease the yang pulses are small when in counterflow, while for a yin disease the yin pulses are large when in counterflow. Therefore, yin and yang, when quiet together or active together, are like being led by a string. When imbalanced, there is disease."

Huang Di said, "The Leg Minor Yin, what is the origin of its movement?"

Qi Bo said, "The Chong Mai Channel (Penetrating Vessel) is the sea of the twelve major channels and is the Great Luo assembly with the

Minor Yin which begins below the kidneys and comes out at the Qi Road. Then it follows the inner side of the leg bone, diagonally enters the middle of the crease of knee, then along the inner side of the shin bone together with the Minor Yin Channel to descend and to enter from behind the inner ankle. Then it enters the bottom of the foot. A separate branch diagonally enters the ankle and comes out to subordinate the top of the instep; it enters the crack of the big toe and goes to all the *luo* channels, then flows to the foot and shin where there is a constant moving pulse."

Huang Di said, "When the nourishing and protective qi travel up and down, they are strung together like a ball without corners. When these suddenly encounter the evil qi, as when meeting great cold, the hands and feet become indolent and idle without strength. The path of the channels of yin and yang transport mutually to meet and also move mutually to lose. This qi, what is its source and return?"

Qi Bo said, "Man's four extremities are assemblies of yin and yang. This qi has great roads in the *luo* channels; in the four streets, qi has wide paths. Consequently, when the *luo* channels are cut off, causing wide penetration by disease, the four limbs release and cause qi to follow and assemble, mutually transporting like a sphere."

Huang Di said, "Excellent. So this is what is meant to be like a ball without corners. A lack of knowledge of these disciplines cuts off the returning and the beginning. This is the meaning."

63. AN ESSAY ON THE FIVE FLAVORS

Huang Di questioned Shao Yu, "The five flavors enter the mouth. Each flavor has that with which it travels. Each has that with which it may be ill. The sour flavor travels the muscles; too much eating of it causes problems of urination in man. The salt flavor travels the blood; too much eating of it causes thirst in man. The pungent flavor travels the qi; too much eating of it causes the heart qi to be hollow in man. The bitter flavor travels the bones; too much eating of it causes man to transform and to vomit. The sweet flavor travels the flesh; too much eating of it causes palpitations, that is, a fearful heart in man. I know these things as a fact but do not know of their origins. I would like to hear about the causes."

Shao Yu replied, "When the sour flavor enters the stomach, its qi is rough and astringent; it ascends the two, middle and upper heaters. If it is not able to come out or go in, by not coming out immediately, it is detained in the middle of the stomach. It mixes and warms in the middle of the stomach and results in a downward flow to the bladder. The bag of the bladder is thin and weak. When it receives this sour flavor, it coils up and binds in difficult circumstances and is obstructed. The water ways not moving causes difficulty in urination. In the yin part of man the sour flavor accumulates in the muscles for which it is the terminus. Therefore the sour flavor enters and travels the muscles."

Huang Di said, "The salt flavor travels the blood, too much eating of it causes thirst in man. Why?"

Shao Yu said, "When the salt flavor enters the stomach, its qi arises and travels the middle heater and flows into the channels where blood and qi travel. Thus, blood and the salt flavor are received together and result in congealing. This congealing causes the saps in the middle of the stomach to flow. This flowing results in the middle of the stomach being empty. This emptiness heats the path of the throat and causes the root of the tongue to dry and be constantly thirsty. The blood channels being the roots for the middle heater make it so that when the salt flavor enters, it travels the blood."

Huang Di said, "The pungent flavor travels the qi; too much eating of it causes the heart qi in man to be hollow. Why?"

Shao Yu said, "When the pungent flavor enters the stomach, its qi travels to the upper heater. The upper heater, when it receives qi, nourishes all the yang. Ginger and onions possess a scorching qi so that the nourishing and protective qi is shortly received, then detained for a long time below the heart, causing a hollow heart. The pungent flavor and qi travel together. Therefore, the pungent flavor enters and comes out together with sweat."

Huang Di said, "The bitter flavor travels the bones; too much eating of it causes man to transform and to vomit. Why?"

Shao Yu said, "When the bitter flavor enters the stomach, the five valley qi all are unable to overcome the bitterness. The bitter flavor enters into the lower channels of the stomach which is the path of the Triple Heater. All is blocked and obstructed. Consequently, there are transformations and vomiting. The teeth, the bones and that which cause their wholeness make it so that the bitter flavor travels the bones. It can enter, return and come out. Thus, we know it travels the bones."

Huang Di said, "The sweet flavor travels the flesh; too much eating of it causes the heart to palpitate and there to be fear in man. Why?"

Shao Yu said, "When the sweet flavor enters the stomach, its qi is fragile and small. It is unable to ascend and to reach the upper heater. So it is detained in the valley qi in the middle in the stomach, which causes man to be soft and moist. The stomach being soft results in slowness; slowness causes a wormlike movement. A wormlike crawling movement results in man having palpitations and fearful heart. This qi as it externalizes, penetrates the flesh; therefore, the sweet flavor travels the flesh."

64. YIN AND YANG AND TWENTY-FIVE TYPES OF MEN

Huang Di said, "I hear there are yin men and yang men; what are they like?"

Bo Gao said, "Between heaven and earth, in the six enclosures nothing is inseparable with the five.[1] Man also resonates with them. Consequently, five times five makes twenty-five states of man, besides the yin and yang configurations of men, whose aspects may be tuned with the five. I already understand this, but I would like to hear about the twenty-five states of men, their physical body type, their blood and qi and that which gives them birth, how they may be separated because of symptoms so that one can follow the external to know the internal. What are they like?"

Qi Bo said, "How comprehensive and final a question. These are the secrets of the ancient teachers. Even Bo Gao is unable to clarify their uniqueness."

Huang Di arose from his throne and made the following observation: "I hear that man without instruction is like strength that is lost, like a leaking which heaven abhors. I would like to obtain clarification of these matters and store them in a golden chest so that they would not dare be scattered."

Qi Bo said, "First establish the five appearances of metal, wood, water, fire and earth. Separate them into the five colors. Differentiate them into the five body types of man, and then the twenty-five types of men as a whole."

Huang Di said, "I would like to hear all of it."

Qi Bo said, "Cautiously, slowly, I will reply with these words. The wood type of man who resonates with the upper *jiao* tone carries the inheritance of the Green Emperor. These men have a greenish color and complexion. They have small heads, long faces, large shoulders and straight backs, small torsos, and good hands and feet. As to their attributes, they labor with the heart and mind. They have sparse strength, worry a lot, and labor in business. Their abilities are in spring and summer. They do not have the ability to endure autumn and winter and are then subject to the beginning of disease. The Liver Channel of the Leg Shrinking Yin is easy and harmonious.

"The man who resonates with the great *jiao* tone, in tune with the left Leg Minor Yang and the upper region of the Minor Yang, is soft and yielding. The man who resonates with the left *jiao* tone, in tune with the right Leg Minor Yang and the lower region of the Minor Yang, is smooth and following. The man who resonates with the *dai jiao* tone[2] in tune with the right Leg Minor Yang and the upper region of the Minor Yang, is pushed and extended. The man who resonates with the *pan jiao* tone,[3] in tune with the left Leg Minor Yang and lower region of the Minor Yang, is straight as a rafter.

"The fire type of man who resonates with the upper *zhi* tone carries the inheritance of the Red Emperor. These men have a reddish color and complexion. They have wide backs, thin faces, small heads, good shoulders, back, buttocks, and abdomen, and small hands and feet. They walk level on the ground. They have quick hearts and minds. They walk swinging their shoulders. Their back and flesh are full. They have qi, easy wealth, few beliefs, much planning and worry. They see business clearly, have good foreheads, and anxious hearts and minds. They will not live to an old age, they die suddenly. Their abilities to counter disease are in spring and summer. They cannot do this in autumn and winter, so in autumn and winter they are subject to the beginning of disease. The Arm Minor Yin is solid as a nut. The man who resonates with the pure *zhi* tone, in tune with the left Arm Major Yang and upper region of the Major Yang, is muscular and fleshy. The man who resonates with the minor *zhi* tone, in tune with the right Arm Major Yang and the lower region of the Major Yang is joyful. The man who resonates with the right *zhi* tone, in tune with the right Arm Major Yang and upper region of the Major Yang, is rough and sharklike. The man who resonates with the pure *pan* tone, in tune with his left Arm Major Yang and lower region of the Major Yang, is supported by a conceited appearance.

"The earth type of man who resonates with the upper *gong* carries the inheritance of the first Yellow Emperor. These men have a yellowish color and complexion. They have round faces, large heads, beautiful shoulders and backs, large abdomen, beautiful thighs and legs, small hands and feet and much flesh. Their upper and lower parts are mutually appropriate. They walk levelly on the ground and raise their feet slightly. They have tranquil hearts and minds, and are good generous men, not happy with authority and power. Virtue adheres to these men. Their abilities are to counter disease in autumn and winter. They cannot do this in spring and summer, so in spring and summer they are subject to the beginning of disease. The Leg Major Yin is excellent and true. The man who resonates with the great *gong* tone, in tune with the left Leg Bright Yang and the upper region of the Bright Yang, is genial and smooth. The man who resonates with the *jia gong* tone, in tune with the left Leg Bright Yang and the lower region of the Bright Yang, is pitted. The man who resonates with the minor *gong* tone, in tune with the right Leg Bright Yang and the upper region of the Bright Yang, is round as a pivot. The man who resonates with the left *gong* tone, in tune with the right Leg Bright Yang and the lower region of the bright yang, is determined and resolute.

"The metal type of man who resonates with the upper *shang* tone carries the inheritance of the White Emperor. These men have square faces, a white color and complexion, small heads, small shoulders and backs, small abdomen, and small hands and feet. The external malleolus is prominent, but in general the bones are light. The body is clear and lean. They have anxious hearts and are quiet and fierce. They are good officials. Their abilities are to counter disease in autumn and winter. They cannot do this in spring and summer, so in spring and summer they are subject to the beginning of disease. The Arm Major Yin is excellent and true.

"The man who resonates with the *dai shang* tone,[4] in tune with the left Arm Bright Yang and upper region of the Bright Yang, is angular and modest. The man who resonates with the right *shang* tone, in tune with the left Arm Bright Yang and the lower region of the Bright Yang, is at ease. The man who resonates with the right *shang* tone, in tune with the right Arm Bright Yang and the upper region of Bright Yang, is vigilant. The man who resonates with the minor *shang* tone, in tune with the right Arm Bright Yang and the lower region of the Bright Yang, is stern and majestic.

"The water type of man who resonates with the upper *yu* tone carries the inheritance of the Black Emperor. These men have a black color and complexion. Their faces are not level. They have large heads, angular chin and jaws, small shoulders, large abdomen, moving hands and feet, a swinging of the body as they begin walking, a long coccyx, and a long back. They have no respect for fear. They are good as swindlers. Death may come from being killed in war or in disgrace. Their abilities to counter disease are in autumn and winter. They cannot do this in spring and summer, so in spring and summer they are subject to the beginning of disease. The Leg Minor Yin is wide and expansive.

"The man who resonates with the great *yu* tone, in tune with the right Leg Major Yang and upper regions of the Major Yang, has good color and cheeks. The man who resonates with the minor *yu* tone, in tune with the left Leg Major Yang and lower regions of the Major Yang, is circuitous. All of the men who resonate with the *zhong yu* tone, in tune with the right Leg Major Yang and the lower regions of the Major Yang pure, are pure and clean. The man who resonates with the pure *yu* tone, in tune with the left Leg Major Yang and upper regions of the Major Yang, is peaceful and tranquil.

"Thus, these are the five physical forms and their twenty-five transformations. This is why all of these men are so limited mutually."

Huang Di said, "We have obtained the physical body, but not the colors. What are they like?"

Qi Bo said, "The physical forms are equal to the colors. The colors are equal to the physical forms. When reached, it is additionally like the equality between time and years. When they are affected by the movement of disease, it must be done away with or the result will be grief. For the physical body and color are received together in the same manner that wealth and nobility are the great joys."

Huang Di said, "A person's physical body and color are together equal in time, but as the years increase, what is known?"

Qi Bo said, "For all of the years of the types of men described above, there are years of dread and magic fear. This great dread is added to seven years.[5] The sixteenth, twenty-fifth, thirty-fourth, forty-third, fifty-second, and sixty-first years, all are years of great dread for man. He cannot be peaceful in himself and is affected by the movement of disease. It must be done away with or result in grief. At these points in time do not make debauched affairs. For they are known as the years of dread."

Huang Di said, "Sir, you have spoken of the upper and lower channels, and the symptoms concerning blood and qi. What is in accord with the knowledge of the physical body and qi?"

Qi Bo said, "When the Leg Bright Yang's upper regions are full of blood and qi, it causes the whiskers to be beautiful and long. If the blood is sparse and the qi plentiful, it causes the whiskers to be short. Therefore, if the qi is sparse and the blood is plentiful, it causes the whiskers to be sparse. When blood and qi are all sparse, then there are no whiskers, and both corners of the mouth look as if they are painted.

"When the Leg Bright Yang's lower regions are full of blood and qi, it causes the lower pubic hair to be beautiful and long, and hair to grow on the chest. If blood is plentiful and qi sparse, it results in the lower hair being beautiful but short, and the hair to grow up to the navel. In walking, it results in high stepping, while the foot and heel will be sparse of flesh, and the feet will be frequently cold. If blood is sparse and qi plentiful, it will cause fleshiness and frequent chilblains. When blood and qi are both sparse, then there will be no hair and there will be a thin, withered and distressed appearance. There will be frequent disease from deficiencies and rheumatism of the feet.

"When the Leg Minor Yang's upper regions are full of qi and blood, it causes the sideburns to be beautiful and long. If blood is plentiful and qi sparse, it results in the sideburns being beautiful but short. When blood is sparse and qi plentiful, it will result in sparse sideburns. When blood and qi all are sparse, the result is no whiskers. The effect of cold and damp is frequent rheumatism. The bones ache and the nails wither.

"When the Leg Minor Yang's lower regions are full of blood and qi, it causes the hair on the legs to be beautiful and long. The external ankle is fat. If blood is plentiful and qi sparse, it results in the hair on the legs being beautiful but short, and the skin of the outer ankle is thick and firm. If blood is sparse and qi plentiful, it results in the hair on the leg being sparse. The skin of the outer ankle is thin and soft. When both blood and qi are sparse, there is no hair on the legs. The outer ankle is emaciated and without flesh.

"When the Leg Major Yang's upper regions are full of blood and qi, it results in beautiful eyebrows. The eyebrows have fine hair. If blood is plentiful and qi sparse, it results in sickly eyebrows, with many little lines on the face. If blood is sparse and qi plentiful, it will cause the face to be fleshly. When blood and qi harmonize, it will result in beautiful color and complexion.

"When the Leg Major Yin's lower regions are full of blood, it causes fullness in the flesh of the heel, and the heel and ankle are firm. If qi is sparse and blood plentiful, it results in emaciation and hollowness at the heel. When both blood and qi are sparse, it will result in frequent cramps in the muscles, and the bottom of the heel will be painful.

"When the Arm Bright Yang's upper regions are full of blood and qi, it will cause the mustache to be beautiful. If blood is sparse and qi plentiful, it causes the mustache to be sickly. When both blood and qi are sparse, it results in no mustache.

"When the Arm Bright Yang's lower regions are full of blood and qi, it results in beautiful hair under the armpit, and the hand's Fish is warm and fleshy. When the qi and blood are both sparse, it results in the hands being thin and cold.

"When the Arm Minor Yang's upper regions are full of blood and qi, it causes the eyebrows to be beautiful and long. The color of the ear is beautiful. When both blood and qi are sparse, it results in the ear being withered with a sickly color.

"When the Arm Minor Yang's lower regions are full of blood and qi, it causes the palm of the hand to be fleshy and warm. When both blood and qi are sparse, it results in the hands being cold and thin. If qi is sparse and blood plentiful, it causes thinness with many veins.

"When the Arm Major Yang's upper regions are full of blood and qi, it causes much facial hair, and the face is fleshy and balanced. When both blood and qi are sparse, it causes the face to be thin with a sickly color.

"When the Arm Major Yang's lower regions are full of blood and qi, it causes the flesh of the palm to be abundant. When both blood and qi are sparse, it results in the hands being thin and cold."

Huang Di said, "For the twenty-five types of men, what are the regulations for acupuncture?"

Qi Bo said, "When the eyebrows are beautiful, the Leg Major Yang Channel is full of qi and blood. When the eyebrows are sickly, blood and qi are sparse. When the body is fat and greasy, blood and qi are excessive. When fat but not greasy, the qi is in excess and blood insufficient. When the body is thin and not glossy, qi and blood are both insufficient.

"Examine and judge the body's appearance and qi to see if there is excess or insufficiency, then harmonize in accord with the understanding of counterflow and smooth flow."

Huang Di said, "How should acupuncture be used on the body according to the above yin and yang?"

Qi Bo said, "With the hand take the pulses at the Inch Mouth and Man's Receptor, and harmonize in accord with yin and yang. Closely follow the major channels of the body to see if they are congealed and rough, or tied up and obstructed. With all these, the body is painful with rheumatism. In extreme cases it results in no movement, which will cause congealing and roughness. When there is congealing and roughness, treat the qi to warm it. When the blood harmonizes, then stop. If the *luo* channels are tied up and the channels are tied up and the blood is not in harmony, break them open so there will be movement. For it is said, when qi is excessive above, guide it lower. When qi is insufficient above, push and detain the needle. When it is not reached by delaying and detaining, then originate and receive again, for one must illuminate the tunnels of the channels; only then can one be supportive. If cold and heat contend, then lead and move them so that the body is yielding and arranged, and so that the blood is not tied up, and results conferred. For it is necessary first to understand the twenty-five types of men and what causes blood and qi to be what they are, as well as where they are located, left or right, or upper and lower, to complete the rules of acupuncture."

Notes

1. "Six enclosures" means six sides of east, south, west, north, the zenith and the nadir. The five means five dynamic elements.
2. The "*dai jiao* tone" is the great fettered *jiao* tone.
3. "*Pan jiao* tone" means demi-tone of great *jiao*.
4. The "*dai shang* tone" is the great tone.
5. The years of "great dread" are numbered by adding nine and its multiples to seven. Nine in the system of yin and yang represents heaven. Six represents earth. Great dread or magic fear in this instance would then be considered as originating in the heavens.

65. THE FIVE TONES AND FIVE FLAVORS

"Right *zhi* and minor *zhi* harmonize the upper regions of the right Arm Major Yang.

"Left *shang* and left *zhi* harmonize the upper regions of the left Arm Bright Yang.

"Minor *zhi* and great *gong* harmonize the upper regions of the left Arm Bright Yang.

"Right *jiao* and the great *jiao* harmonize the lower regions of the right Leg Minor Yang.

"Great *zhi* and minor *zhi* harmonize the upper regions of the left Arm Major Yang.

"*Zhong yu* and minor *yu* harmonize the lower regions of the right Leg Major Yang.

"Minor *shang* and right *shang* harmonize the lower regions of the right Arm Major Yang.

"Pure *yu* and *zhong yu* harmonize the lower regions of the right Leg Major Yang.

"Minor *gong* and great *gong* harmonize the lower regions of the right Leg Bright Yang.

"*Pan jiao* and minor *jiao* harmonize the lower regions of the right Leg Minor Yang.

"*Dai shang* and upper *shang* harmonize the lower regions of the right Leg Bright Yang.

"*Dai shang* and upper *jiao* harmonize the lower regions of the left Leg Major Yang.

"Upper *zhi* and right *zhi* resonate together in the valley qi with wheat; of the domestic meats, mutton; of fruits, apricot; with the Arm Minor Yin, of the viscera, the heart; of colors, red; of flavorings, bitter; of seasons, summer.

"Upper *yu* and great *yu* resonate together in the valley qi with large beans,[1] of domestic meats, pork; of fruits, the chestnut; with the Leg Minor Yin, of the viscera, the kidneys; of colors, black; of flavors, salty; of seasons, winter.

"Upper *gong* and great *gong* resonate together in the valley qi with unpolished rice; of domestic meats, beef; of fruits, jujube; with the Leg Major Yin, of the viscera, the spleen; of colors, yellow; of flavors, sweet; of seasons, long summer.

"Upper *shang* and right *shang* resonate together in the valley qi with sorghum; of domestic meats, chicken; of fruits, the peach; with Arm

212

Major Yin, of the viscera, the lungs; of colors, white; of flavors, pungent; of seasons, autumn.

"Upper *jiao* and great *jiao* resonate together in the valley qi with hemp; of domestic meats, dog; of fruits, the plum; with the Leg Shrinking Yin, of the viscera, the liver; of colors, green; of flavors, sour; of seasons, spring.

"Great *gong* and upper *jiao* resonate with the upper regions of the right Leg Bright Yang.

"Left *jiao* and great *jiao* resonate with the upper regions of the left Leg Bright Yang.

"Minor *yu* and great *yu* resonate with the lower regions of the right Leg Major Yang.

"Left *shang* and right *shang* resonate with the upper regions of the left Arm Bright Yang.

"*Jia gong* and great *gong* resonate with the upper regions of the left Leg Minor Yang.

"Pure *pan* and great *gong* resonate with the lower regions of the left Arm Major Yang.

"*Pan jiao* and great *jiao* resonate with the lower regions of the left Leg Minor Yang.

"Great *yu* and great *jiao* resonate with the upper regions of the right Leg Major Yang.

"Great *jiao* and great *gong* resonate with the upper regions of the right Leg Minor Yang.

"These are the tones: right *zhi*, minor *zhi*, pure *zhi*,[2] *pan zhi*; right *jiao*, *dai jiao*, upper *jiao*, great *jiao*, *pan jiao*; right *shang*, minor *shang*, *dai shang*, upper *shang*, left *shang*; minor *gong*, upper *gong*, great *gong*, *jia gong*, left corner *gong*; *zhong yu*, pure *yu*, upper *yu*, great *yu* and minor *yu*."

Huang Di said, "Women do not have hair on the face. Are they without blood and qi?"

Qi Bo said, "The penetrating channel and conception vessel channel all begin in the center of the uterus, then ascend following the base of the backbone. They are the seas for the major channels. They float to the exterior, following the right of the abdomen and moving up to assemble in the throat, then separate with channels to the lips and mouth. When blood and qi are abundant, it causes a flow to the skin and a warming of the flesh. When the blood only is abundant, it pulsates and seeps to the skin and produces fine hairs. So women at birth have an excess of qi and an insufficiency of blood which may be counted as being stripped of blood in the penetrating and conception channels, so that the mouth and lips are not nourished so that hair does not grow."

Huang Di said, "When a soldier has an injury to his sexual organs, the yin qi is cut off and does not rise. The yin organ is not functioning, but his facial hair does not go away. What are the reasons? Only eunuchs have it go away. Why? I would like to hear about this."

Qi Bo said, "Eunuchs have lost their generative muscles and have been injured in the penetrating channel; the blood has been stripped from it and not returned. The interior of the skin is tied up. The lips and mouth are not nourished. Consequently, facial hair does not grow."

Huang Di said, "There are the celestial[3] eunuchs who have not tasted passivity from wounding. They have not been stripped of blood, yet their facial hair does not grow. What causes this?"

Qi Bo said, "Those celestials have that which is an insufficiency, in that their conception vessel and penetrating channels are not full. The generative muscles have not been established. They have qi but no blood. Their lips and mouth are not nourished. Consequently, facial hair does not grow."

Huang Di said, "How excellent! The sages penetrated the myriad of beings as if the sun and moon lit up the vistas; they heard tones which incited the sounds. I hear these tones and the knowledge of their physical appearance. But is there not a master who can explain the essences of these thousand things? This would be thus a sage who could examine a person's temples and color, whether yellow or red, and much heated qi, or green and white and little heated qi; or a black color with much blood and little qi. Beautiful eyebrows mean the Major Yang has much blood; the full whiskers and sideburns and facial hair mean the Minor Yang has a plentitude of blood. There can be beautiful facial hair which means the Bright Yang is full of blood. These are the constants.

"These are the constant for man: the Major Yang regularly has much blood and little qi; the Minor Yang regularly has much qi and little blood; the Bright Yang regularly has much blood and much qi; the Shrinking Yin regularly has much qi and little blood; the Minor Yin regularly has much blood and little qi; the Major Yin regularly has much blood and little qi. These are the celestial axioms."

Notes

1. "Large beans" are most probably kidney beans.

2. The Chinese characters that translate as "pure zhi" sound like "zhi zhi".

3. Here "celestial" means "congenital."

66. THE BEGINNING OF THE HUNDRED DISEASES

Huang Di questioned Qi Bo, "The hundred diseases' beginning and birth, all are born in wind, rain, winter's cold, summer's heat, clearness and humidity, or joy and anger. When joy and anger cannot be controlled, it causes injury to the viscera. Wind and rain cause injury to the top. Clearness and humidity cause injury to the bottom. These three sections of qi have that which injures a different type. I wish to hear about their meetings."

Qi Bo said, "Each of the three sections is different. At times they arise in the yin, at times they arise in the yang. If you please, I will discuss their rules. When joy and anger are not regulated, it causes injury to the viscera. If the viscera are injured, it causes sickness to arise in the yin. When clearness and humidity hollow the inner lining, it causes sickness to begin below. When wind and rain hollow the inner lining, it causes sickness to begin on top. These are spoken of as the three sections. In regards to these, their debauchery and overflow are impossible to count."

Huang Di said, "I can barely number these obstinate things. Therefore, these are the questions of the first teachers. I would like to hear completely about their way, their Dao."

Qi Bo said, "Sometimes wind, rain, cold, and heat do not obtain hollowness; their evil, singly, is unable to injure man. When suddenly encountering the quick wind and violent rain and there is no illness, it means one is covered and there is no hollowness. Consequently, these evils singly cannot injure man. Disease must originate in the wind's hollow evil and in the body's form. The two hollownesses together form disease and then the guest will appear. Two solid entities meeting each other means the whole of the man's flesh is solid. But he is attacked by the hollow evil which originates from climatic and seasonal influences. The disease appears in the form of a hollowed-out solid, which is a complete and great illness. When the qi has a fixed abode, the origin is named after the location, top or bottom, internal or external. They are divided into three circles of influence.

"When the hollow evil attacks man beginning in the skin, the result is the skin slows and the foundation between skin and flesh and the pores open. These openings allow the evil to follow the hair, to penetrate, and to enter. This entry reaches deeply. This deepness causes the hair to issue upright. The hair issuing upright causes a chilling and causes the skin to be painful because the evil qi is detained and does not go away. This causes a transmission to the locations of the channels. At the time it is located in the channels, there is pain in the muscles and flesh. This pain, at times, stops. When the great channel suffers, it detains and does not go away. At the time it is located in the channels, there are chills and frequent fear. Because it is detained and does not go away, it transmits to the positions of the *shu* acupuncture points. At the time it is located at the acupuncture points the six channels do not penetrate the four limbs, causing pain in the joints of the limbs and stiffness in the loins and backbone. If the evil qi is detained and does not go away, it transmits to the hidden Penetrating Vessel Channel. At the time it is hidden in the Penetrating Vessel Channel, the whole body becomes heavy and painful. If it is detained and does not go away, it transmits to shelters in the intestines and stomach. At the time it is located in the intestines and stomach, there will be an enlarged and swollen abdomen which makes noises. Much cold causes the intestines to rumble and diarrhea of the evening meal; food does not transform. Much heat causes a melting and coming out of dissolved wastes. If it is detained and does not go away, it transmits to shelters to the exterior of the intestines and stomach and among its original membranes.[1] Then if the detaining belongs to the channels of blood and the evil qi is delayed, this detention will fix beneath and accumulate. At times it belongs to the capillaries; at times it belongs to the luo channels; at times it belongs to the major channels; at times it belongs to the acupuncture points; at times it belongs to the hidden Penetrating Vessel Channel; at times it belongs to the back muscles; at times it belongs to the intestines and stomach or the original membranes. When it connects above with the slowed muscles and the evil qi debauches and overflows, one can only speculate as to its origin."

Huang Di said, "I would like to hear completely about the origin and causes."

Qi Bo said, "When the evil qi belongs to the capillaries of the blood channels and completes and accumulates, this accumulation goes and comes, ascends and descends. In the arms and hand where these capillaries dwell it floats and slows, unable to seize the accumulation and to stop it. It will go and come, shift and move, between the intestines and stomach. Like washing water it flows and pours with a 'zo-zo' sound. If there is cold, it causes the diaphragm and abdomen to overflow, inducing thunderous noises; consequently, at this time there is a sharp pain.

"When the evil qi belongs to the Stomach Channel of the Bright Yang, it causes a constriction where it dwells along the navel. Being full of food causes a great increase, hunger causes a small increase. When the evil qi belongs to the relaxed and slow muscles, it remains and accumulates in the Bright Yang. Being full of food causes pain; hunger causes calm. When the evil qi belongs to the intestines and stomach and the original membranes, pain is connected from the exterior to the slowed muscles; thus, being full of food causes calm, hunger causes pain. When the evil qi belongs to the hidden Penetrating Vessel Channel, point out the correspondence and move it with the hand; moving forward with the hand causes the heated qi to descend in both thighs like warm soup irrigating the body. If the evil qi belongs to the back muscles located behind the intestines, hunger will cause a visible accumulation, and being full of food will cause an accumulation which cannot be seen. Massage will not reach it. When the evil qi belongs to the acupuncture points of the channels, they are blocked, obstructed, and impenetrable. The body liquids do not descend. The holes and orifices are dry and clogged. This evil qi travels from the outside and penetrates the insides as well as travelling up and down."

Huang Di said, "When the accumulation begins and is born, then reaches its completion, what then?"

Qi Bo said, "The beginning and birth of accumulations follow the obtaining of cold, which then gives birth to deficiencies which completes the accumulation."

Huang Di said, "This completion of accumulation, what is it?"

Qi Bo said, "Perverse qi gives birth to illness of the foot. When this illness is born, the shins are cold, causing the blood channels to congeal harshly. The blood channels congealing harshly cause cold qi to rise and enter the intestines and stomach. Entering the intestines and stomach causes the abdomen to swell. The abdomen swelling causes the sap and foam external to the intestines to forcefully accumulate, and not be able to disperse. Day by day it completes its accumulation.

"When there is suddenly much eating and drinking, it causes congestion of the intestines. When arising and sleeping are not in order, using force beyond one's normal limits causes the luo channels to be injured. The yang luo channels injured results in the blood to the exterior to be excessive. The blood to the exterior being excessive causes bleeding from the nose. If the yin luo channels are injured, it results in the blood in the interior being excessive. The blood in the interior being excessive causes bleeding after a bowel movement. If the luo channels of the intestines and stomach are injured it results in the blood being excessive to the exterior of the intestines. If the exterior of the intestines are cold, then sap and foam and blood battle each other, causing all jointly to congeal and accumulate so they cannot disperse; so this accumulation is complete.

"However, when the exterior is suddenly attacked by cold, or if the inside is injured by trembling and anger, it causes the qi to ascend in counterflow. The qi ascending in counterflow causes the six acupuncture channels to be blocked, warm qi cannot move, congealed blood collects inside and does not disperse. The body fluids are uneven in seeping away. If delayed and not done away with, then all accumulations are complete."

Huang Di said, "What is it like when disease is born in the yin?"

Qi Bo said, "Worry and thought injures the heart and mind. Severe cold injures the lungs. Anger and vexation injure the liver. Being drunk when having intercourse, and sweating at that point, and being exposed to the wind injures the spleen. Using strength beyond its limits is like sweating profusely after intercourse and results in injury to the kidneys.

"These internals and externals are the three sections which can give birth to disease."

Huang Di said, "Excellent. What are the cures?"

Qi Bo replied, "Examine that which is painful in accord with the knowledge of its correspondences. Is there an excess or an insufficiency? At the point of tonification, tonify. At the point of dispersing, disperse. Do not go counter to climate and season. This is what is meant by the best cure."

Note

1. "Original membranes" are mesentery membranes.

219

67. THE ACTIONS OF THE NEEDLE

Huang Di questioned Qi Bo, "I have heard about the nine needles of the masters and their action and use for the members of the Hundred Families and how the blood and qi of each of these members of the Hundred Families has a different form. At times the spirit moves with the qi at the first action of the needle. At times qi and needle meet together. At times, when the needle is already withdrawn, the qi moves independently. At times there are numerous needlings and then perception. At times the needle is withdrawn and the qi is unruly. At times after several needlings the disease increases and is more severe. The total of this is six; each is a different form. I wish to hear about their rules."

Qi Bo said, "The heavily yang type of man, his spirit is easily moved. His qi goes forward easily."

Huang Di said, "What is meant by the heavily yang type of man?"

Qi Bo said, "The heavily yang type of man is hot and high. His speech and words are often fast. He often raises his feet high. The viscera qi of his heart and lungs is in excess. His yang qi is slippery, abundant, and spreads, which causes the spirit to move when the qi begins to act."

Huang Di said, "If the spirit does not move in the beginning for the heavily yang type of man, what is the reason?"

Qi Bo said, "That man must be inclined towards the yin."

Huang Di said, "What is in accord with the knowledge that he is inclined towards the yin?"

Qi Bo said, "When there is much yang there is much happiness. Where there is much yin there is much anger. When angry numerous times, it is easily released, consequently, this is said to be inclination towards the yin. So when yin and yang are separated and difficult to join, it causes the spirit to be unable to move at the beginning."

Huang Di said, "What is it like when the qi and the needle meet together?"

Qi Bo said, "Yin and yang are harmonized and in tune, so the blood and qi profit from being soft, glossy, and slippery. Thus the needle enters and the qi comes out, and quickly there is a meeting together."

Huang Di said, "When the needle is already withdrawn and the qi moves independently, what manner of qi is this?"

Qi Bo said, "This means the yin qi is abundant and the yang qi small. The yin qi sinks and the yang qi floats in the interior of the viscera; thus, when the needle is already withdrawn, the qi then follows afterwards and so moves independently."

Huang Di said, "Numerous needlings and then perception, what manner of qi is this?"

Qi Bo said, "This man has abundant yin and little yang. His qi sinks and the qi is difficult to move forward; thus it takes numerous needlings until there is perception of action."

Huang Di said, "When the needle enters and the qi is unruly, what manner of qi is this?"

Qi Bo said, "This is qi in counterflow. When several needlings increase and worsen, the disease is not qi of yin and yang, nor understood in the circumstances of floating or sinking. This is spoilage from total stupidity and coarseness. The technique is that of the lost physician. Then the sick person's body and qi cannot pass through its illness."

68. ASCENT INTO THE DIAPHRAGM

Huang Di said, "I already know that when qi makes an ascent in the diaphragm, food and drink which have been eaten come back and out. Also, if parasites have made a descent in the diaphragm, this descent in the diaphragm makes food come back out after a day and night. I have yet to receive the theories and I would like to hear all about them."

Qi Bo said, "When joy and anger are uneven, food and drink are not regulated, cold and heat are not timely, and consequently cold saps flow into the middle of the intestines. The flow into the middle of the intestines causes the parasites to be cold. The parasites being cold causes an accumulation and assemblage. To protect the lower ducts results in the intestines and stomach flowing and filling to the brim. For if the protective qi does not prosper, the evil qi will become settled. If a person's eating causes the parasites to ascend to feed, the parasites ascending to feed causes the lower ducts to be hollow. The lower ducts being hollow results in injury from evil qi, which accumulates, assembles and is detained. This detaining results in the formation of ulcers. The formation of ulcers causes constriction of the lower ducts. When the ulcers are located in the inside of the ducts, immediately there is a deep pain. If the ulcers are outside the ducts, the result is that the external ulcer causes a superficial pain. Also the skin above the ulcer will be hot."

Huang Di said, "What acupuncture can be done?"

Qi Bo said, "Lightly place the hand on top of the ulcer to see how the qi moves. Then begin by needling shallowly from the side. When the needle is slightly in, increase the depth, then come back with the needle and needle again.[1] Do not pass by any of the three actions. Examine to see if the disease has a sinking or floating quality to make a deep or shallow insertion. When the needling is finished, it is then necessary to use the ironing method. Command the heat to enter the middle. Each day, send the heat inside, and the evil qi will gradually lessen and the great ulcer will diminish. Match the five and manage and forbid making a division of the intrinsic.[2] When there is calm, tranquility, and nondoing, then the qi is able to act. Afterwards use salty and bitter herbs. The valley qi and food will transform and descend naturally."

Notes

1. The third part could also mean "revolve," that is, "twist" the needle.
2. Needle in accord with the five dynamic elements, and yin and yang.

69. GRIEF AND ANGER WITHOUT WORDS

Huang Di questioned Shao Shi, "A man who is suddenly grief-stricken and angry speaks without sounds. What blocks the way? What qi, in moving out, sends sounds without form? I would like to hear about these rules."

Shao Shi replied, "The throat and the esophagus are the road for water and food. The throat and the larynx are where air ascends and descends. The meeting place is the cover, the glottis, where sounds and tones have their door. The mouth and lips are the fans for sounds and tones. The tongue is the moving instrument for sounds and tones. The suspended harmonious hanging is the gate for sounds and tones.[1] The nasal passages divide the air where it flows out. The horizontal bone of the tongue is that which sends and controls the spirit qi as it issues from the tongue. Consequently, when a person's nostrils have mucus coming out without stop because the nasal passages are not open, the division of air is lost. There is consequently a cover which is small, with a quick thinness, which causes the air to issue forth quickly. This opens the gates sharply and lets out the air easily. When the cover is big and thick, it causes the gates to be opened with difficulty. The air comes out slowly and thus there is heavy and slurred speech. If a person is suddenly without sounds, cold qi is a guest in the cover, which causes the cover to be unable to issue out and if it issues out, it is unable to descend. So the gate is opened but the qi does not reach it, therefore there are no sounds."

Huang Di said, "What acupuncture can be used for this condition?"

Qi Bo said, "Use the Leg Minor Yin, since it ascends and connects to the tongue and with the *luo* path to the horizontal bone which ends in the meeting place of the cover. Doubly drain the blood channel so that the muddy qi is removed. The meeting place of the Cover Channel is the upper *luo* channel of the Conception Vessel; treat at Celestial Chimney. Its cover then can be forthcoming."

Note

1. The "suspended harmonious hanging" is the uvula.

70. CHILLS AND FEVER

Huang Di asked Qi Bo, "When there are chills and fever and scrofulous swellings in the neck and armpits, what qi is responsible for the growth of them?"

Qi Bo said, "All of these are called 'rat fistula' and the chills and fever are from poisoned qi which is detained in the major channels and does not go away."

Huang Di said, "How can they be made to go away?"

Qi Bo said, "The roots of the rat fistula are all located in the viscera; its branches arise and come out around the neck and armpits. It can float in the middle of the channels; if it does not penetrate internally into the muscles and flesh, and superficially forms pus and blood, it is easily removed."

Huang Di said, "How is it removed?"

Qi Bo said, "Please follow the disease from its roots as it leads forward to its branches. Make what is responsible for it to diminish and go away; then there will be an end to the chills and fever. Use the hand to examine its way and to give treatment. Use slow insertion and withdrawal to remove it. If the swellings are small like wheat grains, one needling treatment to comprehend, then three treatments will finish it."

Huang Di said, "How is life or death decided in these cases?"

Qi Bo said, "For this rebellious disease, examine the eyes. If the center has red veins and strings in the pupil ascending and descending, and one vein can be seen, there will be death in one year. If one and one-half veins can be seen, one and one-half years to death. To see two veins means two years until death. To see two and one-half veins means two and one-half years until death. To see three veins means three years until death. To see red veins which do not descend and pass through the pupil means this can be cured."

71. THE EVIL GUEST

Huang Di asked Bo Gao, "When evil qi is a guest in a person, what causes that person's eyes not to close and insomnia? What qi is responsible for this?"

Bo Gao said, "The five valley qi enter into the stomach. Then the dregs, the body fluids, and the ancestral qi are divided to make three circles. Consequently, the ancestral qi accumulates in the middle of the chest, comes out in the throat and larynx, links together with the Heart Channel, and activates inhalation and exhalation. The nourishing qi is in the seepage of the body fluids and flows into the channels. It transforms to make blood and to nourish the four limbs. Internally, the flow is to the five viscera and six bowels where there is a resonance with the quarterly time intervals of the day. The protective qi comes out, its fierce qi is violent and quick and first moves in the four limbs, in the divisions of the flesh and the gaps of the skin, and is unceasing. During daytime, it travels in the yang. At night, this qi travels in the yin; it follows the divisions and gaps of the Leg Minor Yin as it moves in the five viscera and six bowels. When a perverse and deficient qi is a guest in the five viscera and six bowels, it causes the protective qi to protect only the outside, to move in the yang but not gain entrance into the yin. This movement in the yang causes the yang qi to be abundant. The yang qi being abundant causes the Yang Anklebone Channel to be dense. Not gaining entrance into the yin causes the yin to be hollow so the eyes cannot close."

Huang Di said, "Excellent. What is the cure?"

Bo Gao said, "Tonify the insufficient, disperse the excess. Harmonize the hollow and the solid, penetrate and clear the routes and remove the evil. Drink a dose of medicine made with *Pinelliae ternatae*. When yin and yang are penetrated completely, sleep can be immediately reached."

Huang Di said, "Excellent! This is called to open the blockages. The channels become completely smooth. The harmony of yin and yang is obtained. I would like to hear the formula."

Bo Gao said, "This medicinal recipe uses eight *shen* of water which has flowed for a thousand *li*.[1] Raise and agitate the water vessel myriad times from side to side. Take from this five clear *shen* and boil. For the cooking, use a fire of reeds and firewood. When truly boiling, add one *shen* of millet and five-tenths of a *shen* of prepared *Pinelliae ternatae*, and cook slowly. When it has evaporated to one and one-half *shen*, remove the dregs. Drink of this liquid one small cup three times a day.

There may be a slight increase which is in accord with knowledge of the limits. Consequently, should this disease make a new appearance, a return to the cup will cause sleep. If sweat comes out, it will cause a completion. If the disease has been chronic, three drinks and finish."

Huang Di questioned Bo Gao, "I wish to hear how man's limbs and joints resonate with heaven and earth."

Bo Gao replied, "Heaven is round. Earth is flat. Man's head is round and his feet are flat, making the correspondences and resonances. Heaven has the sun and moon. Man has two eyes. Earth has the nine regions. Man has the nine orifices. Heaven has wind and rain. Man has joy and anger. Heaven has thunder and lightning. Man has tones and sounds. Heaven has the four seasons. Man has the four limbs. Heaven has the five tones. Man has the five viscera. Heaven has the six primary notes of the pitch pipe. Man has the six bowels. Heaven has winter and summer. Man has chills and fevers. Heaven has the ten days of the celestial stems. Man's hands have ten fingers. The earthly branches are twelve. Man's feet have ten toes, plus the penis and testicles make the correspondence. Women lack these latter two sections but can enwomb the human body. Heaven has yin and yang. Man has male and female. The year has three hundred sixty-five days. Man has three hundred sixty-five sections. Earth has high mountains. Man has shoulder and knee caps. Earth has deep valleys. Man has armpits and the crease of the knee. Earth has twelve rivers. Man has twelve major channels. Earth has springs and streams. Man has the protective qi. Earth has grass and greens. Man has fine hairs. Heaven has day and night. Man has sleeping and waking. Heaven has classifications of stars. Man has teeth. Earth has little hills. Man has little joints. Earth has stony mountains. Man has prominent bones. Earth has forests and trees. Man has a curtain of muscles. Earth has an accumulation of cities. Man has an accumulation of flesh at the major joints. The year has twelve months. Man has twelve major joints. Earth in the fourth season cannot produce grass. Man in later years does not produce children. These are the mutual resonances between man and heaven and earth."

Huang Di questioned Qi Bo, "I wish to hear about the management of the several needles, the principles regarding the penetration of the needle, the theory of following or receiving, the guardian of the skin, and the openings to the foundation between skin and flesh. How do the channels curve and bend? How does the qi come out or go in its dwellings? How is the qi reached to come out? How is it reached to stop? How is it reached to slow down? How is it reached to quicken?

227

How is it reached to penetrate? I would like to hear exhaustively about how these relate to the six bowels and the transports, the acupuncture points in the body. I would like to hear about all the rules which make the little but orderly distinction and separation of the dwellings, how it separates to enter the yin, how it separates to enter the yang and how these roads follow and move."

Qi Bo said, "The emperor's question is the complete way, the Dao, of the needles."

Huang Di said, "I would like to hear it all."

Qi Bo said, "The Arm Major Yin Channel comes out in. the tip of the thumb and bends inside, following the border of the white flesh, reaches the base of the wrist joint, and afterwards the Major Abyss where a pulse can be felt. The channel bends to the outside and ascends the lower part of the base of the wrist joint, then bends to penetrate the assembly of all the yin *luo* channels at Fish Border. These several channels flow together and the qi is slippery and smooth. Then the channel is hidden as it moves to descend the bone of the thumb, where it curves out to appear at the Inch Mouth. It moves and ascends to reach the inner side of the elbow. There it enters below the large tendon at Cubit Marsh where it bends in and goes up moving along the yin side of the upper arm until it enters under the armpit, curves inward and travels to the lung. This channel can be smooth flowing in its actions. When it is in counterflow and rebellious, it has numerous bends and curves.

"The Heart Master or Pericardium Channel comes out at the tip of the middle finger, bends inside, follows the inner side of the middle finger as it ascends, is detained in the middle of the palm at Labor's Palace, then is concealed as it travels between the two bones, bends out and comes out between two tendons at Great Mound at the crease made by bone and flesh at the wrist; this qi is slippery and smooth. The channel goes up two *cun* to the outside and comes out and travels between two tendons. Then it continues up to reach the inner side of the elbow where it enters below a small tendon at Crooked Marsh, where it is detained at the meeting of two bones. Then the channel ascends and enters into the middle of the breast where internally it connects with the path of the Heart Channel."

Huang Di said, "The Arm Minor Yin Channel alone is without acupuncture points. Why?"[2]

Qi Bo said, "The Minor Yin is the Heart Channel. The heart is the grand master of the five viscera and six bowels. It is the shelter of seminal essence and spirit. The organ is firm and solid. Evil must not

228

make an appearance. An appearance causes injury to the heart. Injury to the heart causes the spirit to depart. The spirit departing causes death. Consequently, all evil which is located in the heart should be located in the Pericardium Luo Channel. This Pericardium Luo Channel is the major channel of the heart master, or pericardium. Thus it is the Minor Yin alone that does not have the acupuncture *shu* points."

Huang Di said, "Since the Minor Yin alone is without acupuncture points, is it without disease?"

Qi Bo said, "It can be that the external channel can be diseased and the viscera not diseased. Consequently, treat independently the channel beyond the palm at Spirit Door near the tip of the sharp wrist bone. This extra channel comes out and enters, bends, and curves. It moves slow and fast. In actions all is similar between the Arm Minor Yin Channel and the Pericardium Channel. Therefore, the base *shu*, the Spirit Door point, can be used to treat the causes of the qi being hollow or solid, fast or slow. So it is said, if the origin of a disease is qi which is rushing, then disperse. If the origin is weakness, then tonify. So it will be that when the evil qi has departed and the genuine qi is firm and solid, then this is spoken of as the origin of the orderly sequence of heaven."

Huang Di said, "What is the management of the needles in insertion and withdrawal?"

Qi Bo said, "First it is necessary to understand clearly the roots and branches of the twelve major channels, the cold and heat of the skin, the pulses when full or weak, slippery or rough. When the pulses are slippery and full, the disease will progress during the day. If hollow and thin, it will last for a long time. If large and rough, it means rheumatism and pain. When yin and yang are as one, the disease will be difficult to cure. When the roots and branches still are fevered, disease will still be in place. When the fever lessens, then the disease will also depart. One form of management is through the cubit, the elbow, and forearm; examine the flesh to see if it is firm or weak, great or small, slippery or rough, cold or warm, dry or moist. Then inspect the causes by looking at the five colors of the eye to understand the five viscera and to decide whether the future holds death or life. Examine the blood channels, and examine their colors, to comprehend chills and fever and rheumatic pain."

Huang Di said, "The management of the needles to insert or to withdraw, I have yet to obtain the theory."

Qi Bo said, "The Dao of the management of the needle is to be focused and centered. One must be tranquil and quiet. First understand hollow and solid, and the movements, fast or slow. The left hand fixes the bone position, the right hand follows. Do not cause the flesh to fruit (to bunch up). If dispersing, focus and be centered. If tonifying, one must block the skin. Revolve the needle to seize the qi. When the evil qi which is obtained flows away with its debauchery, the genuine qi is obtained and remains."

Huang Di said, "To guard the skin and to open the foundation between skin and flesh and the pores, what is this?"

Qi Bo said, "Disease can originate in the divisions of flesh. Have the left hand separate the skin, slightly insert and slowly move the tip. This is suitable so that the spirit will not scatter and the evil qi will depart."

Huang Di questioned Qi Bo, "Man has eight hollows. Each is symptomatic of what?"

Qi Bo replied, "They may be symptomatic of the five viscera."

Huang Di said, "Symptomatic how?"

Qi Bo said, "When the lungs and heart are diseased, their qi is detained in the two elbows. When the liver is ill, its qi flows to the two armpits. When the spleen is ill, its qi is detained in the two hips. When the kidneys are ill, their qi is detained in the two knees. The total of these are the eight hollows. All are moving gates to the house. The genuine qi is that which passes by; the blood *luo* channels are those which cover. If the evil qi and sick blood harden and cannot be obtained, they stay and detain. This staying and detaining causes injury to the muscles, the channels, bones, and joints. The moving gates are unable to bend or to stretch. Therefore there will be a hunched back and spasm."

Notes

1. A "thousand *li*" is five hundred kilometers.

2. Classically, points were not used on the Heart Channel. Used instead were points on the Pericardium Channel of the Arm Shrinking Yin.

72. PENETRATING HEAVEN

Huang Di questioned Shao Shi, "I have heard man has yin and yang. What is meant by a yin man? What is meant by a yang man?"

Shao Shi said, "Between heaven and earth are the six enclosures (east, south, west, north, the zenith, and the nadir) and an inside; which are inseparable with the five. Man also resonates with them; not merely is one yin and one yang, but the entirety. This is a sketch for it cannot be totally clarified."

Huang Di said, "I would like a summary of this theory. There have been sages and masters. How did their hearts and minds prepare for action?"

Shao Shi said, "There is a major yin man, minor yin man, major yang man, minor yang man, and the balanced and harmonious yin and yang man. This total makes five types of men of different aspect. Their muscles, bones, qi, and blood are all dissimilar."

Huang Di said, "How can I hear about these dissimilarities?"

Shao Shi said, "The major yin man is greedy and without benevolence. He is interested in secular things and income. Sickness is the outcome. The heart and mind keep calm but this does not manifest externally. He does not pay attention to time and his movements are tardy. This is the major yin man. The minor yin man has a little greediness with a thief's heart and mind. Seeing other people's loss, he constantly feels gain. He is fond of injuring and wounding others. Seeing other people to be prosperous, he contrarily feels annoyance and anger. His heart and mind are quick and without mercy. This is the minor yin man.

"The major yang man is always conceited. He is fond of speech of great affairs, but without ability it is hollow talk. His ambitions go into the four wilderness areas. When he has begun and arranged things he no longer cares and becomes negative. In the doing of business he is constant and self-motivated. Although affairs may be spoiled, he is constant and without regrets. This is the major yang man.

"The minor yang man is accurate in examination and is fond of personal honor, like very minor officials, and therefore is high on their personal fitness. They are fond of outside connections and not dependent on intrinsics. This is the minor yang man.

"The balanced and harmonious yin and yang man dwells and stays tranquil and quiet without fear and apprehension and without exuberant joy. He is pleasant and follows the myriad forms. At times without struggle he makes timely changes and transformations. When he is honored, he is modest and retiring. When he is humbled, he does not falter. Boasting does not cure. The reality is said to be the best cure. The ancients skillfully used the needles and *Artemisia*. They examined the five aspects of man, then cured. When full, they dispersed; when hollow, they tonified."

Huang Di said, "What therapy cures men of these five types?"

Shao Shi said, "The major yin man is much yin and no yang. His yin blood is muddy. His protective qi is rough. Yin and yang are not harmonized. The muscles are slow and skin thick. If a quick dispersing method is not used, there will be no ability to change.

"The minor yin man is much yin and a little yang. He has a small stomach and big intestines. The six bowels do not harmonize. His Bright Yang Channels are small, while the Major Yang Channels are large. One must investigate, then harmonize. His blood is easily stripped. His qi is easily spoiled.

"The major yang man is much yang and a little yin. To harmonize carefully, don't strip his yin, but disperse his yang. If the yang is stripped heavily, it can transform to madness. If both yin and yang are stripped, he will become unconscious and suddenly die.

"The minor yang man is much yang and little yin. The major channels are small and the *luo* channels large. Blood is positioned in the middle with the qi to the outside. The yin is solid. The yang is hollow. Individually disperse the *luo* channels to cause a strengthening of the qi, then draw back quickly when the center qi is insufficient, so that disease will not begin.

"The balanced and harmonious man has his yin and yang qi in harmony. The blood channels are in tune. Be attentive in a medical examination of yin and yang. Inspect the evil and the primary qi. There is a peaceful and ceremonious appearance; judge if there is an excess or insufficiency. If full, then disperse. If hollow, then tonify. Neither full nor hollow, then treat the channels; this will harmonize yin and yang. These are the five separate types of men."

Huang Di said, "The five types of men do not have a common beginning, yet suddenly here is a new assemblage. Without knowing their actions, what are the differences?"

Shao Shi replied, "The assembly of men are as follows. If one does not understand these five aspects of man, it is because there are five times five, or twenty-five types of men, which have not been given in these five aspects of men. These five types of men are not inclusive of the rest of the population."

Huang Di said, "How does one separate these five aspects of man?"

Shao Shi said, "The appearance of the major yin man is solemn and earnest and his countenance of a black color. His thought is secular. He looks tall and large. He has protruding muscle but no deformity. This is the major yin man.

"The appearance of the minor yin man is clear and positively full of stealth. He is solid as a thief of the dark. When he is erect, he is jumpy and uneasy. He walks and moves in a crouch. This is the minor yin man.

"The major yang man is satisfied and conservative in appearance. His body is thrown forward, while his knees are bent. This is the major yang man.

"The minor yang man is erect in his appearance, which results in bending easily. His walking causes an easy swaying of both arms and elbows, which results in them swinging behind the back. This is the minor yang man.

"The balanced and harmonious yin and yang man, his appearance is yielding positively and following in a positive manner. He is genial and contented inside. He is a bean of a fellow and of all men he may be said to be a gentleman. This is the balanced and harmonious yin and yang man."

SCROLL ELEVEN
73. SENSE AND CAPABILITIES

Huang Di requested of Qi Bo, "I have heard about the nine needles from you, the master. It is superlative and beyond counting. I recommend that these discussions be made into one record. I will do the recitations. You listen to the principles, for this does not result from announcements of mine, but is from you speaking of the primary and the way of the Dao. I command that this be done so that it may be transmitted forever to future generations to prevent calamity. To do this, man will have what is transmitted; without this, man would be without these words."

Qi Bo kowtowed repeatedly and ceremoniously said, "It is pleasing to listen to the Dao from a sage emperor!"

Huang Di said, "The principles of using the needles, one must know the physical form and qi and their positions: left and right, top and bottom, yin and yang, external and internal, whether blood and qi are plentiful or sparse, whether movement is in counterflow or smoothflowing, whether the qi in coming out or entering is tuned. Then one can plan to attack the excessive. Know how to untie knots. Know how to tonify the hollow and to disperse the solid. Know the upper and lower qi doors. Be clear in penetrating the four seas. Examine what is and its locations, cold and heat, exhaustion from being soaked or ill from exposure, and the different locations of the transporting acupuncture points. Carefully harmonize the qi, to know clearly the channels and tunnels, the roads of the limbs both left and right. Know completely the meeting places. When cold and heat contend, have the ability to tune and harmonize. When hollow and solid are connected, know how to break apart and penetrate. If left and right are not harmonized, one must grasp the movement and know clearly whether the qi is in counterflow or smoothflowing. Then this knowledge can cure. Yin and yang are not oddities; consequently, understand the beginning and the seasons. Examine the roots and branches. Investigate chills and fevers. Know the locations of the evil and then the thousand needlings will not be dangerous. Know how to manage the nine needles. This completes the Dao of needling.

"Be clear about the five *shu* points in using a slow or quick method at their locations. Whether bending, stretching, coming out or going in, all have their principles. When speaking of yin and yang, join them with the five dynamic elements, the five viscera and six bowels, for each also has the viscera which is his, as well as the four seasons and eight winds

234

to have completely the nature of yin and yang. Each has its positions which are enclosed at the Bright Foyer of the nose. Each dwelling has its color and area for the five viscera and six bowels. Examine where it is painful, left and right, high or low. Understand the body's being cold or warm and in what channels it is located. Examine the skin for cold or warmth and to see if it is slippery or rough. Know that which suffers. The diaphragm separates an upper and lower area. Know where the body's qi is located. First obtain the paths to needle sparsely, distantly to detain when deeper, and thus be able to slowly penetrate. When there is great fever in the upper part of the body, push it to descend. Follow the lower and the upper to lead it away. When inspection shows the front is painful, that must be treated first. When there is great cold in the external parts, detain the needle and tonify. If cold has entered the middle, follow by dispersing the sea or confluence acupuncture points. If needling does reach it, moxibustion is then appropriate. When the upper qi is insufficient, 'accumulate and follow' by detaining the needle. When yin and yang are both hollow, fire is appropriate. If there is a perverse flow and extreme cold and the flesh to the side of the bone is depressed and low, then cold has gone through the knee. Treat Three Distances. If the yin *luo* channels are excessive, obtain the qi by detaining the needle to stop. When cold has penetrated to the middle, 'push and move' the needle to scatter the evil. When the channels are depressed and sinking, fire is appropriate at that point. When channels are knotted firm and solid, fire is that which will cure. Some excellent therapeutics would be missed if one did not understand disease and pain in the two Anklebone Motility Channels. One can use a method of reversal for the lower points, for men the yin channel and for women the yang channel. This is the forbidden rule for the superior technique. This is the completion of the essay on needling. To use the needle in practice one must know the rules and consequences. Above, one sees the bright lights of heaven. Below, one sees the seasonal administration of the eight primary periods. In order to avoid the strange evils, one must inspect the Hundred Families. Examine the hollow and solid to negate the violations of evil. Thus, by obtaining the dew of heaven, even though encountering years of hollowness, one can be saved and not be overcome. Reverse the suffering of misfortune. Therefore, it is said one must know the astrological avoidances to speak about the theory of acupuncture.

"Act according to the laws of the ancients. Examine what may come from what is in the present. Inspect the depths and obscurities; penetrate without limit. The coarse doctor does not see. The excellent doctor is honored. Not to understand the physical being is being a spirit of dishevelled hair.

"When evil qi attacks man, chills agitate the body, and the primal evil attacks man. A little may be first seen in the color, but not knowing the body it is like to be or not to be, like losing or remaining; there is form and no form without knowing the circumstances. There is thus the superior therapy which treats the qi and releases its germination and sprouting. The common therapy handles what is already completed and originates with injury to the body.

"Therefore, for the techniques to use the needles, know where the qi is located. Protect the gates and doors. Be clear on how to harmonize the qi, the locations, and that which should be tonified or dispersed, and the theory of the slow or fast needle, so that one can treat the dwelling. To disperse, one must use the circular method, insert and twist; the body's qi then will move. Quickly insert and slowly withdraw the needle, the evil qi then will come out, deepen to meet, agitate the hole greatly and the qi will come out quickly. To tonify, one must use a square method. From the outside draw up the skin. This point is the door. The left hand must induce the pivot, the right hand pushes the needle to the skin, a little twist and a slow push. It is necessary to be correct and straight, to be tranquil and quiet, to be of firm heart and mind, and not unraveled. The desire should be a little detention of the needle, and then when the qi descends, quickly withdraw the needle. Press on the skin to cover the outside doors. The genuine qi then will remain. These are the necessities of using the needle; do not forget the spirit."

Lei Gong questioned Huang Di, 'The Essay on the Needles' says 'To do this man will have what is transmitted; without this, man would be without these words.' What knowledge can be transmitted?"

Huang Di said, "Individual attainment is according to the person; conception of these possibilities causes the ability to be clear and intelligent concerning these affairs."

Lei Gong said, "I wish to hear about these senses and capabilities. What are they?"

Huang Di said, "Bright eyes are responsible for the seeing of color. Clever ears are responsible for the hearing of sounds. Smart and quick words and speech are responsible for the transmission of discussions and speech. Slowness with tranquility and quiet, and the skill of the hands and the accurate judgement of heart and mind are responsible for the actions of acupuncture and moxibustion, the principles of blood and qi and the harmonization of all that is in counterflow or smooth flowing, as well as the examination of yin and yang, together with all the methods.

"Slow joints and pliable muscles, with the heart and mind harmonized and in tune, are responsible for guiding and leading the movements of qi. Quick and poisonous words and speech of the frivolous man are responsible for spit, ulcers, and disease from curses. Withered nails and poisoned hands make for frequent injury to affairs and are responsible for the pressure and accumulation and restraints of rheumatism.

"Each has and attains according to his ability. The rules which make the actions are practical, then their names become famous. That man who does not attain, his ability is incomplete and his teachings are nameless. Thus it is said, 'The man of attainment has speech, the man who is without transmits nothing.' This is the meaning. If a poisoned hand is responsible, examine it by placing it on a tortoise. Place the tortoise under a vessel and place the hand on top. In fifty days there will be death. If the hand is sweet, there will be a return to life as before."

74. AN ESSAY ON DISEASE AND ON THE EXAMINATION OF THE CUBIT, THE ELBOW, AND THE FOREARM

Huang Di questioned Qi Bo, saying, "I call to mind that without investigating the colors or taking the pulse, the individual's harmonics may be examined at the elbow and forearm. How does this location tell about disease in following the outside to know the inside?"

Qi Bo said, "Examine the cubital area and skin to see if it is slow or anxious, small or large, slippery or rough, and whether the flesh is firm or weak, to establish the form of the disease.

"When inspection shows a person to have a little swelling above the lower part of the eye socket, like just getting up from sleep, and in addition, the pulses on the neck are agitated, and there is coughing, press on the hands and feet. If they are sunken and do not rise, wind and water cause the swelling of the skin.

"The cubital skin being slippery, slushy and marshlike, the disease is from the wind. When the cubital flesh is weak, there is fatigue and drowsiness, and there is emaciation and stripped flesh and chills and fever, there is no cure. When the cubital skin is slippery, glossy and greasy, it is the wind. When the cubital skin is rough, it is wind rheumatism. When the cubital skin is coarse like the scales of a dried fish, it is because water is dissipated in drinking. When the cubital skin is extremely hot and the pulses are full and hasty, it is a disease of warmth. If the pulses are full and slippery, the disease will then come out. When the cubital skin is cold and the pulses small, there is diarrhea and shortness of breath. When the cubital skin is twisted like a torch made of reeds, first there will be fever and afterwards chills, it is disease of chills and fever. If the cubital skin is first cold, and remains a long time greatly chilled, and then hot, it is also chills and fever.

"When the area around the elbow alone is hot, then there will be heat above the loins. When the hand alone is hot, there will be heat below the loins. When the area to the front of the elbow alone is hot, it is also chills and fever. When the area around the elbow alone is hot, then the front of the breast is hot. When the area to the back of the elbow alone is hot, then the shoulders and back are hot. When the middle of the outer arm alone is hot, then the loins and abdomen are hot. When the area to the back of the elbow is coarse and the area three or four *cun* down from it on the arm is hot, then there are parasites in the intestines. If the middle of the palm is hot, the middle of the abdomen is hot. If the middle of the palm is cold, the middle of

238

the abdomen is cold. When the white flesh on top of the Fish has greenish blood channels, the middle of the stomach is cold.

"When the cubital skin is twisted like a torch of reeds, and hot, and the pulse at Man's Receptor is large, the blood should be drawn. If the area of the elbow is firm and large and the pulses are extremely small, there is shortness of breath and increasing depression. This means immediate death.

"If the eyes are of a red color, disease is located at the heart; white, it is at the lungs; green, at the liver; yellow, at the spleen; black, at the kidneys. When there is a yellow color of the eyes which cannot be named or described, disease is located in the middle of the chest.

"Upon examination, if the eyes are painful and there are red veins going up and then down in the eyes, the Major Yang Channel is diseased. If the veins go down, then up, the Bright Yang Channel is diseased. If the veins travel from the outside to the inside, then the Minor Yang Channel is diseased.

"Upon examination, if there are chills and fever and there are red veins which go up and down to reach the pupil, the sight of one vein means death in one year. The sight of one and one-half veins means death in one and one-half years. The sight of two veins means death in two years. The sight of two and one-half veins means death in two and one-half years. The sight of three veins means death in three years.

"Upon examination, if the gums and teeth are painful, massage the Arm and Leg Bright Yang channels as they come to the area. As it passes through, the individual locations will be hot. If located on the left, the left will be hot. If located on the right, the right will be hot. If located on the top, the top will be hot. If located on the bottom, the bottom will be hot.

"Upon examination, when the blood channels in an area are very red, there is much heat; very green, there is much pain; very black is made by chronic rheumatism. When the area is very red, very black, and very green, it means chills and fever.

"When the body is painful and the color is slightly yellow, and the teeth are dirty and yellow and the upper part of the fingernails and toenails are yellow, it means yellow jaundice. If a person sleeps peacefully, but his urine is yellow and red and the pulses are small and rough, he is not desirous of food.

"When a person is ill and the pulse at the Inch Mouth and the pulse at the Man's Receptor are small and large and in agreement, and they are floating or sinking and in agreement, the disease will be difficult to cure.

"If a woman's Heart Channel of the Arm Minor Yin pulse is very agitated, it means she is pregnant.

"When children are ill and the hairs on the head all stand up and go the wrong way, it means death. If between the ears blue veins rise up, there is a pulling pain, there is diarrhea of the evening meal which is red and melon-like, the pulses are small, and the hands and feet are cold; this illness will be difficult to cure. If there is diarrhea of the evening meal, the pulses are small, but the hands and feet are warm, the diarrhea will be easy to finish.

"In the changes of four seasons, winter's cold and summer's heat alternate. When yin is heavy, there must be yang, and when yang is heavy, there must be yin. Thus yin controls cold, and yang controls heat. Consequently, when cold reaches an extreme, it will cause heat, and when heat reaches an extreme, it will cause cold. Thus it is said, cold gives birth to heat and heat gives birth to cold. These are the transformations of yin and yang.

"Therefore, it is said winter injuries from cold will produce diseases from fatigue and fevers in spring. Spring injuries from the wind will produce diarrhea of the evening meal and a washing out of the intestines in summer. Summer injuries from summer's heat will produce emaciation and fever in autumn.[1] Autumn injuries from humidity will produce coughing in winter. This is what is meant by the order of the four seasons."

Note

1. Fever here probably refers to malaria.

75. ACUPUNCTURE METHODS, GENUINE AND EVIL QI

Huang Di asked Qi Bo, saying, "I have heard acupuncture has five methods. What are they?"

Qi Bo said, "There indeed are five methods. One is called 'to shake the dirt.' Two is called 'to pierce blindness.' Three is called 'to remove the claw.' Four is called 'to take off the clothes.' Five is called 'to untie the doubts.'"

Huang Di said, "The sages speak of the five methods, but I do not understand the theory."

Qi Bo said, "'To shake the dirt' is to needle the external channels to remove yang illnesses. 'To pierce blindness' is to needle the acupuncture points of the hollow organs to remove their diseases. 'To remove the claw' is to needle the gates and the joints and the *luo* channels of the limbs. 'To take off the clothes' is to needle exhaustively all of the unique yang acupuncture points. 'To untie the doubts' is to understand completely the harmonizing of the yin and yang, to tonify or to disperse the effects of excess or insufficiency, and how they are mutually inclined and move.

Huang Di said, "For the method of acupuncture called 'to shake the dirt,' the sages said to needle the external channels to remove yang illnesses. I do not understand what this means. I would like to hear more."

Qi Bo said, "Shake the dirt when the yang qi is in great rebellion. It ascends and overflows in the chest which makes the chest congested and the person stare and shrug the shoulders. The great qi ascends in counterflow, causing coughs and dyspnea, a sitting down, and prostration. The disease is from the evils of dirt and smoke, causing a blockage of the throat which makes eating and breathing difficult. If you please, this is an explanation of 'to shake the dirt,' as well as of the illnesses of to shake the dirt."

Huang Di said, "Excellent. What is the treatment?"

Qi Bo said, "Use Celestial Appearance."

Huang Di said, "When there is coughing, ascending qi, extreme stammering, and pains in the breast, what do you use?"

Qi Bo said, "Take Angular Spring."

Huang Di said, "This treatment should take how long?"

Qi Bo said, "In treating Celestial Appearance, not as long as it takes to walk one *li*.[1] In treating Angular Spring, wait until the blood changes in the face, then stop."[2]

The emperor said. "Truly excellent!"

Huang Di said, "The acupuncture method called 'to pierce blindly,' I do not understand its theory, for in order to pierce blindly when the ear is without hearing and the eye is without sight, the sages said to needle the acupuncture points of the hollow organs in order to remove the ills of the hollow organs. What acupuncture points do this? I would hear of these methods."

Qi Bo said, "How excellent are your questions. This acupuncture method has a grand record. This is the epitome of needling, with the aspects of the bright spirit. The mouth which speaks from books and scrolls alone cannot reach it. If you please, the piercing blindness method is applicable to piercing the dimness of the ear."

Huang Di said, "Excellent. I wish to hear all."

Qi Bo said, "The acupuncture for this must be done in the middle of the day. Needle Listening Palace, which attacks the pupil of the eye. For sounds which are in the ear, tinnitus, this is the acupuncture point."

Huang Di said, "Excellent. What is meant by 'sound in the ear'?"

Qi Bo said, "To needle this evil, use the hand, firmly press on both nostrils. This will quickly stop the sounds, and must be done in correspondence with the needling."

Huang Di said, "Excellent. So this is what is meant by not seeing and without eyesight, but you can see and grasp mutually with the bright spirits."

Huang Di said, "For the method of acupuncture spoken of as 'to remove claws,' the sages spoke of needling the gates and joints on the channels on the limbs. I wish to hear all about this."

Qi Bo said, "On the loins and backbone, the human body has large gates and joints. The legs and shins are the governors of man when he is running or roaming. The hanging stalk[3] is the moving power in the center of the body which is the governor of yin essences, the path through which the body saps are ferried. When food and drink cannot be regulated, and joy and anger are not timely, this condition causes the ferrying of the liquids to overflow to the insides. These liquids then descend and detain in the marshes[4] making the blood paths to be obstructed. Day by day this condition enlarges without rest. Bending and bowing are not easy. Running and roaming are not possible. This disease prospers with the accumulation of water. There is no ascending or descending of water. Treat with the stone probes. The appearance cannot remain hidden, it cannot be constantly concealed; therefore, it is named 'to remove the claws'."

The emperor said, "Excellent."

Huang Di said, "For the acupuncture method which is spoken of as 'to remove the clothes,' the sages spoke of totally needling all of the yang unique acupuncture points, for the problem is without a fixed dwelling. I wish to hear all."

Qi Bo said, "When there is an excess of yang qi and yin qi is insufficient, the yin qi being insufficient allows the insides to heat up. The yang qi being in excess causes the exterior to heat. The insides being heated causes a mutual battle. The heat is carried in the bosom like a burning coal. The exterior fears the approach of even silk and cotton fabrics. Nothing is allowed to approach the body, even a mat. Between the skin and flesh the pores are blocked and obstructed; thus, sweat does not come out. The tongue is hot, the lips withered like salted meat. The throat is dry and scorched. Drink and food are unappetizing in this illness."

Huang Di said, "Excellent. How is it treated?"

Qi Bo said, "Use the acupuncture points Celestial Mansion, and Big Shuttle, three bruises each. Also needle Middle of the Back. This is in accordance with moving fever. Tonify the Leg And Arm Major Yin channels, which will make and remove the patient's sweat. The fever is gone and the sweat lessened with this method of 'removing clothes'."

Huang Di said, "Excellent."

Huang Di said, "For the acupuncture method called 'to untie doubts,' the sage's words were: 'Understand totally the harmonization of yin and yang, to tonify or to disperse. To have an excess or deficiency know how they are mutually inclined and move.' But the doubts, how are they untied?"

Qi Bo said, "When there is great wind in the body, the blood pulses are inclined to be hollow. Hollow means insufficient, solid means excess, lightness and heaviness are not balanced. A tilting is like lying down. One does not know east or west, south or north with a feeling of sudden movement upward and downward. One is suddenly in one thing, suddenly in another. Things are upside down or reversed without stability. There are extreme errors and doubts."

Huang Di said, "Excellent. How do you treat this?"

Qi Bo said, "Disperse when there is an excess, tonify when there is an insufficiency. Return yin and yang to balance. Use the needle like this, and the doubts will untie quickly."

Huang Di said, "Excellent. Please store this theory in the fragrant chamber. Don't dare to be reckless and let it out."

Huang Di continued, "I have heard acupuncture has an effect on the five evils. What is meant by the five evils?"

Qi Bo said, "Diseases holding swelling, or the shape of bigness, or narrow smallness, or heat or cold. These are spoken of as the five evils."

Huang Di said, "How is acupuncture used for these five evils?"

Qi Bo said, "All acupuncture for the five evils has rules. Do not go beyond the five sections or methods. For weariness and fever, melt and extinguish. For swellings and accumulations, scatter and lose. For cold and numbness, cover and warm. The small should be covered with yang. The big must be removed. This is the way of these rules.

"In general, needle the evil of swellings by not welcoming the blockages. Clear it with the usual movements for its nature.[5] If there is no pus, delicate is the road in changing its actions and removing it from its established site. When its dwelling is not peaceful, it will scatter and disperse. When all yin or yang are excessive, accompanied by swellings, treat through the acupuncture points by using dispersion.

"In general, needle large evils daily to reduce them. Disperse and grasp what is in excess. Fill in that which is hollow. Puncture in the penetration. Needle its evil. Examine muscle and flesh to distinguish what is real and what is not. Needle all the yang in the divisions between the flesh.

"In general, needle small evils daily to strengthen the body. Tonify the insufficient, then there will be no injury. Investigate that which stays, that which comes, and the limits it reaches. Remove the problem both near and far. If it is not drawn outside, penetrate and move it so the self will not be weakened. Needle the acupuncture points in the divisions between the flesh.

"In general, when needling the hot evil, pass over and cool. When it swims out and does not return, then there is no disease. Make openings and penetrate the perverse gates and doors. Dispatch the evil so that it goes out. The disease then is finished.

"In general, needle the cold evil daily to warm it. Slowly go forward and slowly return (with the needle) to reach the spirit. When the gates and doors have been blocked, the qi is no longer divided. Hollow and solid are harmonized, and the patient's qi can rest."

Huang Di said, "What needle instruments are there?"

Qi Bo said, "To needle swellings, use the sword needle. To needle the big, use the lance needle. To needle the small, use the round and sharp needle. To needle the hot, use the chisel needle. To needle the cold, use the hairfine needle.

"If you please, an explanatory essay would go like this. Heaven and earth are mutually resonant, the four seasons are mutually set by one another. Man is a triad with heaven and earth. These causes can make an explanation. When there is a seepage and dampness underground, it gives birth to water plants and rushes above. This is what may be used to compare the body's qi, being plentiful or sparse, yin and yang, like winter and summer. Heat causes the nourishing rain to remain above so that the base and roots have little nourishing sap. Man's qi stays exteriorly, the skin is slow, the pores are open, blood and qi are lessened, the sap is greatly drained. Cold causes freezing of the earth and water so that man's qi stays in the center, the skin is dense, the pores are blocked, sweat does not flow, the blood and qi are strong, and the flesh is solid and rough. At this point in time, if there is virtuous movement of water, it is unable to flow forward through the ice. If there is a good covering to the earth, it is unable to break through the freeze. Good needling also is unable to grasp the four deficiencies, for the blood channels are congealed and tied up. There are blockages and transmission does not go or come. Also the body cannot immediately soften. The movement of water must depend on heaven's warmth to release the ice and the frozen ground so that water can flow and the earth can be penetrated. Man's channels are like this. To cure deficiencies, one must begin to warm, to tune and to harmonize the channels. The palm and the armpits, the elbows and the feet, the nape of the neck and backbone should be made harmonious. When the fire qi completely penetrates the blood channel, it then moves. Then investigate the disease afterwards, if the pulses are slippery and marshy, needle to balance. If the pulses are hard and tight, use the stone probes to scatter. The qi descends, then stops. This is spoken of as a release of the ties.

"Use the needles with these rules is to harmonize the qi. When the qi accumulates in the stomach, make a penetration with both nourishing and protective qi. Each walks his path. The ancestral qi remains in the seas. It descends and flows into the streets of qi. It ascends and travels in the path of breath.[6] Because of a deficiency in the foot, the ancestral qi will not descend, the blood in the middle of the channels congeals, is detained and stopped. Without the fire of moxibustion to harmonize, it would not be possible to grasp the illness.

"In the use of the needles, one must begin by examining the patient's major channels, whether they are solid or hollow. Investigate closely, and follow. Press with the hand and feel, like playing a musical instrument. Observe the correspondences and the movements. Afterwards, use the manual techniques to grasp what has been felt below. When the six channels are harmonized, both hand and foot, it is said there is no disease. Although there may be disease, it is said to be self-finishing.

245

A channel where the top is solid, but the bottom is hollow and obstructed, means one must use the horizontal luo channel to fill, to add to, and to assist the major channel. For these obstructions, see that there is a draining. This is spoken of as untying knots.

"When the upper part is cold and the lower hot, begin by needling the Major Yang Channel at the nape of the neck, and detain the needles for a long time. When the needling is finished, heat as if ironing the nape of the neck, the shoulder, and shoulder blade. When the heat which is lower joins the upper, stop the therapy. This is what is spoken of as pushing from lower to upper. When the upper part is hot and the lower cold, examine to see if the pulses are hollow and sinking in the channels. Treat. When the qi descends, then stop. This is what is spoken of as leading from upper to lower.

"When there is a great heat everywhere on the body, with madness making the patient see, hear, and speak of absurdities, look to the Leg Bright Yang Channel and The Great Luo Channel. Treat them. If hollow, tonify; if the blood is solid, disperse. Have the patient recline and lie down. Since the problem dwells in the front of the head use the four fingers on both hands. Hold them close together, and press and massage the moving pulse on the neck. Press for some time. Gather and push tightly. Press and descend until the Broken Dish is reached at the center of the clavicle. Stop, return to the front of the head, and repeat. When the heat is dissipated, then stop. This is what is spoken of as pressing and scattering."

Huang Di said, "In one channel, there can begin as many as ten diseases. There can be pain or obstructions, fever or chills, itching, numbness or paralysis. These transformations have not been thoroughly covered. What are their causes?"

Qi Bo said, "All of these are begun by evil qi."

Huang Di said, "I have heard of qi. There is the genuine qi, there is the primary qi, there is the evil qi. What is the genuine qi?"

Qi Bo said, "The genuine qi is that which is received from heaven, and the valleys are forthwith filled up with qi in the body. The primary qi are the primal seasonal winds. They each follow a quadrant in coming. They are neither a hard nor a hollow wind. The evil qi is a hollow wind which robs and injures man. If it attacks man deeply, then the body itself is unable to make it go away. The primary wind attacks man shallowly. When it meets genuine qi it goes away itself. If evil qi comes softly and feathery, then it is unable to overcome the genuine qi so that the individual can make it go away.

246

"The hollow evil qi attacks man, washes and seeps in moving into the body. It commences at the fine hairs and penetrates the pores. It enters deeply and battles internally to the bones. Consequently, the bones are numbed. When it attacks the muscles, the muscles become knotted and tight. When it attacks the center of the channels, the blood is blocked. Blockages then cause and make obstructions and swellings. If the hollow evil qi attacks the flesh and defeats the protective qi and the yang overcomes, it causes fever; but when the yin overcomes, it causes chills. Chills cause the genuine qi to move away. This moving away causes hollowness. Hollowness causes cold to attack the skin and the openings. This qi issues to the outside, opens the pores, shakes the fine hairs. The qi moves with a going and coming, thus causing itching. When detained and not departing, it causes numbness. The protective qi not moving causes numbness.

"When the hollow evil is contained in half the body, it enters deeply. Internally it dwells with the nourishing and protective qi. The nourishing and protective qi become thin and sparse, causing the genuine qi to move out. The evil qi alone is detained. This issues forth and withers the side of the body. When this evil qi is shallow, one side of the body's channels are painful.

"When the hollow evil enters deeply into the body, cold and heat revolve around each other. If this remains for a long time internally and the cold overcomes the heat, then the bones become painful and the flesh withers. If the heat overcomes the cold, then scorched flesh and muscle rot to make pus. Internally the bones are injured. Internally when the bones are injured, it is as if they are eaten up slowly by insects. When there is disease beginning in the muscles, the muscles are bent and unable to stretch. The evil qi dwells in between and does not recede. It makes a swelling in the muscles.

"When there is that which is knotted from the evil qi, the qi returns inside. The protective qi is detained, and cannot obtain a receding. Ferrying the body fluids is delayed for a long time. This shutting down makes swelling in the intestines for a long time; in this case, it means to count in years until the end, so use the hand to press softly. When it is finished, if there is still a knotting, the qi returns. Ferrying of the body liquids is delayed. Evil qi remains in the center, congealed and tied up. In the process of time there are extreme changes. It connects and accumulates at the location to make a swelling tumor. Use the hand to press hard. That which is knotted deeply attacks the bones, for the qi relies on the bones. The bones and the qi are together. In the process of time the overflowing and excess cause bone disease. When that which is knotted attacks the flesh, the ancestral qi returns. The evil is detained and does not depart. There is heat, which causes transformations to make pus. Being without heat causes and makes the flesh diseased. This is the sum of the different qi. They come forth without a fixed dwelling place, but they have constant names."

Notes

1. About seven minutes.
2. Also about seven minutes.
3. The "hanging stalk" is the penis and testes.
4. The "marshes" refer to the testicles.
5. That is, to disperse.
6. The breath as used here may be a secret reference to one's will.

Huang Di asked Qi Bo, saying, "I desire to hear of the movement of the protective qi, its exits, entrances, and convergences. What are they like?"

Qi Bo replied, "The year has twelve months. The day has twelve *chen*.[1] Zi Wu North and South (constellations) make the warp. Mao Yu East and West (constellations) make the woof. The celestial cycle is twenty-eight constellations, with each face (quarter) being seven stars (constellations). Four times seven is twenty-eight stars.

Fang (Scorpio) and *mao* (Pleiades) make the woof. *Xu* (Aquarius) and *zhang* (Equuleus) make the warp. This results in the *fang* (Scorpio) reaching to *bi* (Hyades and Taurus) making yang. *Mao* (Pleiades) reaching to *xin* (Scorpio) making yin.

"Yang controls daytime. Yin controls nighttime. Thus, the movement of the protective qi in one day and one night makes fifty revolutions in the body. The yang movements in daylight are twenty-five revolutions. The yin movements at night are twenty-five revolutions. These are the revolutions in the five viscera.

"Consequently, yin exhausts at daybreak and the yang qi comes out in the eyes (in the Bladder Channel of the Leg Major Yang). The eyes opening causes the qi to ascend to the top of the head. The protective qi then following the neck descends along the Leg Major Yang Channel. The channel follows the back in descending, until it reaches the tip of the little toe. The protective qi spreads and separates in the canthus of the eye, descends the Arm Major Yang Channel to the hand until it reaches the acupuncture gap at the tip of the little finger on the external side.

"The protective qi spreads and separates in the canthus of the eye, descends the Leg Minor Yang and flows to a point adjacent to the little toe on the next (fourth toe). Also, it ascends, follows the Arm Minor Yang Channel section along the side of the little finger and the next (the ring finger), and descends reaching the acupuncture gap at the finger. A separate line also ascends and reaches the front of the ear, and converges with the carotid collateral channel of the neck, flows to the Leg Bright Yang, makes a descent, and moves and reaches the top of the foot, where it enters the five toes to the middle toe.

"The protective qi spreads, follows the lower ear, then descends into the Arm Bright Yang Channel, enters the thumb's cuticle point, then enters the center of the palm.

"When the protective qi reaches the foot, it enters the heart of the foot and comes out at the inner ankle. The lower movements are of the yin part, which then returns and converges in the eye. This causes and makes one revolution.   Consequently when the sun moves one constellational station, man's qi moves 1.8 revolutions in the body. When the sun moves two stations, man's qi moves 3.6 revolutions in the body. When the sun moves three stations, man's qi moves 5.4 revolutions in the body. When the sun moves four stations, man's qi travels 7.2 revolutions in the body. When the sun moves five stations, man's qi travels nine revolutions in the body. When the sun moves six stations, man's qi moves 10.8 revolutions. When the sun travels seven stations, man's qi moves 12.6 revolutions in the body. When the sun moves fourteen stations, man's qi travels 25.2 revolutions.[2]

"When the yang is exhausted in yin, the yin receives the qi. The protective qi commences to enter into yin, and is constant in following the Leg Minor Yin, which flows into the kidney. From the kidney, the flow is to the heart. From the heart, the flow is to the lungs. From the lungs, the flow is to the liver. From the liver, the flow is to the spleen. From the spleen, it returns and flows to the kidney, making one revolution. Consequently, when the night moves, for each station, man's qi moves in the yin viscera, 1.8 revolutions in the visceral channels and is similar to the above yang movements. Then having made twenty-five revolutions, it returns and joins in the eyes. Yin and yang, one day and one night, when joined have a unique remainder of .4 revolutions in the body, while there is a unique remainder of .2 revolutions in yin viscera. Thus, there is for man a time for lying down and for arising. There is dawn and there is evening. But there are unique remainders and, consequently, no exhaustion of the protective qi."[3]

Huang Di said, "The protective qi situated in the body ascends, descends, goes and comes, with differing time periods. What symptoms of this qi are needled with acupuncture?"

Bo Gao said, "The divisions may be full or sparse. The day may be long or short. There are spring, autumn, winter, and summer. Each has its divisions and principles. Certainly there is a fixed progression of the levels of daylight in making a schedule, likewise nighttime in its completions and beginnings. Thus, there is one day and one night, water drops (the clepsydra) in one hundred (quarters) units. Twenty-five units make and complete one-half of daylight, a constant time which is immutable, for the sun rises and sets. Following the sun, its shadows are long or short. Each can be used to make a record for acupuncture. Be prudent and wait for the appropriate time to needle the protective qi in

250

relation to which disease and what period. To miss the time or to be mistaken in method means the hundred diseases cannot be cured. Consequently, it is said, to needle the solid, needle the protective qi as it comes. To needle the hollow, needle the protective qi as it goes. This speaks of the qi which stays or is lost within time. Attend the hollow or solid with acupuncture methods. There is reason to be attentive and wait for the qi so that it is in position to be needled. This is spoken of as the meeting time. When disease is located in the three yang, one must attend that qi located in the yang and then needle. When disease is located in the three yin, one must attend that qi positioned in the yin divisions and then needle.

"When the (clepsydra) water drops one unit, man's qi is located in the Major Yang. When water drops two units, man's qi is located in the Minor Yang. When water drops three units, man's qi is located in the Bright Yang. When water drops four units, man's qi is located in the yin division. When water drops five units, man's qi is located in the Major Yang. When water drops six units, man's qi is located in the Minor Yang. When water drops seven units, man's qi is located in the Bright Yang. When water drops eight units, man's qi is located in the yin division. When water drops nine units, man's qi is located in the Major Yang. When water drops ten units, man's qi is located in the Minor Yang. When water drops eleven units, man's qi is located in the Bright Yang. When water drops twelve units, man's qi is located in the yin division. When water drops thirteen units, man's qi is located in the Major Yang. When water drops fourteen units, man's qi is located in the Minor Yang. When water drops fifteen units, man's qi is located in the Bright Yang. When water drops sixteen units, man's qi is located in the yin division. When water drops seventeen units, man's qi is located in the Major Yang. When water drops eighteen units, man's qi is located in Minor Yang. When water drops nineteen units, man's qi is located in the Bright Yang. When water drops twenty units, man's qi is located in the yin division. When water drops twenty-one units, man's qi is located in the Major Yang. When water drops twenty-two units, man's qi is located in Major Yang. When water drops twenty-three units, man's qi is located in the Bright Yang. When water drops twenty-four units, man's qi is located in the yin division. When water drops twenty-five units, man's qi is located in the Major Yang. This completes one-half of daytime.

"Subsequently, when the constellation measure reaches a total of fourteen stations, water has dropped fifty units. The sun has travelled one-half of its limits. The turning action of one station is water dropping three and four-seventh units, that is 100 - 28 (=3.5714). The remainder is 4 - 7(=.5714).

"The essay 'The Great Essentials' says, 'Three is a constant. As the sun increases in the constellations above, man's qi is positioned in the Major Yang. Therefore, as the sun moves one mansion, man's qi moves through three yang and one yin interval like a constant being without an end. Heaven and earth are together and connected, in chaos and order. In the end, the result is to return, to begin. One day, one night, measured by the water clock is one hundred units to completion.'"

Notes

1. *Chen*, one of the twelve earthly branches, here designates a two-hour time period. It usually refers to the hours between 7 a.m. and 9 a.m.

2. This chapter presents an ancient analogue of the movement of qi energy on the three levels of heaven, man and earth. Yang light and yin dark were divided by mathematics into a schematic progression of cycles which incorporated the sophisticated notion of remainders to express the theory of noncompletion.

The idea of noncompletion is that the universe is never-ending. The use of the magic number five and its multiple of fifty (5 X 10) in this essay infers a familiarity with the use of time. The ancient water clock, a clepsydra, divided time into fifty time units. Here remainders are used to express continuance. In the use of yarrow stalks for division with *Yi Jing (Book of Changes)*, one begins with fifty yarrow stalks and puts one aside before the ritual counting, probably to express the reverse of the remainder symbolism that time can never complete and that in divination one cannot totally manipulate and control time. (Wu, Jing-Nuan. *Yi Jing*. University of Hawaii Press, 1991.)

These presentations of the circular cycles of heaven and man in this chapter and chapter 77 seem to me to justify the title of this part of the Yellow Emperor's Great Classic, *The Spiritual Pivot*.

3. The theory of remainders and fractions in this chapter posits an ongoing revolution of heaven time, man time and earth time. Man is influenced by the time cycles of both celestial and terrestrial movement, but man's own cyclical activity is slightly different. Because of this, all three clocks point to different time readings on a numerical scale if they are read at the very same moment. Philosophically, this proposes a triad

of finals which can never occur simultaneously. Thus, there is no end: time and protective qi continue indefinitely.

A Commentary on the following diagram: The diagram at the beginning of chapter 77 depicts the nine temples or enclosures. The one in the very middle is name Zhong Yang, the Center. Each of the remaining eight temples is named after one of the eight trigrams of the *Yi Jing (Book of Changes)*.

qian	heaven
kun	earth
zhen	thunder
li	fire
dui	marsh
xun	wind
kan	water
gen	mountain

The modifiers of the Center: inciting and shaking, may show the constant movement of a rotating wheel, the eight temples forming a circle around a central hub.

In this progression of the seasons, an earlier, more ancient cycle of transformation and change than the Wu Xing, the Five Dynamic Elements, is revealed.

<blockquote>
To swing and
The Center
To cause
</blockquote>

Other possibilities:
to swing and to cause
to shake and to incite
to swing and to incite
to shake and to proclaim.

For further information see my translaton of the *Yi Jing*.

77. THE NINE TEMPLES AND EIGHT WINDS
"The Primary, Evil, Solid, and Hollow Winds and the Eight Enclosures"

Note: The Chinese words in the middle of the eight circles are the eight trigrams which surround the center.

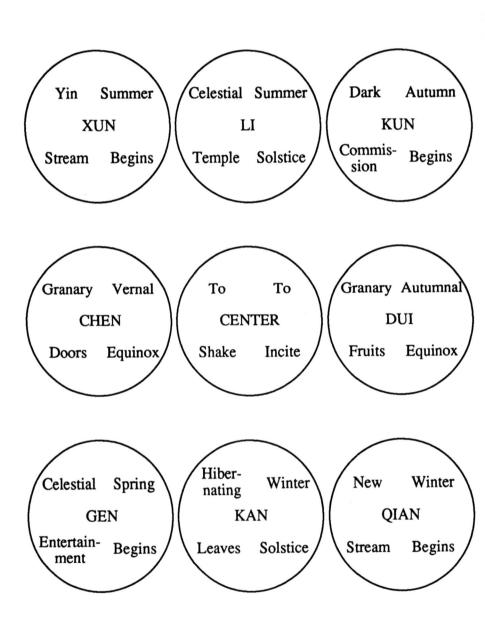

"In the constant of the Great Unity, when the winter solstice reaches its day, they dwell in the Temple of Hibernating Leaves, for forty-six days.[1] In the next day they dwell in the Celestial Entertainment for forty-six days. Then in the next day they dwell in the Granary Doors for forty-six days. Then in the next day they dwell in the Yin Stream for forty-six days. Then in the next day they dwell in the Celestial Temple for forty-six days. Then in the next day they dwell in the Dark Commission for forty-six days. Then in the next day they dwell in the New Stream for forty-six days. Then in the next day they again dwell in the Temple of the Hibernating Leaves, which is called the winter solstice.[2]

"The Great Unity progresses every day. Reaching the day of the winter solstice, they dwell in the Temple of the Hibernating Leaves. In addition to the placement of this day sequentially, there is a dwelling place reached by the nine suns. It then returns to the opposite in the Unity, continually, a beginning without end, an end which returns to the beginning.

"In the Great Unity, due to movements of the sun, heaven resonates to make wind and rain. When the days of wind and rain result in good fortune, the year will be beautiful, the people will be peaceful, there will be little disease. However, if there is much rain earlier, then afterwards there will be much sweating.

"When the Great Unity is at the winter solstice, to predict the sun's transformations, the divinations should be placed with the princes.[3] When the Great Unity is at the spring division, to predict the sun's transformations, the divination should be placed with ministers of state. When the Great Unity is at the Central Temple, to predict the sun's transformations, the divinations should be placed with the officials. When the Great Unity is at the autumn division, to predict the sun's transformations, the divinations should be placed with the generals. When the Great Unity is at the summer solstice, to predict the sun's transformations, the divinations should be placed with Hundred Families.

"What are called changes or transformations? In the Great Unity they are located in the five temples of the sun. The sudden wind can bend trees and can throw around sand and stones. Each temple makes that which it controls. Divine the noble and the mean. The origin and the appearance of the wind and that which follows or comes is the divination. The wind which comes from its dwelling and its homeland makes the solid wind. It controls birth, growth, and nourishment of the myriad creatures. The wind that follows and clashes after it comes, makes the hollow wind. It injures man, controls death, and controls suffering. Respectfully attend and avoid the hollow wind, for the sages said avoid hollowness and evil ways, like avoiding arrows and stones. Then evil will not be able to injure. This is the saying.

"These are the causes which can make the Great Unity enter and change its position in the Central Temple or in the Court of the Eight Winds and make the divination auspicious or inauspicious. The wind which follows and comes from the southern direction is named and called the great feathery wind. It can injure man in the inner dwelling, the heart, and externally in the channels. Its qi controls heat. The wind which follows and comes from the southwestern corner is named and called the scheming wind. It can injure man in the inner dwelling, the spleen, and externally in muscles. Its qi controls and makes weakness. The wind which follows and comes from the western direction is named and called the hard wind. It can injure man in the inner dwelling, the lungs, and externally in the skin. Its qi controls and makes dryness. The wind which follows and comes from the northwestern corner is named and called the breaking wind. It can injure man in the inner dwelling, the small intestine, and externally in the Arm Major Yang Channel. The channel can be cut off, and thus overflows. When the channel is blocked, is cut off and cannot flow, frequently there will be an abrupt death. The wind which follows and comes from the northern direction is named and called the great hard wind. It can injure man in the inner dwelling, the kidneys, and externally in the bones and in the shoulder and back muscles. Its qi controls and makes coldness. The wind which follows and comes from the northeastern corner is named and called the unfortunate wind. It can injure man in the inner dwelling, the large intestine, and in the outer on both sides of the ribs and armpits, in the lower bones and the joints of the limbs. The wind which follows and comes from the eastern direction is named and called the children's wind. It can injure man in the inner dwelling, the liver, and the outer in the thick muscles. Its qi controls and makes the body's dampness. The wind which follows and comes from the southeastern corner is named and called the feathery wind. It can injure man in the inner dwelling, the stomach, and the outer in the muscles and flesh. Its qi controls the body's weight.

"These eight winds all follow the hollows which come from their homeland and so can injure man. When three emptinesses revolve together they cause cruel illness or sudden death. With two solid winds and one hollow wind, the illness results from showers and dews and cold and heat. When two humidities are earthborn, the violations cause paralysis. These are the reasons the sages avoided the winds like avoiding arrows and stones. If the person has three hollows and is attacked by evil wind, he will be struck down with one side withering."

Notes

1. The "Great Unity" is the polestar and its Little Dipper Stars. "They" refers to the Little Dipper Stars.

2.¹ Hibernating Leaves, Celestial Entertainment, Granary Doors, Yin Stream, Celestial Temple, Dark Commission, and New Stream, are poetic seasonal names for each of these forty-six periods.

3. From sun's transformation, the social transformation and individual transformation can be predicted.

Huang Di said, "I have heard of the nine needles from you, the all and the abundant, the extensive and the great, but I am still unawakened from my sleep. May I dare ask how the nine needles began? What are their origins, and how are they named?"

Qi Bo said, "The nine needles, heaven and earth, possess this great numerology. It begins with one and ends with nine, causing the saying: 'One is in accordance with the laws of heaven. Two is in accordance with the laws of earth. Three is in accordance with the laws of man. Four is in accordance with the laws of seasons. Five is in accordance with the laws of the tones. Six is in accordance with the laws of the pitch pipes. Seven is in accordance with the laws of the stars. Eight is in accordance with the laws of the wind. Nine is in accordance with the laws of the regions.'"

Huang Di asked, "Why do the needles correspond to this numerology of nine?"

Qi Bo said, "The sages, men who possessed the beginnings of heaven and earth, possessed the numerology, one to nine. Consequently, this was used to establish the nine regions. Nine with nine moves to nine times nine or eighty-one, which is in accordance with the beginning of numbers of the Yellow Tube and in accord, the needles correspond to this numerology.[1] One is heaven; heaven is yang. Of the five viscera, the lungs resonate with heaven. The lungs are the canopy of the five viscera and six bowels. The skin resonates with the lungs and both belong to man's yang. Therefore, to effect a cure made with acupuncture of these regions, one must use the big needle with a head whose tip is sharp. Do this without going deeply. Enter shallowly and the yang qi will flow out.

"Two is the earth. Man's flesh resonates with the earth. Thus, to effect a cure the needle must be straight with a round tip. Do this without penetrating the divisions of the flesh, or the qi will be exhausted.

"Three is man. Man becomes alive through blood channels. Therefore, to effect a cure the needle must be large with round tip. Use it to massage the channels without penetrating so that it can reach the qi and cause the evil qi to go uniquely.

"Four are the seasons. The qi of the four seasons and eight winds can be harbored in the center of the major channels and make chronic diseases. Therefore, to effect a cure with acupuncture, one must use the needle with a tubular body and lance-like tip. This can be used to drain fevers, to draw blood, and to exhaust chronic diseases.

"Five are the tones. The tones are the center (1-5-9), as winter and summer are divided, as division has a start and an end, as yin is separate from yang and cold and heat contend, and as the two qi mutually revolve. A shutting down makes ulcers and pus. Therefore, to effect a cure with acupuncture, one must use that needle whose point is like a lance. This can be used to treat the swellings of pus.

"Six are the pitch pipes. The pitch pipes harmonize yin and yang, the four seasons, and are in tune with the twelve major channels. When the hollow evil is guest in the major channels, it makes cruel rheumatism. Therefore, to effect a cure with acupuncture, one must use the needle which is pointed like hair from a horse's tail, one that is both round and sharp, and whose body is slightly large. Use it to grasp the cruel qi.

"Seven are the planets. For the planets, man has seven openings in the head. When evil is a guest in the channels it makes painful rheumatism while sheltered in the major channels. Therefore, to effect a cure with acupuncture, one must use the needle whose tip is like the beak of a mosquito or gadfly. Use it quietly, go forward slowly. Though slight, the needle is effective when detained a long time. The primary qi moves to the causes (that is, the seven openings). The genuine qi and evil qi both move forward. After the needle comes out, there is a nourishing.

"Eight are the winds. For the winds, man has the eight joints of the legs and arms (hip, knee, shoulder and elbow). The eight primaries, the beginning and the middle of each season, can possess hollow winds. These eight winds can injure man. When sheltered in the inner being, they make deep rheumatism in the bones, and may be released among the loins, the backbone, the joints, and in the area between skin and flesh. Therefore, to effect a cure with acupuncture, one must use the needle with a long body and a sharp tip. This can be used to grasp the deep evil and distant rheumatism.

"Nine are the regions. For the regions, man has the articulations and the divisions of the skin. The debauched evil flows and overflows in the body in appearance like wind and water, and warmth is unable to penetrate the muscles, the gates, and the large joints. Therefore, to effect a cure with acupuncture, one must use the needle whose tip is like a plane, its lance point slightly round. Use it to grasp qi which is unable to pass through the gates and joints."

Huang Di said, "How many of these long or short needles are there?"

Qi Bo replied, "The first is called the chisel needle. It is patterned after a sewing or cloth needle. To its tip, the handle is one and one-half *cun*. Its end is sharp. Its length is 1.6 *cun*. It controls fevers in the head or body.

"The second is called the round needle. It is patterned after those needles for working cotton. Its body is tubular and its tip like an egg. The length is 1.6 *cun*. It controls and cures the qi which is between the flesh.

"The third is called the spoon needle. Its pattern is a tip like a grain of millet. The length is 3.5 *cun*. It controls by massaging the channels and by grasping the qi. This causes the evil to flow out.

"The fourth is called the lance needle. It is patterned after the needles used for working cotton. Its body is tubular. Its point is a lance. The length is 1.6 *cun*. It controls obstructions, fever, and the drawing of blood.

"The fifth is called the sword needle. It is patterned after a sword or lance. The width is 0.25 *cun*. The length is four *cun*. It controls great swellings, pus, and the contending of two fevers.

"The sixth is called the round and sharp needle. It is patterned after the hair from a horse's tail. Its tip is slightly large, its body is small. It can be used to penetrate deeply. The length is 1.6 *cun*. It controls by grasping swellings and rheumatism.

"The seventh is called the hair-fine needle. It is patterned after a fine hair. The length is 1.6 *cun*. It controls fever and chills, and painful rheumatism in the *luo* channels.

"The eighth is called the long needle. It is patterned after needles for embroidery. The length is seven *cun*. It controls by grasping deep evils and distant rheumatism.

"The ninth is called the big needle. It is patterned after the lance needle. Its tip is slightly round. The length is four *cun*. It controls by grasping the great qi, which is unable to flow through the gates and joints.

"These are the different types of needles. In total, nine needles large and small, long and short, and their laws."

Huang Di said, "I hear the body's shape corresponds to the nine regions. How?"

Qi Bo replied, "You request an explanation of how the body's shape has correspondences to the nine regions. The left leg corresponds to the beginning of spring. Its days are Wu Yin and Ji Chou. The left ribs correspond to spring equinox. Their day is Yi Mao. The left arm corresponds to the beginning of summer. Its days are Wu Chen and Ji

Si. The chest, throat, face and head correspond to the summer solstice. Their day is Bing Wu. The right arm corresponds to the beginning of autumn (beginning of yin). Its days are Wu Shen and Ji Wei. The right ribs correspond to the autumn equinox. Their day is Xin Yu. The right leg corresponds to the beginning of winter. Its days correspond to Wu Xu and Ji Hai. The loins, buttocks, and anus correspond to the winter solstice. Their day is Ren Zi. Of the six bowels below the diaphragm, the three viscera (liver, spleen, kidney) all correspond to the central region. They are under great prohibitions. A great prohibition for the Great Unity is placed there during the day every time it reaches Wu Ji. All these equal nine, and thus attend the eight primaries in their dwellings. It is that which controls left and right, top and bottom of the human body when they have obstructions and swellings. When desiring to cure, do not use that which is straight to the corresponding day; scatter to cure. This is spoken of as the day of the Celestial prohibition.

"When the body is tranquil but the will suffering, the disease begins in the channels. Cure by using moxibustion and acupuncture. When the body suffers but the will is tranquil, the disease begins in the muscles. Cure by using heat to iron it away. When the body is content and the will is content, but there is disease, it starts in the flesh. To cure, use the stone needles. When the body suffers and the will suffers, the disease starts in the throat. To cure, use sweet medicines. When the body is prone to fright and fear, the qi in the muscle channels does not circulate. Disease begins from this negativity. To cure, one must use the hands to massage and the lees of wine as medicine. These are spoken of as the appearances of disease in the body.

"Concerning the qi in the five viscera: the heart controls belching, the lungs control coughing, the liver controls speech, the spleen controls swallowing, the kidneys control yawning.

"Concerning the qi in the six bowels: the gallbladder makes anger, the stomach makes the qi flow backward and makes vomiting, the large intestine and small intestine make diarrhea, the bladder, when uncontrolled, makes difficulties in urination, the lower heater, when overflowing, makes water (edema).

"Concerning the five flavors: sour penetrates the liver, pungent penetrates the lungs, bitter penetrates the heart, sweet penetrates the spleen, saltiness penetrates the kidneys, blandness penetrates the stomach. These are spoken of as the five flavors.

"Concerning the five combinations: the essence and qi working together in the liver cause anger, in the heart cause joy, in the lungs cause grief, in the kidneys cause fear, in the spleen cause pensiveness.

This is spoken of as the qi of the five essences working together in the viscera.

"Concerning the five foulnesses: the liver is fouled by the wind, the heart is fouled by heat, the lungs are fouled by cold, the kidneys are fouled by dryness, the spleen is fouled by humidity. These are the five viscera's qi and that which can foul them.

"Concerning the five secretions: the heart controls sweat, the liver controls tears, the lungs control mucus, the kidneys control water saliva, the spleen controls the digestive saliva. These are the five secretions and that from which they flow out.

"Concerning the five labors: to look excessively injures the blood, to lie down excessively injures the qi, to sit excessively injures the flesh, to stand erect excessively injures the bones, to walk excessively injures the muscles. These are the five labors which in excess are ills.

"Concerning the five travellers: sourness travels the muscles, pungency travels the qi, bitterness travels the blood, saltiness travels the bones, sweetness travels the flesh. These are spoken of as the five travellers.

"Concerning the five lacks: a disease of the muscles is a lack of eating sour things; a disease of the qi is a lack of eating pungent things; a disease of the bones is a lack of eating salty things; a disease of the blood is lack of eating bitter things; a disease of the flesh is a lack of eating sweet things. The mouth desires to drink and eat but cannot, so these are self-made lack. These are called five lacks.

"Concerning five symptoms: in yin diseases, there are beginnings in the bones; in yang diseases, there are beginnings in the blood; in yin diseases, there are beginnings in the flesh; in yang diseases, there are beginnings in winter; in yin diseases, there are beginnings in summer.

"Concerning the five evils: evil which enters the yang will cause madness; evil which enters the yin will cause blood stasis; evil which enters the yang will cause insanity and illness at the top of the head; evil which enters the yin revolves and will cause mutism. Yang penetrating into yin causes a quiet disease; yin flowing out of yang causes a disease with frequent anger.

"The five viscera are storehouses: the heart is the storehouse of the spirit. The lungs are the storehouse of the human soul. The liver is the storehouse of the animal soul. The spleen is the storehouse of thought. The kidneys are the storehouse of the essence and will.

"Concerning the five masters: The heart is the master of the veins and arteries. The lungs are the master of the skin. The liver is the master of the muscles. The spleen is the master of the flesh. The kidneys are the master of the bones.

"The Bright Yang with an abundance of blood and abundance of qi; the Major Yang with an abundance of blood but little qi; the Minor Yang with an abundance of qi but little blood; the Major Yin with an abundance of blood but little qi; the Shrinking Yin with an abundance of blood but little qi; the Minor Yin with an abundance of qi but little blood, result in the saying: 'Needle the Bright Yang to let out blood and evil qi. Needle the Major Yang to let out blood and evil qi. Needle the Minor Yang to let out qi and evil blood. Needle the Major Yin to let out blood and evil qi. Needle the Shrinking Yin to let out blood and evil qi. Needle the Minor Yin to let out qi and evil blood.'

"The Leg Bright Yang and Major Yin reach the exterior and interior. The Leg Minor Yang and Shrinking Yin reach the exterior and interior. The Leg Major Yang and Minor Yin reach the exterior and the interior. This is spoken of as the leg possessing both yin and yang.

"The Arm Bright Yang and Major Yin reach the exterior and interior. The Arm Minor Yang and the pericardium reach the exterior and interior. The Arm Major Yang and Minor Yin reach the exterior and interior. This is spoken of as the arm possessing both yin and yang."

Note

1. Yellow Tube was a standard of measurement in ancient China and also probably a standard for sounds, that is, a pitch pipe.

79. AN ESSAY ON THE SEASONAL DEWS

Huang Di said to Qi Bo, "The classics say summer's sun can injure through summer's heat so in autumn there will be illness and fevers. Fevers which arise because of a season, how can this be?"

Qi Bo replied, "When there is an evil guest in the Wind Mansion, disease will follow the back and descend. The protective qi during one day and one night always circulates and makes a great assembling in the Wind Mansion. From one bright day to another, there is a descent of one section (vertebra), as each day the sun descends to make the evening. Here the evil begins as a guest in the backbone. Consequently, each vertebra is reached by the Wind Mansion which causes the section between skin and flesh and pores to be open and allows the evil qi to penetrate. The evil qi entering causes and makes disease. This is in accordance with the sun's descent, which makes evening.

"The protective qi travels the Wind Mansion. Each day it descends one section, or vertebra. In twenty-one days it descends and reaches the coccyx. By the twenty-second day it enters the interior of the back and flows into the Penetrating Vessel Channel. It travels nine days and comes out in Broken Dish in the middle of the clavicle. This qi ascends as it travels. Therefore, this disease attacks slightly earlier. If it goes in and is transmitted to the five viscera, it links horizontally to the viscera's membranes. Then its path is far. Its qi is deep. Its movement is slow. It cannot be affected in one day. Therefore, it is the following day before there is enough accumulation to make an effect."

Huang Di said, "The protective qi, each time it reaches the Wind Mansion, begins to open the section between flesh and skin and the pores. This begins the penetration of the evil qi. The protective qi descends one section each day, but this is not at the anatomical acupuncture Wind Mansion point. What is this about?"

Qi Bo said, "The Wind Mansion is not a fixed location. It corresponds to wherever the protective qi by necessity has opened the pores and the foundation between skin and flesh. Where the qi is housed amongst the vertebrae sections, there is its Mansion."

Huang Di said, "Excellent. Therefore, wind movements and fever are similar in type. But a wind which is fixed in place and the fevers which are special and made at the time of rest, what are they?"

Qi Bo said, "The wind qi which is detained in its dwelling is like fever qi in the tunnels of the major channels. It sinks and fights in the interior. This causes the protective qi to respond, then to act."

Huang Di said, "Excellent."

Huang Di questioned Shao Shi, "I have heard the four seasons and eight winds attack man. Consequently, when there is cold or heat, cold will cause the skin to quicken and the foundations between skin and flesh and the pores to be blocked. Heat will cause the skin to slow and the foundations between skin and flesh and the pores to be open. This is why the thieving wind and the evil qi can enter. How does one compare the essential appearances of the eight primary hollow evils, and how are they able to injure man?"

Shao Shi replied, "On the contrary, when the thieving wind and evil qi attack man, it does not have to be in accordance with a season. When the origin of the disease is the body being open, the body can be entered deeply. Its interior is the axis of disease. This illness of man is sudden and cruel. When the origin of the disease is the body being blocked, enter shallowly and detain. Its disease loiters in accord with slowness."

Huang Di said, "When the cold and warmth harmonize suitably, the foundation between skin and flesh and pores are not open, yet there is a sudden disease, how is this caused?"

Shao Shi replied, "The emperor does not know how evil enters? Although dwelling peacefully, the body's foundation between flesh and skin may be open or closed, slow or fast. These are causes. They are constant and have their season."

Huang Di said, "How can I hear about this?"

Shao Shi said, "Man, heaven and earth are a triad. Man and the sun and moon are in resonance. So when the moon is full, then the seas and waters of the West are full. Man's blood and qi accumulate. The muscles and flesh fill up. The skin is dense. The hair issues firmly. The foundation between the pores is close together. Mist and earth are in place. At the time, if one encounters the thieving wind, it enters shallowly and not deeply.

"On the other extreme, when the moon is rimmed and empty then the waters and seas of the East are full. Man's qi and blood are hollow. The protective qi goes forth. The body dwells in solitude. Muscles and flesh are reduced. The skin loosens. The foundation between skin and flesh and pores is open. Hair issues thinly. The foundations of metabolism are thinned. Mist and earth drop away. At this time, if one meets the thieving wind, it enters deeply. This sickness of man is sudden and severe."

Huang Di said, "When one has a very abrupt death or abrupt illness, what causes it?"

Shao Shi replied, "The three hollows, its death is cruel and quick. By having the three solidities it means that evil cannot injure man."

Huang Di said, "I would hear of the three hollows."

Shao Shi said, "To be ridden by a year of scarcity, to encounter the moon's emptiness, to lose the seasons of harmony, these are the conditions which allow the thieving wind to injure. They are called the three hollows. Consequently, if one does not know about the three hollows, the work of opposing them is very difficult."

Huang Di said, "I wish to hear about the three solidities."

Shao Shi said, "To encounter the year of plenty, to meet the full moon, to obtain the seasons in harmony. Although there would be thieving wind and evil qi, they do not cause danger."

Huang Di said, "What a joyful discussion. How bright the road! Please store this in the golden cupboard. It is commanded to be named the three solidities, so that each man may possess this essay!"

Huang Di said, "I would hear of the year and how it is in correspondence with all diseases. What are the origins of this theory?"

Shao Shi said, "There are the eight primaries and those forces attendant upon them."[1]

Huang Di asked, "What are the attendants?"

Shao Shi said, "The attendants are these. They are constant and in accord with the following: The day of the winter solstice. The Great Unity stands in the Temple of Hibernating Leaves. When it reaches there, heaven must respond to make wind and rain. This wind and rain follows and comes from the southern quarter. It makes a hollow wind, which can rob and injure man. If it comes at the time of midnight when the multitudes of people all are lying down, it does not violate, and consequently for this year, the people have little disease. If it comes at noontime when the multitudes of people are languid and idle, then all are attacked by the hollow wind, causing the multitudes of people much disease.

"When the hollow evil enters and is harbored in the bones and does not issue forth to the exterior, this condition is reached at the beginning of spring when the yang qi starts to grow. This opens the foundation between skin and flesh and pores. The cause is the day of the beginning of spring, the wind follows and comes from the western quarter and the multitudes of people are all attacked by the hollow wind. These double evils mutually circulate, the channel qi is tied up for long time.

"Consequently, all who encounter this wind and meet this rain are said to have met the seasonal dews, for when the year is in harmony and there is little of the thieving wind, the people will have but little disease and little death. When the year has an abundance of the thieving wind and evil qi, cold and heat do not harmonize; therefore, the people have much illness and death."

Huang Di said, "The wind of hollow evils, how does it injure the bountiful and the mean? What are the attendant signs?"

Shao Shi replied, "The first month, the first day, the Great Unity in its celestial abode is detained in the temple. If it is a day of northwest wind and there is no rain, there will be much death for man.

"The first month, the first day, if it is a tranquil morning with a north wind, in spring there will be many deaths for the people. The first month, the first day, at daybreak with a north wind there will be many diseases, up to fifty percent, for the people. The first month, the first day, if there is wind from the north at midday, in summer there will be many deaths among the people. The first month, the first day, if there is a wind from the north at evening time, in autumn there will be many deaths among the people. A north wind at the end of the day means great sickness and death reaching sixty percent. The first month, the first day, the wind follows and comes from the southern quarter, this is called the Dry Village. When the wind follows and comes from the western quarter it is called Bleached Bones. The country in general will have misfortune, for men many deaths and losses.

"The first month, the first day, when the wind follows and comes from the eastern quarter, it shakes the rooms and houses. It scatters sand and stone. The country will have great calamities. The first month, the first day, if the wind follows and moves from the southeastern corner, spring will bring death and losses. The first month, the first day, if the heavens profit from warmth and there is no wind, grains will be cheap, the people will be without disease. On the contrary, if the heavens are cold and windy, grain will be dear and the people will have much illness. This is what is spoken of as attendant upon the year's winds, the injuries and sufferings of man.

"The second month, the second day, if there is no wind, the population will have much illness of the heart and abdomen. The third month, the eleventh day, if there is no warmth, the population will have many chills and fevers. The fourth month, the sixth day, if there is no summer heat, the people will have a wasting disease. The tenth month, the ninth day, if there is no cold, there will be many abrupt deaths for the people.

"All of this is said of the winds; all this affects dwellings. They bend trees and wood, scatter sand and stone, raise up fine hair on the body and affect the foundations between skin and flesh and the pores."

Note

1. For a discussion of the eight primaries, see the discussion in the notes to chapter 77 as regards the eight trigrams.

80. A DISCUSSION OF GREAT DELUSIONS

Huang Di questioned Qi Bo, saying, "I have tried to mount the clear cold lofty stage, taken the middle step with care, kowtowed and crawled forward on hands and feet, and yet am still deluded! For the longest time, there has been no unravelling for me of the secret differences, the stolen inner wonders. What is unique to blindness? What is unique to sight? What makes the tranquil mind, the arrangement of qi. What is unique to achievement. What is unique to dizziness? How can it appear or be covered over from long kneeling? In bowing down to see for a long time afterwards it still is not clear. This extreme upper part of the self, what qi is responsible for it?"

Qi Bo replied, "The five viscera and six bowels possess essential qi. All ascend and flow to the eyes to make the essences. The essences move to the nests which make the eyes. The essence of the bones makes the pupils. The essence of the muscles makes the purple black of the eyes. The essence of the blood makes the channels, veins, and arteries. The nest qi and essence make the white of the eye. The essence of the flesh makes the collecting and binding. The wrapping and the taking up of the eyelids are from the essences of the muscle, bone, blood and qi. The channels of qi together also make a binding. The qi ascending subsequently goes to the brain. Posteriorly, it comes out in the center of the nape of the neck. Therefore when evil attacks at the nape of the neck, it meets the hollow of the body, the evil enters deeply, then follows the eyes' connections to penetrate the brain. It enters into the brain, making the brain spin. The brain spinning induces the eyes to relate anxiously.

"The eyes relating to this anxiety causes the eyes to be dizzy in response to the spinning. The evil and the body's essences, those essences which are those attacked, are in dissonance, and so the essences are scattered. When the essence is scattered, then vision is forked. When the vision is forked, then all things in general are seen with double images.

"The eyes, the five viscera and six bowels' essences, the nourishing and protective qi, the human soul, and the animal spirit are constantly nourished by the spirit qi which is the source. Therefore, when the spirit is overtaxed, the human soul and animal spirit are scattered, will and thought are confused.

"These are the reasons the pupil and the black of the eye are regulated by yin, while the white of the eye and the red channels are regulated by yang. When the yin and yang join and transmit the essences clearly, the eyes are the mind's envoys. The mind is the spirit's shelter. Thus, when the spirit and essence are disordered, there is no transmission. When sight suddenly does not have a focal position, the essences, spirit, human soul, and animal spirit scatter and are not mutually obtainable, then it is called delusion."

Huang Di said, "I doubt this, for each time I have gone to the Eastern Garden, I have not yet not had delusions. Leaving, I recover. How is it that I have overtaxed my spirit only in the Eastern Garden? Can there be a difference?"

Qi Bo said, "No, the heart or mind has that which is joyous, the spirit has that which may be ill. Suddenly they may mutually be deluded. When the essences and qi are disordered, vision may be impeded, causing delusions. So when the spirit moves, then returns, in the middle is confusion, while at the extremes there are delusions."

Huang Di said, "Man at times is forgetful. What qi is responsible?"

Qi Bo said, "When the upper qi is insufficient, the lower qi is in excess. The intestines and stomach are full, the heart and lungs are hollow. Hollowness causes the nourishing and protective qi to be detained in the lower part for a long period. It does not have the time to go up, and thus causes forgetfulness."

Huang Di said, "Sometimes man has hunger but does not desire to eat. What qi is responsible for this?"

Qi Bo said, "The essences and qi are combined together in the spleen; however, hot qi is detained in the stomach. The stomach being heated causes melting in the valleys; the valley qi melting causes hunger. The unruly stomach qi ascends, causing the stomach channels to be blocked or cold, which causes a loss of appetite."

Huang Di said, "The disease of insomnia, what qi is responsible?"

Qi Bo said, "The protective qi cannot enter and is not received by the yin, but is constantly detained in the yang. When it is detained in the yang, then the yang qi is overflowing. The yang qi overflowing causes the Yang Anklebone Channel to be full. Not entering nor being received by the yin causes the yin qi to be hollow and causes the eyes not to close."

Huang Di said, "The disease where the eyes do not receive vision, what qi is responsible for this?"

Qi Bo said, "The protective qi detained in the yin and not moving nor received by the yang causes the yin qi to be filled. The yin qi filled causes the Yin Anklebone Channel to overflow. Not entering nor receiving in the yang causes the yang qi to be hollow and causes the eyes to be blocked."

Huang Di said, "The man who needs much sleep, what qi is responsible?"

Qi Bo said, "This man's intestines and stomach are enlarged, his skin is humid, and division of the flesh are knotted. When the intestines and stomach are enlarged, then the protective qi is detained there for a long time. When the skin is humid, the divisions of flesh are knotted. He moves slowly, for the protective qi during dawn and daylight always moves in the yang, and at night moves in the yin; therefore, the yang qi exhausted causes sleep. The yin qi exhausted causes wakefulness. When the intestines and stomach are enlarged, then the movements of the protective qi are detained there for a long time. The skin becomes humid, the divisions of flesh knotted, so motion is slow. If detained for a long time in the yin, the yin qi is not clear, thus the desire to shut one's eyes, which in turn causes too much sleep. When the intestines and stomach are small, the skin is smooth and slow, the divisions of the flesh relax and the protective qi is detained for a long time in the yang, which results in only a brief closing of the eyes in sleep."

Huang Di said, "There are those without a constant course, but suddenly they are very sleepy. What qi is responsible?"

Qi Bo said, "When evil qi is detained in the upper heater, the upper heater is blocked and cannot be penetrated. After eating, it is as if one had drunk hot soup. The protective qi is detained for a long time in the yin and does not move. This causes much sleepiness suddenly."

Huang Di said, "Excellent. How may all of these evil diseases be controlled?"

Qi Bo said, "Begin with the viscera and bowels. Put to death minor excess. Afterward, harmonize the qi. If full, then disperse, if hollow, tonify. One must begin by clearly understanding the physical body and the will and spirit, the bad and good circumstances. When certain, then treat the illness."

81. SWELLINGS AND SUPPURATIONS

Huang Di said, "I hear the intestines and stomach receive the valley qi while the upper heater is the opening for qi which warms the divisions of the flesh, nourishes the bones and joints, and penetrates the foundation between skin and flesh. The middle heater is the exit of the qi which is like the dew. It ascends and flows into the narrow valleys. It seeps into the minor channels, ferries the fluids and harmonizes. It transforms that which is red to produce blood. When the blood is harmonized, the minor channels begin to brim over and overflow, thus flowing into the *luo* channels. When all is full, it flows into the major channels. Then yin and yang are strong and will move with the breath. Movement has regulated flow which spirals with the principles of the Dao in conjunction with heaven which has no rest or stop.

"Inspect to harmonize. Follow the hollowing technique to do away with the solid. Disperse to cause a lessening which quickly causes the qi to diminish. Detaining will result in beginning again. Follow the solidifying technique to do away with the hollow. Tonify to cause an augmenting. If the blood and qi have been harmonized, the physical body and qi will be balanced.

"I also would like to know whether blood and qi are balanced or not balanced. I do not understand swellings and suppurations and that which follows their birth, the time of their success or defeat, the period of their death or birth. What is near or far? What is in accord with the limits? How can I hear about this?"

Qi Bo said, "The major channels may be detained in their movements but they do not stop, for they together with heaven have the same rules and they together with earth have joint regulations. Therefore, when heaven's constellations are beyond limit, the sun and moon are but thinly eclipsed. Because the earth's channels are beyond measure, the waterways flow and overflow. When grass and the fabulous ming plant are limited, the five valleys cannot multiply, this is why there are obstructions on the width and surface of the roads.[1] This is why people cannot go and come at the same time. This is why lanes accumulate amidst towns and dwellings. Therefore separate and define the different positions, why blood and qi are like this. If you please, I will speak of causes.

"Man's channels of blood nourish and protect; they circulate and flow without stop. They resonate above to the stars and constellations. They resonate below the numerous rivers. When the cold evil is harbored in the middle of the major channels, it causes blood to settle. The blood

272

settles, thus there is an obstruction. An obstruction causes the protective qi to reverse, so it cannot recirculate to oppose the evil, therefore ulcers and swellings. When the cold qi is transformed and made hot, the heat overcomes, which causes putrefaction of the flesh. The corrupted flesh thus makes pus. The pus not drained causes a rotting of the muscles. The muscles rotting causes injury to the bones. The bones injured causes the marrow to melt, so it does not occupy the hollows of the bones, so that it cannot drain. The blood shrivels to emptiness and hollowness. This causes the tendons, bones, muscles and flesh to be unsuitably malnourished. The major channels are defeated and leak. Smoke is in the five viscera. The viscera injured causes death."

Huang Di said, "I want to hear all about the appearance of swellings and suppurations and the superstitious fear of speaking their name."[2]

Qi Bo said, "Swellings which arise in the middle of the throat are named and called 'savage swelling.' Savage swellings, when not cured, transform and make pus. The pus does not drain. It blocks the throat after which, in half a day, death. When it transforms and makes pus, drain and shut it with lard. Only eat cold food. In three days it is finished.

"When swellings arise in the neck, it is called the 'to die young swelling.' This swelling is large and red and black. If not quickly cured, it causes hot qi to descend and penetrate the armpits. In front it injures the Conception Vessel Channel. Internally it smokes the liver and lungs. When the liver and lungs are smoked, then in ten days, death.

"Yang detained with a large eruption, which melts the brain and is detained in the neck, is called a 'melting of the brain.' Its color is not auspicious. The nape of the neck swells with pain like the pricking of a needle. The heart goes into palpitations. Death; it cannot be cured.

"When it starts in the shoulder, then reaches the upper arm, it is called the 'flawed swelling.' Its appearance is red and black. At this point it may be quickly cured, for this one forces the body to sweat even to the feet so that the five viscera are not injured. After the swelling arises, it may be finished in four or five days if acted on by using cauterization.[3]

"When it arises in and below the armpit and is red and solid, it is called the 'rice swelling.' It is cured by using the stone probes, which should be thin and long. Scatter by use of the probe. Smear on an ointment of lard. It is finished in six days. Do not wrap a swelling which is solid and does not leak. When it makes a horse bean clenched like a goiter, at this point it must be quickly cured.

"When it arises in the chest, it is called a 'well spring swelling.' Its

273

form is like a large bean. Three or four days after it begins, if not cured early, it descends and penetrates the abdomen. In seven days death results if not cured.

"When it arises in the breast, it is called 'solid swelling.' Its color is green. Its appearance is like the hard seeds of *Juniper* or *Artemisia*. Frequently there is suffering from chills and fever. At this point quickly control it by doing away with its chills and fever. But in ten years there will be death, and after death, a flowing out of pus.[4]

"When it arises in the ribs, it is called 'putrid blemishes.' It is a disease of women. Use moxibustion. It is a disease of large swelling and pus. To cure, attack where it begins in the flesh when its size is as large as a small red bean. Cut *Forsythia* and grass roots of one pint each.[5] Use water equalling one peck and six pints and cook. Have the patient drink three pints. Force the patient to drink. At that point cover the patient with a thick blanket. Have the patient sit above the steaming pot to force sweat to come out even reaching the feet to finish it.

"When it arises in the legs and shins, it is called swelling of the leg and shin. There is not much change in appearance, but the ulcer and pus are close to the bones. If not quickly cured, death results in thirty days.

"When it arises in the coccyx, it is called the 'pointed swelling.' Its appearance is red, firm, and large. It must be quickly cured for if it is not cured, death comes in thirty days.

"When it arises on the yin (inside) of the thighs, it is called 'the red exhibit.' If not quickly cured, death results in sixty days. When it is located on both thighs' inner surface and not cured, then the point of death is in ten days.

"When it arises in the knees, it is called 'the blemished swelling.' Its form is large. The swelling's color is not different from normal skin. There are chills and fevers. When it is solid like a rock, do not use the stone probe. The stone probe at this time will cause death. When its appearance is soft, then using the stone probe will mean life.

"For every swelling and suppuration which arises in the joints and is mutually responsive, it cannot be cured if it arises in the yang, in a hundred days there will be death; if it arises in the yin, in thirty days there will be death.[6]

"When it arises in the shins, it is called 'the rabbit gnawing.' Its form is red and reaches to the bone. If not quickly cured, it will injure the patient.

"When it arises in the inner ankle, it is called 'the slow travellers.' Its appearance is ulcerous, but its color is not different from normal skin.

Several times use the stone probe at its acupuncture points. If the chills and fever are stopped, there will not be death.

"When it arises on the top and bottom of the feet, it is called 'the four debaucheries.' Its form is a large ulcer. It must be quickly cured, or in a hundred days there will be death.

"When it arises on the side of the feet, it is called 'the grinding swelling.' Its form is not large. In the beginning, it is like a small finger. As it starts, it must be quickly cured. Remove the blackish part. If not melted away, it abruptly becomes severe. If it is not cured, death comes in a hundred days.

"When it arises in the foot and toes, it is called the 'sharp swelling.' Its appearance is red and black. There will be death and no cure. If not red and black, death does not result from it. If it does not diminish quickly, cut it out so it will not cause death."

Huang Di said, "The sages spoke of swellings and suppurations. What did they use to define them?"

Qi Bo said, "When the nourishing and protective qi are delayed and detained in the middle of the major channels, it causes the blood to settle and not move. Not moving causes the protective qi to follow and become obstructed. These clogs and hindrances and not being able to move cause heat. When great heat is not stopped, the heat is overpowering and causes a corruption of the flesh. The rotting flesh makes pus. Then the qi is unable to descend and penetrate, the bones and marrow are not viable. They become scorched and withered. The five viscera are not injured, so they are named swellings."

Huang Di said, "What is spoken of as suppurations?"

Qi Bo said, "The hot qi which is clear and abundant descends and sinks into the muscles and skin. The muscles and marrow wither. The inner ties of the five viscera, the blood and qi are exhausted. At this point the suppuration descends to the muscles, bones, and good flesh, all these without end, so it is called suppuration.

"In the case of suppuration, the top of the skin dies while young and hardens. The surface is like the leather color of oxen. As for swellings, the upper skin is thin and marshy. These are their symptoms."

Notes

1. When the fabulous ming plant occurs and is seen it means well-being in the society.

275

2. I use swelling here, but the text may have been referring to cancer, which may have been so feared that referring to it by name would have been similar to a curse.

3. Cauterization is moxibustion.

4. Ten years may be a mistake in the text. Ten days would be more likely.

5. Other ancient sources use pine alder instead of *Forsythia*. A Chinese pint, *shen*, equals 31.6 cubic inches, which equals one-tenth of a Chinese peck, *dou*.

6. Mutually responsive means "if in all the major joints."

Appendix A. The Five Actions and Shen Ke Cycles

The Wu Xing, commonly translated as the "Five Elements," is an ancient Chinese concept used to explain the universe. "Element" is not a good translation of Xing, for the Chinese character means "to walk, to move, to act," so we translate Xing as "action" to denote dynamic movement rather than material element.

The Five Categories of Things Classified According to the Five Elements

| Five Elements | Viscera | Bowels | Human Body | | | | Seasons | Environmental Factors | Nature | Colors | Tastes | Orientations |
			Five Sense Organs	Five Tissues	Emotions			Growth & Development			
Wood	Liver	Gall Bladder	Eye	Tendon	Anger	Spring	Wind	Germination	Green	Sour	East
Fire	Heart	Small Intestine	Tongue	Vessel	Joy	Summer	Heat	Growth	Red	Bitter	South
Earth	Spleen	Stomach	Mouth	Muscle	Meditation	Late Summer	Dampness	Transformation	Yellow	Sweet	Middle
Metal	Lung	Large Intestine	Nose	Skin & Hair	Grief & Melancholy	Autumn	Dryness	Reaping	White	Spicy	West
Water	Kidney	Urinary Bladder	Ear	Bone	Fright & Fear	Winter	Cold	Storing	Black	Salty	North

Shen Ke Cycles

Generative Cycle (Shen)

Fire creates Earth: When volcanos erupt or Wood burns out, the ash remains and becomes part of the Earth. Therefore, Fire is the mother of Earth, and Earth is the child of Fire.

Earth creates Metal: Metal is usually found in the Earth. Therefore, Earth is the mother of Metal, and Metal is the child of Earth.

Metal creates Water: Ancient Mirrors were made of Metal. Water condensed on their surface overnight, thus Metal creates Water by condensation.

Water creates Wood: Wood grows by absorbing Water. Water is the mother of Wood, and Wood is the child of Water.

Wood creates Fire: Fire can be made from Wood. Therefore, Wood is the mother of Fire, and Fire is the child of Wood.

Destructive Cycle (Ke)

Wood destroys Earth: Wood and its rooting systems can break apart soil and Earth.

Earth destroys Water: Earth dams can stop Water.

Water destroys Fire: Water can put out Fire.

Fire destroys Metal: Metals can be melted by Fire.

Metal destroys Wood: Metal tools can cut Wood.

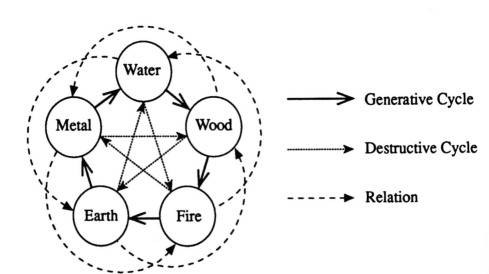

Appendix B. Ten Celestial Stems and Twelve Earthly Branches

The ten celestial stems and twelve earthly branches is a traditional Chinese system of time keeping.

A complete cycle using ten and twelve items equals sixty.

There are ten celestial stems. They are Jia, Yi, Bing, Ding, Wu, Ji, Geng, Xin, Ren, and Gui.

There are twelve earthly branches. They are Zi, Chou, Yin, Mao, Chen, Si, Wu, Wei, Shen, You, Xu and Hai. Each of these corresponds to an animal, a constellation, and the hours in a day. It is also called a duodecimal cycle (see Table 1).

Table 1. The Twelve Earthly Branches (The Duodecimal Cycle)

	Branches	Animals	Zodiac	Hours
子	Zi	Rat	Aries	11-1 a.m.
丑	Chou	Ox	Taurus	1-3 a.m.
寅	Yin	Tiger	Gemini	3-5 a.m.
卯	Mao	Hare	Cancer	5-7 a.m.
辰	Chen	Dragon	Leo	7-9 a.m.
巳	Si	Serpent	Virgo	9-11 a.m.
午	Wu	Horse	Libra	11-1 p.m.
未	Wei	Sheep	Scorpio	1-3 p.m.
申	Shen	Monkey	Sagittarius	3-5 p.m.
酉	You	Cock	Capricorn	5-7 p.m.
戌	Xu	Dog	Aquarius	7-9 p.m.
亥	Hai	Pig	Pisces	9-11 p.m.

Appendix C. Acupuncture Points Mentioned in the Text

Lung
L-2 Cloud Door
L-3 Celestial Mansion
L-5 Cubit Marsh
L-7 Crack of Lightning
L-8 Channel Ditch
L-9 Major Abyss
L-10 Fish Border
L-11 Minor Shang

Large Intestine
LI-1 Shang Yang
LI-2 Second Interval
LI-3 Third Interval
LI-4 Joining Valleys
LI-5 Yang Stream
LI-6 Side Passage
LI-11 Crooked Pond
LI-13 Five Distances
LI-14 Outer Side of the Arm
LI-15 Shoulder Bone
LI-18 Supporting Chimney

Stomach
S-2 Lower Gate
S-5 Great Welcome
S-6 Jaw Carriage
S-8 Head Border
S-9 Man's Receptor
S-12 Broken Dish
S-25 Celestial Pivot
S-30 Qi Road or Qi Rushing
S-31 Thigh Gate

S-32 Crouching Rabbit
S-35 Calf's Nose
S-36 Three Distances
S-37 Great Hollow Upper
     Passage
S-39 Great Hollow Lower
     Passage
S-40 Abundant Mound
S-41 Lower Mound or
     Released Stream
S-42 Rushing Yang
S-43 Sinking Valley
S-44 Inner Court
S-45 Tip Exchange

Spleen
Sp-1 Hidden White
Sp-2 Great Capital
Sp-3 Pure White
Sp-4 Grandfather Grandson
Sp-5 Shang Mound
Sp-6 Three Yin Junction
      or Three Yin Crossing
Sp-9 Yin Mound Spring
Sp-21 Big Envelope

Heart
H-5 Penetrating Inside
H-7 Spirit Door
H-8 Minor Mansion
H-9 Little Capillary

Small Intestine

SI-1 Little Marsh
SI-2 Front Valley
SI-3 Back Stream
SI-4 Wrist Bone
SI-5 Yang Valley
SI-6 Caring for the Old
SI-7 Branch Regulator
SI-8 Small Sea
SI-16 Celestial Window
SI-17 Celestial Appearance
SI-19 Window Basket or
      Listening Palace

Bladder

B-1 Eyes Bright
B-2 Drilling Bamboo
B-5 Five Places
B-6 Receiving Light
B-7 Penetrating Heaven
B-8 Connect and Withdraw
B-9 Pillow Bone
B-10 Celestial Pillar
B-11 Big Shuttle
B-29 Middle of the Back
B-39 Yielding Yang
B-40 Yielding Middle
B-57 Supporting Mountain
B-58 Flying About
B-59 Footbone Yang
B-60 Kun Lun Mountain
B-64 Level Bone
B-65 Bound Bone
B-66 Penetrating Valley
B-67 Extremity of Yin

Kidney

K-1 Gushing Spring
K-2 Blazing Valley
K-3 Major Stream
K-4 Big Bell
K-6 Shining Sea
K-7 Returning Stream
K-10 Yin Valley

Pericardium

P-1 Celestial Pool
P-3 Crooked Marsh
P-5 Messenger Go-Between
P-6 Inner Gate
P-7 Great Mound
P-8 Labor's Palace
P-9 Middle Capillary

Triple Heater

TH-1 Capillary Gate
TH-2 Fluid Door
TH-3 Middle Islet
TH-4 Yang Pond
TH-5 Outer Gate
TH-6 Brand Ditch
TH-10 Celestial Well
TH-16 Celestial Shutters
TH-18 Convulsions Channel or
      Ear Clear Channel
TH-20 Minor Corner
TH-21 Ear Door
TH-23 Silk Bamboo Hollow

Gallbladder

Gb-2 Hearing Center
Gb-3 Master of Man or Upper Gate
Gb-5 Skull Suspension
Gb-12 Final Bone
Gb-15 Above the Tears
Gb-16 Eye Window
Gb-17 True Management
Gb-18 Receiving Spirit
Gb-19 Brain Hollow
Gb-20 Wind Pond
Gb-22 Abyss of the Armpit
Gb-30 Ball Joint
Gb-31 Wind Market
Gb-34 Yang Mound Spring
Gb-37 Bright Light
Gb-38 Yang Support
Gb-40 Mound Dwellings
Gb-41 Descending Tears
Gb-43 Narrow Stream
Gb-44 Cavity of Yin

Liver

Li-1 Big Stump
Li-2 Walking In Between
Li-3 Great Rushing
Li-4 Middle Seal or Center Seal
Li-5 Insect Grove
Li-8 Bending Spring
Li-13 Chapter Gate

Conception Vessel

Cv-4 Gate of Origin
Cv-6 Throat of the Umbilicus or Sea of Qi
Cv-12 Great Granary or Middle Duct
Cv-15 Dove Tail
Cv-17 Center of Breathing
Cv-18 Beautiful Jade or Jade Foyer
Cv-19 Purple Palace
Cv-22 Celestial Chimney
Cv-23 Middle of the Throat or Angular Spring
Cv-24 Receiving Fluids

Governing Vessel

Gv-1 Long and Strong
Gv-8 Contracted Muscle
Gv-13 Kiln Path
Gv-14 Big Vertebra
Gv-15 Mute Door
Gv-16 Wind Mansion
Gv-17 Skull Gathering
Gv-19 Posterior Summit
Gv-20 Hundred Meetings
Gv-21 Anterior Summit
Gv-23 Upper Star
Gv-26 Middle of Man

Lightning Source UK Ltd.
Milton Keynes UK
11 April 2011

170730UK00001B/15/A